RETURN TO OZ

❖ ❖ ❖

George M. Radcliffe, Jr.

ISBN 978-1-62806-426-1 (print | hardcover)

Library of Congress Control Number 2024919342

Published by Salt Water Media
29 Broad Street, Suite 104
Berlin, Maryland 21811
www.saltwatermedia.com

Salt Water
MEDIA

Cover design by Brian Robertson

Return to Oz

CONTENTS

OZ REVISITED

Nestled in northern Baltimore in the 1950s, there was a magical land, sheltered from the harsh realities of the world around it, where children could blossom as they coped with the challenges of growing up. I am far removed from the Oz of my childhood, but I still need to revisit it. This isn't nostalgia for better days because the best days always lie ahead. To think otherwise is to begin to die. However, we are a composite of our experiences and those we have known.

There are aspects of Oz I would not care to revisit: the racial prejudice, the false elitism that higher society often engenders, and the prevailing view at the time of women as secondary in importance. As a card-carrying member of the baby boomer generation, I grew up in a fascinating period of history, after World War II but before the significant changes of the late 1960s: the anti-war movement, racial integration, and the country's tragic obsession with drugs. Our childhood in Oz was bliss; it prepared us for life but not to face the reality presented by the 1960s and beyond.

This is the companion volume to *Growing Up in Oz* (2023), primarily covering my early life. The following essays continue the story and stretch into my early adult years, or at least when I was struggling to be an adult. And stumble, I did. They also document my often feeble attempts to move from Oz to the real world. Although somewhat chronological, many stories cover a range of time, and each can stand on its own and doesn't have to be read sequentially. I grew up in a family of six, of which I alone remain, and returning to Oz allows me to keep that remarkable assemblage alive. The essays are authentic and capture not only the essence of each of my family members but also how a family is far more than the sum of its parts. No sugar coating needed.

I often refer to my family as lovingly dysfunctional: six flawed individuals bonded tightly by love. That should be every family. I am now the lone survivor of that colorful menagerie. When my brother and sister died in a car accident in 1982, my mother refused to talk about them; it was too painful for her. Years later, I could talk about them but only in the most favorable light. I loved them both dearly, but neither was a saint. To keep them alive, I had to talk about their frailties and idiosyncrasies, not just the wonderful things they did. In revisiting Oz, I remember all of them as genuine individuals. Thus, they live on: my mother's selfless love and strength in the face of indefinable tragedy, my father's continuous battle to keep his family afloat, my brother Bill's infectious laugh and love of life, Gussie's giggle and joyous mischief-making, although suffering unimaginable pain, and my little sister Kim, only with us briefly, but so much a part of who I am to this day. And there could never have been an Oz for me without four remarkable grandparents who provided family stability and added colorful ornaments and stability to our family tree.

If life is a series of trials and errors, I have lived a full life. There is no majestic story of redemption here, just an ordinary individual trying to find his way. You won't read about me in the annals of history. I am simply one of the billions who resulted from the chance union of a sperm and ovum, a temporary housing of atoms created billions of years ago in stellar furnaces. But I have indeed been one of the lucky "accidents" of nature.

"The Good Old Days"

I often heard my grandfather reminisce about "the good old days." He spoke of the love of family, community celebrations, Christmas memories, and childhood adventures. I loved to listen to his stories, and he almost had me convinced he had grown up in a better time—until he spoke of walking out to the family outhouse, stopping to pull a corn cob out of a barrel before entering.

S oon after dinner, the phone rang in Dad's study. When it was evident that no one upstairs would answer, I picked up the receiver. "Yes, can I help you?" My stuttering prohibited me from saying "hello," but I had a repertoire of responses that wouldn't trip me up. I immediately recognized my grandfather's voice.

"George, how are you? Have you got some free time this evening?"

"Sure, Grandfather, I'll be right down."

I knew what this was about; this scene played out every few weeks. Two years earlier, my grandmother had passed away, and my grandfather lived alone now in his sizeable three-story house two blocks from us. He had been a United States senator, a close friend of two US presidents, and undoubtedly the most educated person I knew. However, to me, he was just a lovable grandparent, full of marvelous stories and family history.

Grabbing a textbook, I headed out in the evening chill. It was a short walk down the hill to his house, and I had only put on a light jacket. Knocking on the door, I waited for him to answer, often a long wait since the sound of a door knock could get swallowed up in that immense cavern. I could hear him shuffling, and soon, he opened the massive door.

"My, my, my, it's good to see you. Thank you for coming down to help."

We climbed the large staircase to his room, passing a series of portraits of ancestors I could never name. He led me into his bedroom and sat down in an oversized chair. I walked across the room to a small black-and-white television set and turned it on.

"Thank you, George. You can turn it off in an hour."

He was the most highly educated US senator when he was in office, but he never learned how to operate the small television we had given him. As surprising as that was to some, I understood. He had been born years before the advent of radio and only got a TV set at eighty-eight. The telegraph using Morse code was the advanced technology of his early years. Until age forty, he had no access to a car, a relatively new commodity, yet he lived to see a man land on the moon.

Bill, Gussie, and I considered him a dinosaur, much like my grandchildren laugh at my comparatively limited technological expertise. My grandfather grew up in the age of horse and carriage. As a child, a technology upgrade for him was getting a better mule. The world was changing rapidly, and I couldn't imagine the world of his childhood: no cars, televisions, radios, indoor plumbing, and ... NO electricity! His home on the Eastern Shore was not electrified until he was seventy-one! It was a different time and less complicated, but a corn cob instead of toilet paper?

Education was less accessible for him, but he immersed himself in an ocean of books. Paper was scarce, and a small chalkboard was essential school equipment. My generation had typewriters, salvation for one who could never get above a "C" in penmanship—but it might have helped if I had taken a typing course. My hunt-and-peck style was slow but still an improvement over my alien-looking cursive. There was one drawback, however... correcting a mistake. With word processing and speech-recognition software today, most have forgotten the horrors of erasing and retyping.

Today, kids use software, apps, scientific calculators, and spreadsheets to perform sophisticated calculations. When I was in school, there were no calculators. For more sophisticated calculations, we were taught to use slide rules, movable rulers based on a logarithmic scale. I'm not sure I could get much today for my slide rule on eBay.

Baby boomers, of which I am a charter member, thought television was miraculous when we were kids. As a six-year-old, I wanted to take a TV apart to find the people inside. Dad tried to explain that the picture traveled through the air to the set; I routinely searched the air for the pictures flying by. There was nothing automatic about a 1950s TV set: multiple adjustment knobs to manipulate if the image was blurred or unstable. There were only three channels, and these went off the air at 11 p.m. with the playing of the Star-Spangled Banner. Life was difficult for insomniacs then. The set had an antenna one could adjust to get a decent signal, and we learned to adorn it with tin or aluminum foil to improve reception. Remote controls had not been invented, meaning one had to get up off one's butt and burn an extra three calories to change the channel.

There was no streaming or recording of shows. Movies were seen on the big screen in a theatre, but in the evening on TV, we could sometimes see an older film, even if we had to view it on a tiny black-and-white set that almost required binoculars. Every parent told their child they would go blind if they sat too close to the set, which we did as soon as they left the room.

There were no microwave ovens, but at least we had a refrigerator and stove. Because my grandfather's Eastern Shore home had no electricity, cooling was done in an ice box, a sealed cabinet where one could put a block of ice. Our family always had a refrigerator, but we still called it an "ice box." Wood-fueled stoves handled the cooking in that home, a little more work, but they never broke down. Vegetables came in a can, but there was no fancy opener. On several occasions, I saw my grandfather open a can with a knife, something he did efficiently. Without an opener, I, a clumsy excuse for a human, would have lived in the emergency room. And there was no packaged or processed food; every dish was prepared from scratch. Think of all the unnecessary chemicals we were spared, but one needed to read, measure, and follow a recipe. Shocking!

Toys were simple, made with metal or wood—no plastic! Today's toys are programmed to self-destruct; those old metal trucks, soldiers, and gadgets lasted an eternity. Electronic devices were a few years down the road, but electric trains were the rage. Our generation learned a lifetime of electrical knowledge by completing circuits, installing switches and rheostats, and manipulating voltage. Troubleshooting a short circuit in the layout required expertise and patience. Without electricity, my father, as a child, had to push his train around the track.

Nothing, however, surpassed dolls and teddy bears. Dolls today can carry on a conversation and have more computer memory than the earliest personal computers; my bears talked, fueled by my imagination, not a microprocessor. However, for us, almost all our play required creativity. We built forts out of wooden blocks, cabins out of Lincoln Logs, and skyscrapers out of Erector Sets by fastening metal beams with nuts and bolts. There was always a construction project underway somewhere in the house. We constantly raided our dad's tools and scrap lumber to build unrecognizable structures, accumulating an impressive array of cuts, bruises, and sore thumbs—it might have helped if we had planned what we would build in advance. My father spent half his life trying to find the tools I never returned to his cabinets.

In the summer, all play was outside … ball games, biking, and roller skates that we attached to our shoes. The creativity continued as we built forts and go-carts out of scrap lumber, wooden boxes, and spare wagon wheels or roller skates. There was no downtime, no one was ever bored, and we were always thinking and planning. Every day was a new adventure, and rarely was electricity involved. Of course, we all wore an impressive array of bandages and drove our parents crazy with all we left lying around for them to trip on.

Math skills have deteriorated for the average American, but who uses math daily today? As children, we measured to make a meal, sew, and do construction projects; although frequently engineering disasters, our numerous projects made a tape measure an essential daily tool. And we actually used fractions—cutting that eight-foot board into three equal lengths. Without calculators, we were constantly calculating change. Try giving a fast-food worker today $2.11 for a $1.86 charge to get a quarter back and avoid pennies.

Things took more time, and considerable thought was involved. We learned to amuse ourselves and work with a group to solve problems. However, I'm not giving up my laptop, cell phone, or internet service. Marvelous advances today enhance our lives and make us more efficient. I'm starting to feel like my grandfather must have; I have the best of both worlds. I grew up in a less advanced world and had to learn to be more self-reliant, but I can make the most of the technological miracles surrounding me today.

My students are amused at their technological superiority over me. I tell them their grandchildren will laugh at their cell phones, laptops, and big-screen televisions. Only one thing is certain—we will continue to advance, and the rate of change will increase. My grandfather used a horse and carriage to get into town, so he likely never thought he would watch a human land on the moon on a television set. Artificial intelligence will open the door for advancements we can't even imagine. My grandchildren will be laughed at when they tell their grandchildren that humans were once the most intelligent entities on the planet.

THE BIG APPLE

At seven, I had rarely been out of my neighborhood, but on this day, I was in Jersey City, ready to board a ferry to visit New York City. I accompanied a friend and his family for a day trip to the Big Apple. The family was moving quickly to make the ferry, and I followed the mother, fixating on her green dress. She stopped, and I looked up. Horrified, I was now looking at a stranger. I was lost in a crowd of thousands in an alien land.

I grew up in Baltimore, but I was never truly a city kid, protected from the negatives of a big city; I was only exposed to the positives. The city to me was my neighborhood, the world I could quickly and safely navigate with my bike. My friends and I staked out all the great places to explore and play ball. We had our corner pharmacy where we could buy baseball cards, gum, and an occasional soda. There was an alley where we could roller skate and bike and a tiny vacant lot, which made a poor but usable ballfield. On a nearby property, we discovered a small fishpond, a giant lake to us, and a tree we could climb nearby. However, I rarely ventured out "into" the city except when my father would take me down to watch trains and ships come and go. Memorial Stadium, where the Orioles and Colts played, was only several blocks away. It was an excellent, carefree existence for a child: friends, relatives, entertainment, and recreation within a short walk or bike ride.

Baltimore was not one city but a series of middle and lower-class neighborhoods, many ethnic, communities for the wealthy that the rest of us could only drive through, and sadly, segregated communities for the black population. Most cities were this way to an extent. Going through the city, it was easy to tell whether one was in a Polish, Jewish, or Italian community. It was all the same city in name, but the other neighborhoods were foreign territories. I lived in a small neighborhood near Johns Hopkins University, and this was a middle-class area skewed toward the intellectual side due to the professors housed among us. I lived in a large city; Baltimore was the sixth largest city in the US then, with a population hovering around a million. The city had boomed during the war with the port and the many Bethlehem Steel projects. But I didn't know a big city until my first visit to New York.

At age seven, I accompanied a friend and his family for a day in New York City. I was going from one city to another, no problem. I had never been out of Maryland before, and I'm not sure I had even been out of Baltimore. The family had decided they would not drive into the city; this sounded strange because, in Baltimore, one could drive anywhere with relative ease. We were going to take a ferry from New Jersey into the City. After the long drive through New Jersey, we parked the car and headed toward the ferry. I remember standing in line with a sea of adults towering around me. The line moved slowly, and finally, we reached the ticket counter. I had lost my friend in the ocean of people, but I was close to his mother.

As a young child, one can't see faces when in a crowd, but you can follow their clothing. I had been in long lines before, waiting to buy a ticket for an Oriole game, but I was in a strange land now. When we got to the head of the line, I looked up at my friend's mom for guidance, and that's when I realized that the green dress I was following belonged not to his mom but to a total stranger. I glanced around and then became frantic. I was LOST!

Frantic begat terror begat hysteria. I remember being led eventually to an office where I sat and waited and sat some more. I have no memory of how long I was there. It could have been ten minutes; it could have been hours. My brain froze on one thought: I'm lost and will never see my family again. I sat by myself while the crowds filed in and out. All people look the same when one is lost and terrified; they're just strangers. Finally, I remember seeing a familiar face; someone had returned and somehow found me. After a long conversation, I went off with my friend's father, and he and I ferried into the city. I remember nothing else of the day. I don't know what landmarks we visited; I only remember the terror and fear that I would be lost again. I had seen the City, and I was never going back. I'm reminded of my adventure when I watch the movie *Home Alone 2*, where the kid is lost in New York City for a couple of days. It's a cute movie, but it evokes a memory of that terror I experienced that day. But realistic, it is not! My day in the Big Apple was anything but fun.

Three years would pass before I returned to the Big Apple, and three years made all the difference in the world. I went with my grandmother, aunt, and cousin. It was billed as a holiday shopping trip. My parents were having serious difficulty with my little sister Kim, who had been diagnosed with severe mental impairment. I suspect everyone thought my getting away for a few days would benefit me. My memory of my last visit was front and center, but we were driving into the City; there would be no ferry ride. This had to be better. My grandmother, Ma, as I called her, was like a mother to me, and I always felt as safe with her as in my own home. I was the oldest of Ma's grandchildren, and my cousin was the second most senior, a few months younger than me. The city I had blocked out before came alive for me this time: the sights, sounds, and smells. We did the usual sightseeing: the Empire State Building and St. Patrick's Cathedral, but my cousin and I had already decided what would be number one on our list: FAO Schwarz, the world's largest toy store. Who cared about the world's tallest buildings, cathedrals, and monuments? Ten-year-old kids are all about toys, and we were not disappointed. We wandered through a world of stuffed animals larger than we were, model planes whizzing around us, and train sets that spanned what seemed like a football field in size; there was a North Pole, after all.

But the landmark event came one night as we journeyed to Broadway. The lights of the billboards and theatres awed this kid, outdoing even the best Christmas lights I had ever seen. We had seen the tree at Rockefeller Center, but these lights were amazing. I had never seen Times Square or Broadway before, and this was like nothing I had seen in my city. I was lukewarm about seeing a Broadway play even though I had never seen one, not even in Baltimore. Although only ten, I was very familiar with the popular musicals of the day. I had grown up listening to my parents' record albums: *The Student Prince, The Desert Song, Show Boat, Carousel, The King and I,* and most recently, *My Fair Lady,* the one I had wanted to see. Sadly, *My Fair Lady* was sold out, and Ma had gotten tickets to some play that had only come out the month before. I had never heard of it; I could only remember that the word "music" was somewhere in the title. I remember thinking how "brilliant" that was; what musical didn't have music? The show was at the Lunt-Fontanne Theatre, but I had to admit the theatre was "cool" looking, much fancier than our neighborhood theatre.

We walked into the theatre amidst the crowds. To my shock and dismay, I quickly discovered that this theatre didn't even have popcorn. An unknown musical with no popcorn would be a long evening. We took our seats midway in the theatre, and my aunt handed me a *Playbill.* My spirits lifted slightly as I recognized the lead in the musical, Mary Martin. She had played Peter Pan in the live TV presentation of *Peter Pan* a while back; maybe there was some hope; she might fly across the stage singing a song. Flying sounded good!

The lights dimmed, and an orchestra started up. I had never heard an orchestra before, and this caught my attention. Music sounded quite different coming from a real orchestra, not from a scratched 33

RPM record playing over a tiny monaural speaker. The curtain lifted, and a woman was on the stage; I guessed this was Mary Martin, but she wasn't flying. Then everything changed when she launched into the first song, "The hills are alive, with the sound of music;" I was entranced. The unknown musical that became our backup play was *The Sound of Music*, in its opening month on Broadway in 1959. I'm unsure if there has ever been a moment when I was so surprised and transformed. Disappointment became rapture, and as the musical progressed, I sat on the edge of my seat, savoring each wonderful song and line. The story moved me; the songs were incredible, and I felt like the only person in the theatre. I left the theatre with "Climb Every Mountain" repeatedly playing in my head. So, this was what a Broadway musical was all about. *My Fair Lady* was all but forgotten. To this day, *The Sound of Music* is still a favorite, and so much of that is due to its impact on me that evening. That still is the only musical I've ever seen on Broadway; I can't imagine anything topping it.

I made one more trip to the Big Apple as a child. There was no longer a feeling of terror as we neared the City; FAO Schwarz and *The Sound of Music* had cured that. This time I went with my family. Kim had been institutionalized, and our family now had the freedom to go somewhere. Finances were still an issue as Kim and my sister Gussie's medical expenses were crippling, but this was a business trip for my father. I assume this meant many of the costs were covered. He had to attend meetings, and he and Mom had one formal evening event they would attend. I was thirteen then, my sister Gussie was twelve, and my brother Bill was nine. We went sightseeing and got Broadway tickets, but not to a musical. It was a Jack Benny revue with some other performers: singer Jane Morgan, who had me squirming in my seat, and the Clara Ward Singers, a gospel group that got my attention after Jane had almost put me to sleep. While Benny was one of my favorite comedians, this was not a musical, and the show paled compared to *The Sound of Music*.

Unlike the trip three years earlier, I was acutely aware of the prices in the City: $4.00 for a Coke! While that might not seem extreme by today's standards, $4.00 would have fed our entire family of five at what were then the precursors of today's fast-food joints. We found cheaper places to eat but ate one meal in the hotel. This was one of those places where the prices were left off the menu; I shudder to think about the bill. I know our family did not have the money. Then came the evening when my parents were to go to the business social. Mom and Dad had debated the whole trip as to how to deal with the three of us. I finally convinced them that I was not a child and could handle the "babysitting." I promised not to leave the hotel, and we were given a sizeable amount of money to get dinner there. Unbeknownst to them, however, Gussie and I had developed a devious plan before they even left.

We had eaten two meals at a Horn and Hardart automat, and the food there was reasonable. This may have been the precursor of fast food. The walls were covered with little slotted windows. One could look at the food through the mini-windows, and by inserting a coin or two, one could lift the window, pulling out the plated food item. This was a dream for both parent and child—inexpensive for the parent and no wait time for the child.

When my parents left, we planned to escape the hotel, buy a cheap meal at Horn and Hardart, and pocket the remainder to spend on toys at FAO Schwarz the next day. We could each get an entire meal here for less than half the price of a soda at the hotel. My parents left us in the room, with us promising to be good and stay in the hotel. I was an honest kid, but this was FAO Schwartz we were going to the next day.

Once we were sure they were in a cab and on the way to their function, we left the hotel, turning in the <u>wrong</u> direction. I hadn't noticed how we had gotten to the automat for lunch the day before, but I knew it was only about three blocks from the hotel. We trudged along the streets, looking for the familiar sign. Maybe it was on a parallel road, so we returned a block and continued our search. Unlike the fear of being lost years before, this was an adventure. Naïve beyond description, we walked along, joking and marveling at the signs and unusual stores: novelty stores, an occult shop, and a jewelry store with more bars than a prison. Still, no Horn and Hardart. And which way was the hotel from here? We walked for an hour and somehow made it back to the hotel. Undaunted and determined to pocket some good change, we charged off in the other direction. Now, I can only imagine what my mother, with her doctoral degree in worrying, would have thought if she had known her children were wandering the streets of New York City at night.

We somehow managed to find the Horn and Hardart and, feeling so proud of ourselves, went in for our feast. Returning to the hotel, which we thoroughly explored, we returned to the room well before they returned. It's mandatory child behavior at a hotel to ride all the elevators, stopping at every floor, even the darkened basement. I wonder if my parents ever figured out what we had done, but we each produced the money we had "saved at home from our allowances" the next day at FAO Schwarz. Mom clearly was not thinking straight because my allowance was only a quarter, a significant increase from the previous year's dime. Proud that her children had saved so much money, she matched our "saved" cash, allowing us to make an even better purchase. We grinned the whole way through the store. Victory! The life-sized stuffed bear exceeded my price range, but a smaller version sufficed.

Many years later, I repeated this experience when visiting New York as a part of a teacher institute I attended. We spent the morning on a behind-the-scenes tour of the Museum of Natural History, where we got to hold an Ivory-billed Woodpecker (skin) and handle a herbarium specimen mount cataloged by that famous botanist, George Washington. We were each given a nice sum of money to buy lunch and dinner. Whether we spent it all or not, the cash was ours to keep. There was no automat, but Chinatown filled the bill. The one hundred dollars given to me for meals was overkill as ten dollars purchased a tremendous oriental meal. I made a nice profit that day; some things never change. The only hall of fame I will ever enter is the American Cheapskate Hall of Fame; I'm a charter inductee. I still wonder why Jackie hasn't divorced me after all these years.

While many love the excitement of a city, it is not my idea of how to live a quality life. I'm very content living in the country, where a traffic jam is defined as having to slow down for a tractor or combine. But I will carry those fantastic memories of the Big Apple forever: getting lost, FAO Schwarz, the search for the automat, and that glorious musical.

Jingle Bells in the Summer

As a child, my two favorite people drove vehicles character-
ized by the tinkling of bells. At Christmas, bells announced
the coming of the Jolly Old Elf, but in summer, another set
of bells highlighted our day as that blessed little white truck
made its way up our narrow street.

All decided many years ago that I was not the brightest bulb on
the cosmic Christmas tree. Exhibit A for that statement rests
in my childhood interpretation of that beloved, over-sung holiday
classic, "Jingle Bells." When I listened to that song as a young child, I
heard the lyrics as, "One horse soap and sleigh." That seemed an illog-
ical pairing of items for a Christmas song, but then I connected the
"soap" part with the one Christmas negative for me … the dreaded
Christmas bath. No young boy is a fan of baths, but Christmas Eve
at our house began with the bath to top all baths, with my mother as
Chief Inquisitor. This bath was only a notch below being dipped in
boiling oil since the tub was only a few degrees below boiling. I did
bathe regularly, against continuous protest, but this bath contained a
prolonged scrubbing and shampoo, which probably could have mer-
ited Mom a charge of child abuse. But "soap and sleigh?" Any moron
could have figured out this was an incorrect song interpretation, but I
wasn't just "any" moron. However, I digress; jingle bells in the summer
took on the most positive meaning imaginable.

It's amazing how, during summers today, so many live inside, coming out only for an occasional sporting event or barbecue. It's always too hot or buggy, and all one hears about is how dangerous the Sun is. Has anyone ever shared this danger with the plant world? As children, we lived outside during the summer, not because we were more rugged but because it was hotter than Hades inside. Air conditioning for the home was unaffordable for the masses. One could buy a small metal fan, but that only moved more hot air past you. (Cheap plastic, thankfully, was in its infancy.) Granted, the fan still felt heavenly, but you can't fit six people in front of a tiny fan without your body heat trumping the minuscule cooling of the fan. If the fan oscillated, you either had to suffer while waiting for the heavenly breeze's return or shove the person beside you out of the way. Summers in the 1950s were always spent outdoors. We'd charge out the door soon after breakfast and remain outside until bedtime, coming in only for meals. (If you doubt my story, look at how many in the baby-boom generation are now contracting skin cancer.) It was hot, but hot was our only option. Summer meant bicycling, playing ball in the street, and swimming. Now, I don't mean swimming as you might think. Picture six little kids climbing into a five-foot diameter pool, one foot deep. The sheer volume of our bodies emptied the pool, but wet was all we needed to combat the excessive heat. Any water shortages today must result from continually refilling those kiddie pools years ago. We weren't as smart as kids in the inner city, as we never figured out how to open a fire hydrant. Summer was still heaven because, after all, there was no school.

While children today have their summers planned for them with camps, programs, and vacations, summer for us was just one hot day after another. There were no programs, and it was too hot for most sports. A simple one or two-week vacation to the family farm was our only reprieve, and camps were rare and expensive. We had no schedule; each day was an unplanned adventure. Living on a street with row houses, we had plenty of kids to join our escapades. We, of course, had our token block bully, who terrorized us. I was lucky; only once did he leave me dangling upside down on a rope from a tree, and I only had to hang suspended for an hour before the neighbors discovered and cut me down. The morning was a time to explore on our bikes, although we were limited to two blocks from the house. The early afternoon after lunch was time to lay out on the small porch with a book, and reading during the summer was the best if one could avoid the required reading for school. I always wondered how the educational powers-to-be managed to choose required summer reading books that no children in their right minds would ever pick off a shelf. I visited the library frequently but never returned with a book on the required list. I'd always wait until a week before school started to read those books.

The late afternoon always saw a baseball game materialize, but the evening was the high point of every day. While our houses were still over 100 degrees, the evenings outside were heavenly as the air cooled to a comfortable ninety degrees. This was when everyone, adult and child, piled out of their houses to garden, play, and just hobnob. (Exactly how does one hobnob anyway?) The air was filled with the odor of grilling hot dogs and burgers, and the dogs who had laid low in the day's heat came out to see who could bark the loudest. A giant game of neighborhood tag would inevitably materialize. Playing tag at night was much more fun because there were so many more things to trip over and run into. My brother once ran into a moving car, but happily, the vehicle was not damaged. Catching fireflies was the second most popular activity, and occasionally, a nighttime baseball game would occur. Baseball is a sport that requires a high degree of skill, but in the dark, it escalates to a whole new level. One must time a swing based on the perceived motion of the pitcher since seeing the ball is an impossibility. Fielding was reduced to trying to find the ball in someone's yard after hearing the ball land. Everyone ducked when the bat made contact with the ball lest you end up with a bloody nose.

However, the high point of every day, the moment we all waited for, was marked by the jingling of bells in the distance, which signaled the coming of the "Good Humor Man," the ice cream truck that made it onto our little street once each afternoon or early evening. At the first sound of the bells, every game immediately stopped while every child sprinted home to beg their parents for enough change to buy a treat. The little white truck had a freezer on each side and one in the back and was loaded with Popsicles, Creamsicles, Fudgesicles, ice cream sandwiches, and "Good Humors," ice cream on a stick covered with chocolate. The latter was the caviar of the ice cream world for us, but usually, we were only given a nickel for a Popsicle. One could also get a little cup of ice cream that you could eat with a stick. Eating ice cream with a flat wooden stick is the American equivalent of chopsticks. I've mastered neither in my lifetime.

The real challenge was to be able to, upon hearing the first sound of the bells, get to one's house, wake one's mother, nervously pace while she searched for her purse, use a metal detector to find any loose change that may have fallen to the bottom of her handbag, and then sprint back to the street ... before the Good Humor Man passed by. It was a sad day when one returned with a nickel or dime, only to see the truck disappearing in the distance. Then came the athletic part of the event, sprinting uphill to catch the truck before it left the street. One could only hope that some other kid would flag down the truck before it moved on to another neighborhood.

I often wonder why, knowing the truck was coming eventually, we never got the needed change in advance. We weren't the brightest inhabitants of the planet, and this never occurred to us even once. Instead, we sprinted toward our houses, screaming for change before getting to our front door. Maybe it was because getting change from our moms was not a given. We were always told that if we were bad, there would be no ice cream, and even though we were often bad, the ice cream money was always forthcoming. My mother could never find her purse, even though it was big enough to carry most of the contents of our house. My sister, brother, and I would madly race around the house searching for the phantom purse. Hurdling furniture, opening every cabinet drawer, and communicating with panic-laden screams, we would search every niche in every room in record time. We could chart the movement of the Good Humor Man by the progression of the bells, and as he moved by the house, the search would escalate in fervor. It always amazed me how my mother never knew where her purse was—the time she left it in the freezer meant an afternoon without ice cream.

Upon reaching the truck, we had a tough decision, although the amount of money we had usually limited our choices. We'd sit on the curb, eating our treat, and all was well with the world. The truck would move up the street, jingling its bells as we knew we had won the race that day. To this day, those bells send a delightful chill up my spine, and the fact that similar bells also marked Santa's approach made these the most heavenly sounds. Santa and the Good Humor Man were my two favorite people. The bells would fade in the distance, but we knew another day meant the truck's return.

After finishing the Popsicle or ice cream, we are always left with the ultimate trophy, a popsicle stick, and this was where the less desirable Popsicle paid out its bonanza—two sticks. The popsicle sticks became a treasure and often served as the currency of choice on our little street, being traded away for baseball cards and silly trinkets. The sticks could be used for a myriad of projects, from mini construction timbers to paste applicators to tombstones for toads, and they were retrieved from the ground along with deposit soda bottles. Every kid had a collection of sticks bound with a rubber band. Popsicle sticks, marbles, sticks of gum, and baseball cards were our prized possessions. What else could a kid possibly need?

One doesn't see an ice cream truck often now; inflation and gasoline prices would make that treat expensive. Likely, few children would see the truck today on a summer afternoon since few are out-side, and no one could hear the jingle of little bells over the sound of air conditioning and television. But how sad that today's kids miss out on that heavenly afternoon event, which punctuated each long, hot summer day when all activity would cease briefly. I won't say kids today are spoiled; it's just a different world. Those long, hot summer days taught us to be creative as we became masters of our domain. We learned to socialize, to make do with what we had, and to make that mad dash when we heard those beloved bells. There was no TV, air conditioning, water bottles, or plan for our day, but we had the freedom that few have today. I often subconsciously listen for the bells while working in the heat on a hot July day. We could endure any day, no matter how hot, because we knew the Good Humor Man was coming.

FREEDOM

At the age of eight, I was under strict orders to stay within two blocks of home, but this day, I decided to throw caution to the wind and bike two miles into the city. Unlike many my age, I was not brave, always trying to be the well-behaved son, but that day, something motivated me to risk it all.

In 1957, I was in third grade in a small parochial school in Baltimore, and I had my first crush on a girl in that class. In fact, every boy in the small class had a crush on her. After checking over all the girls in the class, I decided that Virginia was the prettiest. At least, I think that was her name; sixty-five years has eroded more than just my looks. Playing ball and collecting baseball cards were still my passions, but age made me curious about those creatures who used the "other" bathrooms. I can still picture her sitting across the room, working studiously. I never wrote her a note or approached her and mostly kept my mild infatuation to myself. I looked down if I had to pass her desk. "Shy" was my middle name.

We noticed girls more because they were different than because we were attracted to them. My mother had put my sister and me in the same bathtub many times when we were very young, and I did realize that she was missing a vital body part. Being a genius, I concluded that all girls must lack that anatomical feature. Breasts were not the obsession they would later become since Gussie and I had matching chests at that young age. I was so clueless that I had no idea what breasts were for—probably just something that evolved so companies could sell bras. We eight-year-olds were curious because no one talked about the apparent differences between us and the girls, and curiosity is a powerful motivator.

I was not alone with my eight-year-old crush, as my good friend Jack was also smitten. He and I had learned Morse code to communicate in school, figuring this was much safer than notes. Notes could be intercepted and read while our desktop tapping of "dots" and "dashes" evaporated into the air. Morse code, which had been developed in conjunction with the use of the telegraph, was not widely used anymore, and we were virtually positive that no kid we knew, or the nuns who taught us, could decode it. The school had to be boring for two kids to take the time to learn Morse code, but I attacked it with a passion. I developed a great technique of drumming lightly on my desk, and soon, I would break into a pattern of taps: "dashes" were followed by a slight pause, and "dots" by no pause. When I would hear Jack tapping, I would write down the pattern of dots and dashes and then decode the message. SOS, meaning "help," was three dots, flowed by three dashes, and then with another three dots. I'm amazed now that I was able to learn it, as years later, learning a foreign language proved to be an impossible task. It's probably the only thing I learned in third grade.

This day, classwork was especially uninspiring. I had learned my times tables the year before, but here we were, drilling them for the umpteenth day in a row. At around noon each day, our teacher, a cloistered nun, had to leave for ten minutes, and this unsupervised time allowed Jack and I to perfect our craft. Tapping away, we decided to go for a long bike ride after school. He would tell me the destination later in the day. How I could tell he was excited from his tapping, I do not know, but it was all I could do to focus on any work for the remainder of the day. He had a big plan, and I was ready for the adventure. I was painfully shy, but Jack more than made up for my reluctance to "step out." There's virtually nothing he wouldn't do. His family life was far more stressful than mine, and although he lived five houses away, I could often hear his parents' reaction as they discovered something else their son had done. He was a good kid, and I sometimes felt sorry for him.

We lived on the narrowest one-way street ever constructed in Baltimore, and since cars could also park on one side of the road, there was no need for the fifteen-mile-per-hour street sign. If one went faster than five mph, the car would probably nick the curb or a parked car. It was an excellent street for riding bikes as there was no traffic on it. The road had enough of an incline to build up some speed going downhill on a bike but allowed us to climb it with minimal effort. There was an alley behind our house, paralleling the street, and this allowed us to make a loop, which we rode incessantly. I had just learned to ride a bike the year before, and I felt like I was breaking the bonds of the Earth when I rode my old, dilapidated two-wheeler. No respectable kid today would ever allow themselves to be seen on such a vehicle.

After getting home, I immediately ran for my bike. I always completed my homework in school, between moments of perfecting my Morse code skills. I rode down to Jack's house, and he was already sitting on his bike, eager to start.

"What's this great adventure you have planned?" I asked.

"We're going to see Virginia," he replied.

I was shocked as I knew that she lived almost two miles away. We knew her address and had gotten out a map to find her street several days earlier. Both of us had been discouraged to see she lived so far away, but it never occurred to me to think of visiting her. Jack had already figured we could get there and back, returning in plenty of time before we were called in for dinner. I was under strict orders not to venture more than two blocks from my house and obeyed that edict religiously. Being a Catholic and attending a parochial school, I was well-versed in the many things I could do to warrant a ticket to Hell. The nun's description made Dante's hell seem like a vacation resort. I had burned myself several times; telling a child not to use matches is all the motivation needed to try it. Trying to extrapolate from one burn to roasting for eternity was more than this child could comprehend.

Now, Jack was coercing me to commit two sins: disobedience and the inevitable lie that would be necessary when later asked where I had been. Would either qualify as a mortal sin, an automatic ticket to the ultimate weenie roast? Unlike many my age, I believed my mother and the nuns. It was too big a risk to gamble that they were wrong. Jack laughed at my reluctance; he figured his ticket to Hell had already been punched. I had been a good kid, in action if not in thought, but the potential of seeing Virginia out of school uniform was tempting. What iced the cake was the thrill of breaking our neighborhood's bonds and doing something prohibited.

The classic angel vs. devil argument was playing out in my cerebrum. The devil won out for the first significant moment in my life: the thrill of freedom with the added plus of seeing Virginia. Without hesitation, I mounted my trusty cycle, and we took off, neither thinking of the potential pitfalls or whether Virginia would even be home. We were both excited as we headed north in the city and suddenly realized that two miles was farther than we thought when dealing with busy streets, stop signs, and traffic lights. And it was only two inches on the city map! While the street was our highway in our little neighborhood, we wisely stayed on sidewalks on this journey.

We finally reached her street and began searching for her house number. We found the house, but neither of us had the nerve to stop and approach her door. I was relieved when we saw no one. Dogs were barking away, but everyone let their dogs run loose in those days. This forced one to perfect riding skills as dogs chased beside you, trying to bite the bicycle tire. We learned to accelerate quickly, leaving the barking beast to eat our dust. Jack decided to pass by the house several times in case we saw her. I remember praying she would not appear; I might have to say something. I was shy anyway, but what would I say to the prettiest girl in our class? Finally, on that last pass, Virginia appeared in her front yard. Jack pulled to a stop with me right behind him.

"Hi, Virginia," Jack yelled.

"What are you all doing here? I know you all don't live near here."

Jack replied, "Oh, we were just out for a bike ride. I didn't know you lived here?"

I seriously doubted that she bought that line.

Finally, I summed up the nerve for a feeble "Hi."

Then Virginia spoke her first and last word to me ever. "Hey."

The only girl I had ever had a crush on in the first eight years of my life looked at me and said something. This was the high point of my social life in third grade. Then came the painful, extended silence, finally broken by Jack saying, "We've got to go. See ya'."

And off we rode. It was the most pathetic encounter in the history of human interaction, but we felt like Kings of the Universe. We did it, although I wasn't sure what we had done. We floated on air the whole way home. We were in rush hour traffic and making poor time as we headed south; we didn't care. I arrived home just as my mother was calling me in for dinner.

"What have you been doing, George?"

"Oh, just out riding bikes with Jack."

"Where did you go?"

"Just around." Eight-year-olds never volunteer more than minimal information. The more one said, the greater the chance of digging a verbal hole.

There would be no further interrogation, and this would remain my secret. I shudder to think about her reaction if she had known her eight-year-old son had ventured two miles from home. Jack and I never ventured in that direction again, and the next school year saw me in a new school without Jack and Virginia. What a wonderful, uplifting day that had been.

Today, if a young child ventured two miles away from their house in Baltimore, the parents would be charged with neglect. People no longer allow their children to roam, and there are some excellent reasons for this. One only needs to watch the news to hear the latest horror story, but as a child, I experienced a degree of freedom that few kids today ever experience. My mother was overprotective by the standards of that time. She had a doctor tell her that my stuttering might have resulted from her not letting me cross a busy street alone until I was almost seven. The busy street was 39th Street, a "monstrous" two-lane road with limited traffic. I needed to cross it because the pharmacy at the base of our street sold baseball cards, my passion then. Five cents would purchase a large pack of cards with a stick of gum, and we could easily coax an adult into giving us a job for a nickel or, at worst, pick up enough deposit soda bottles to get the needed change. The pharmacy was on the first floor of the Ambassador apartment building, and going there alone was the supreme "cool thing" for a young kid. Once allowed to cross this street, we discovered a giant parking lot behind the Masonic Temple, which was great for bike-riding stunts. One is somewhat limited riding along a narrow street or alley, but this vast parking lot was the ultimate freedom in bike riding. And soon, we discovered the "Field of Dreams" behind this lot, an open space large enough to play ball on. It had no grass or room for an outfield, but this was Memorial Stadium compared to our fifty square foot yards.

Our relative freedom allowed us to discover the world, learn independence and initiative, and make small mistakes from which we would learn. As pitifully small as my neighborhood was, I learned a sense of ownership and responsibility. I learned to explore and understand boundaries (although I ignored them that afternoon). We learned early to feel what it was like to be a part of a family, but in the neighborhood, we knew what it was like to be a part of a community. We learned to care about our little world; we picked up deposit bottles and bent down to pick up a piece of trash. This was OUR neighborhood.

We learned how to entertain ourselves. Seldom did our parents have to invent an activity for us. This allowed them to do the adult chores that invariably pile up. Parenting today is so much more difficult as parents rarely get a break. They plan every day of the summer, every weekend day, and almost every spare moment of every day. Summer for us was one day after another of exploring, bike riding, street games, and reading. Those were glorious days filled with adventure and surprise. But the feeling of just breaking out of the confines of one's house, then one's yard, and eventually one's neighborhood prepared us so well for the life to come.

Sixty-five years after that memorable bike ride, I am blessed to live on a large family property in Dorchester County. We first visited the property that summer when I was eight. There were no roads to ride bikes on, but no property line was in sight. We explored different worlds: corn fields, forests, and marshes. The sights, sounds, and smells differed, but the freedom and sense of adventure were the same. And we were allowed to explore. Yes, we returned covered with poison ivy and soon learned to avoid it. We learned that the snakes were generally not poisonous, and bees would only bother us if we got too close to a nest. My children grew up in this environment, and all four grandchildren are growing up on farms.

When teaching, I noticed a difference between kids who grew up in towns and neighborhoods and those who grew up in the country. The country kids were invariably more responsible as they were required to do more jobs or help take care of animals. They could entertain themselves better and seemed just ... well, happier. I like to think this was because of the freedom they experienced and learned to adapt to. Every child should be so lucky.

Today, we yearn for a world where accidents, no matter how small, never happen. Parents keep their kids reined in for fear that an accident will occur, and the community will consider them irresponsible. Accidents are a part of life and learning. One does not let a three-year-old child play in a busy street, but children must be given increasing degrees of freedom as they age. Granted, it was a different world in the 1950s, but I thank my parents for trusting me enough to let me out of their sight. I shudder to think what my overprotective mother would have been like in today's world, but I thank her for caring enough to turn me loose. And while a two-mile bike trip through the city would have set her off, the risk we took was minimal. Life involves taking small risks, and minor accidents are a part of life. To deprive a child of virtually any freedom is to take a far greater risk; someday, that child will take off into the world, and instead of experiencing a gradually expanding freedom, they'll get it all in one dose. Will they know what to do with it, how to set limits and boundaries, and embrace the responsibility that comes with freedom? We learned the basics in our little neighborhood world in the 1950s. I enjoy my freedom regularly as I still "explore" my property, building trails, finding new "special" places, and acting as a steward of my little world. Those lessons learned long ago have served me well. I don't know where life has taken Jack or Virginia, but it has been good to me. I worry about age one day taking away my freedom, but as I did years ago, I'll still find little worlds to explore.

"Is He Going To Die?"

The sounds in my parents' room were muffled. A television show on our recently purchased set sounded miles away. The doctor had been called to the house, and he and my parents were talking.

"Gus, there's nothing else I can do right now. You've given him aspirin, and wiping his forehead with a washcloth is comforting to him, but it isn't lowering his temperature. He's registering 108 degrees now, and we've got to bring that down somehow. I'm afraid to move him now, and he seems relaxed."

Mom asked, "But will he be all right? Is he going to die?"

"Time will tell. I'll check back in the morning."

"But the temperature is so high."

"He seems to be getting delirious at this point. Just let him sleep. He needs sleep."

It was like someone was turning down the volume, and voices blended. Sleep was overtaking me, and as I saw my mother leaning over me, all suddenly went black.

(Spoiler Alert: I didn't die.)

Maybe I'm too dramatic here, and I've never really flirted with death. This was one moment, however, when I at least had a balcony view of the Grim Reaper. I grew up in a much safer time than in the past. Most of the horrible diseases that took out so many children years earlier had vaccines in the 1950s: whooping cough, diphtheria, and scarlet fever, to name a few. However, there were still the big three: measles, mumps, and chicken pox.

In the early 1950s, Poliomyelitis (Polio for short) was the dreaded disease, crippling and killing many children. I remember images of people in "iron lungs," antique ventilators, being treated for the disease. My grandfather was involved most of his life in raising funds to help find a treatment for the disease since he was a close personal friend of Franklin Roosevelt, who had been stricken by the disease. Our whole family was involved with the March of Dimes, which raised funds for the treatment, a "dime" at a time. The summer I was six, many stayed out of swimming pools for fear of contracting polio. I had to relearn how to swim at age seven because I had missed a summer in the pool. Fortunately, Jonas Salk developed a vaccine in the mid-1950s, which was beginning to be widely distributed late in my childhood.

If you look at ancestry trees from even the nineteenth century, there was seldom a family that didn't lose at least one child. Seven of my great-grandfather Radcliffe's thirteen children from his two marriages died young. Today, that would be considered the ultimate tragic family, but sadly, it was closer to the norm; survival of the fittest had an actual workout years ago.

One disease that had no vaccine in the 1950s was measles. I had already survived mumps and chicken pox, and although I felt lousy, they did get me out of school for a few days. So, I had no fear of the measles: quick fever, getting waited on by my mother, and a week or so off school. Bring it on. German measles (rubella) hit our family initially, with everyone except my father and me contracting it.

When my mother had the disease, she did not know she was in the very first stages of pregnancy. Sadly, we discovered several years later this may have caused my youngest sister's mental retardation.

That tragedy aside, my father and I had to hold down the fort while the others recuperated. The immediate disaster was my father's cooking. My mother was generally regarded as the world's worst cook, but that was because my father didn't cook. Only my mother could ruin instant mashed potatoes and burn meat until one couldn't tell whether we were eating pork, chicken, or beef. My father could barbecue a steak, but that wasn't on that week's menu. The only thing he knew how to cook was something he claimed to have learned in the military. He called them "Birmingham eggs," a name that no one on the planet ever seems to have heard. Some call the dish "eggs in a basket." One cuts a hole in a piece of bread and drops in an egg, frying it on both sides. They were good, but, as I said, this was all he knew how to cook. We saw this delicacy appear on our plates for breakfast and dinner day after day. School lunches were my only salvation. My mother's gourmet tuna on a leaf of lettuce with canned peas was a welcome sight once she recovered.

I started feeling poorly the first night my mother was back on her feet. The following morning, I was running a fever, and our family doctor was called in. He was a friend of the family and a pediatrician with an excellent bedside manner. He had saved me many times, sparing me from an overprotective mother. "For God's sake, Augusta, just take the damn eyelash out of his eye!" After a quick survey that day, he concluded it was my time to weather German measles. It was comforting to have a doctor who would make house calls. No one can afford this "luxury" today, but it was the norm in the 1950s for even middle-class families.

I did appreciate the fact that I was missing school. I moved to my parents' bedroom on a lower floor; the bed was more comfortable, and there was a TV. I could handle a slight fever and discomfort to lie in the lap of luxury. Several days passed, and I wasn't getting any better. It was a Sunday, and the novelty was wearing thin; even school started sounding appealing. Later that afternoon, my temperature climbed, and I concluded that this was no fun. The doctor had been called back to reassess his patient, and he concluded that I also had measles. Was it even possible … to have both diseases at the same time? And can you believe that you could get a doctor to make a house call on a Sunday afternoon? The fever progressed, and suddenly, TV didn't hold any appeal to this patient. The fever was so high by dinner that the good doctor was called back again. At this point, things become a little fuzzy.

I remember getting delirious, unsure of what was real or dreamed. It was 7 p.m., and *The Wonderful World of Disney* had just come on, but there was no way I could even turn to look at the set. The TV's sound receded as if someone continually moved the set farther away. I heard the doctor enter the room, but I was too far gone to follow most of the discussion. I heard him say, "Temperature is 108", and I was alert enough to remember my mother once answering "108" when I had asked what the highest human temperature possible was. The voices and TV were continuing to fade, and the last thing I remember hearing was the doctor saying, "I'm worried; let's keep our fingers crossed." My next thought occurred thirty-six hours later.

When I awoke, I was dazed and not entirely coherent. My mother was sitting there stroking my head, and I was disoriented. I was greeted with a "Honey, you gave us a scare," but I still was not processing well. My fever had dropped to 104 degrees the day before and was stable. It took a while to open my eyes, and the light was almost blinding. Only later did I find out that I had missed an entire day. When my eyes finally adjusted to the light, I noticed these black splotches on my arms. When the doctor arrived, he explained that I now had Black Measles, something no one else had ever heard of. I have since found that they are more commonly called hemorrhagic measles, a severe form of measles where blood vessels erupt under the skin, creating patches of dried blood and giving them a black appearance. Within a few days, I was a sight to look at: a large, overdone, toasted open-face cheese sandwich.

The fever continued for another week, but because of the severity of the measles and looking like one of my mother's cooking disasters, I was to stay out of school for at least another month: a child's dream come true. I quickly learned that my initial joy was unwarranted; no one wants to play with a burnt cheese sandwich. It was a long, lonely month. Happily, or sadly, I guess, I went back to school after an almost two-month absence and was not behind, a testament to the less-than-challenging parochial school I attended. I survived three cases of measles at the same time. Only later did I fully comprehend that I had been closer to death than I realized. It was not a life-changing event, and I resumed being my magnificently mediocre self—no rebirth here.

My illness's severity was not unusual, especially before the advent of vaccines. Do these illnesses make the body stronger? My immune system got a great workout those few days. No one should have to go through such a disease; there are much safer ways to build up an immune system. When I hear of people today skipping the measles vaccine because their child might have some reaction to it, I know our collective memory of the disease is almost gone. My parents shared stories of the horrors of scarlet fever and diphtheria; we have vaccinated children against those for years. I can attest to the severity of measles; no one wants to endure it. Get a vaccine!

I was lucky and blessed to have parents and an attentive and caring doctor. So many did not have the care that I did—loving parents who would sacrifice anything for their children. Mom may have been the worst cook in the world, but she was at my side every moment during that illness—the head rubs, unrelenting smile, and patience. I did get tired of her recipe for any illness: milk toast, buttered toast drowning in warm milk. However, I saw her smile as I lost consciousness and returned to the world thirty-six hours later. You might be reading my obituary rather than this at a different point in history. But then you will be reading my obituary someday, ... just not any time soon. Sorry! I always get my vaccines.

THE YEAR CHRISTMAS CAME TWICE

Dec. 28, 1958

Every child dreams of having two Christmases in a year, and in 1958, that dream came true for this nine-year-old child. However, it didn't come without considerable trauma. It was one of only two times my father lost control and launched some of his well-buried Army Air Corps vocabulary. It had been an unusual Christmas as the true nature of the jolly elf from the North Pole had been revealed. Christmas lost some of its magic, but I acquired the status of assistant elf, thus allowing my mother to make it to bed on Christmas Eve. But the talk in our house on Christmas Day quickly transitioned to what would happen three days later. For the first time, the Baltimore Colts had made it to the NFL Championship Game, which would later be voted "The Greatest Game Ever Played."

While I was hardly an athlete, pro football was in my blood as we lived in the shadow of Memorial Stadium in Baltimore for my first nine years. With the opening of that stadium in 1954, the Colts and Orioles came to town. My grandfather had led the city parade to the first Oriole game in 1954, dressed as Lord Baltimore. He was a connoisseur of history but never could pronounce the name of everyone's hero, Colts quarterback Johnny Unitas, always putting the accent on the last syllable (saying "uni TASS" instead of "u NITE us"), but then pro football was a largely unknown sport for most of his life.

My father was an avid Colt fan, holding season tickets. My mother always accompanied him, but to her, the games were a social event as they always sat with friends. I never understood why my mother got to go when I was the real football fan. While she could hardly name a player, she knew which team to root for. It would be several more years before I would discover why they took two flasks to the game. Sunday home games would completely disrupt our area of Baltimore as the small streets were hardly designed for the influx of 50,000 people, and local kids made a fortune finding parking places for fans on the primarily narrow streets. I lived for these Sundays even though I had never been to a game.

This Colt fan's Christmas had started several weeks earlier as the team held a neighborhood Christmas party for the local kids. Getting to "hang out" with Art Donovan, Lenny Moore, and Raymond Berry was a dream. They were our heroes, but they were just local folks with real jobs who happened to suit up on Sundays for gridiron warfare for less than what a pro football player would get now for 5 minutes of playing time. This was only the second winning season for the Colts, and they had qualified for the championship game by beating Y.A. Tittle and the San Francisco 49ers in a fantastic come-from-behind game. Their opponent for the championship game was the New York Giants, with multiple winning seasons under their belt and the World Championship in 1956. In my lifetime, no Baltimore pro sports teams had ever gotten into a playoff game; this was uncharted territory for a young kid.

The game was televised since it was played in New York, and our home became a veritable theatre that day as many of the neighborhood dads and their sons packed into our living room, where Dad had set up our only TV. This was not some 96" flat screen Ultra HD system; it was a little 19" black and white set with an antenna adorned with tin foil to give us better reception ... supposedly. That meant that if you squinted, you might see the numbers on the back of the jerseys, but then we knew every player by profile and position. These televisions took forever to come on while the tube heated up, and one needed to constantly adjust the focus and the vertical adjustment to keep the picture from flashing upwards at a rapid rate, making it impossible to see.

The beer was put on ice, and the crowd was boisterous when the game started. My mother wisely gave up her seat for one of the men, and she and a couple of the moms retreated to the kitchen for more consequential conversation. My job was to relay scores to them, giving me time to grab a snack. My mother did not bake (it must have been against her religion to cook on Sundays ... or any other day), but several neighborhood moms had brought goodies. There was also a monstrous bag of Little Tavern hamburgers. One could get a hamburger for ten cents, even if it was barely larger than the pickle. Our beagle Dixie stood guard over these in case one jumped out of the bag.

The game started frustratingly as the Colts turned the ball over twice and failed to score on one drive. The Giants went ahead 3 – 0 on a field goal, eliciting some "colorful" language from one of the dads; however, my education was just beginning. The officials and Giants' players had been officially declared "dem bums" by this point. I was sent out to get food for the group, and the Colts scored while I was out. The dads decided that my absence was good luck, and I was soon sent out again, with the same result; the Colts scored again and went up 14 – 3. Half time saw another round of beers. My father even offered me a sip, but one sip sent me running for another Coke. My favorite beverage only came in six-and-one-half-ounce glass bottles then, and for the first time, I was allowed a second bottle. Extra Coke and the Colts ahead – life was bliss.

Having missed two scores, I was not about to leave anymore, and sure enough, the Giants would score twice, leading 17 – 14 with two minutes left in the game. The Colts had the ball deep in their territory, and all looked bleak. Unitas was early in his Hall of Fame career and began what became his trademark: his precision two-minute drill in which he would make maximum use of timeouts, stopping the clock, and short plays to march down the field ... and march they did. The Colts entered the Giants' territory as time was ticking off. The dads were on their feet, screaming ... any civility was long gone. The Colts had a chance now, albeit a remote one ... and that's when IT HAPPENED.

The living room lights and TV suddenly blinked off as the Colts were moving in for a potential score. Screaming, the dads all rushed to the TV to turn the blooming thing back on, but the appearance of the moms at the door told us that all the power was off. We were to find out later that our section of Baltimore blacked out. The screaming and cursing crescendoed, and I could never figure out why continually banging the TV set would suddenly turn it on when there was no power. Sports do not always bring out the best qualities of the male of our species. Beer was trumping logical thought. Somebody ran for a radio, forgetting briefly that this also needed electricity. The Lord was called upon many times in those minutes in less than complimentary ways. Even my father let loose a couple of choice expletives. I only heard him curse one other time, for which he was assuredly forgiven. Our beloved beagle, Dixie (although less than beloved that day), had somehow gotten the large grease can off the kitchen counter. Dragging it into the living room, she lay down and started woofing it down on the oriental rug my father had just inherited from his godmother. By the time Dad discovered this, Dixie had somehow covered herself with the rancid bacon grease and was now rolling on the carpet to remove the excess. Dad's exclamation was undoubtedly heard up and down the entire East Coast. From that moment on, he referred to Dixie as "auch gammitz," which Dad explained was German for "get out." My father's one semester of German in college was clearly of questionable consequence as no one had ever heard of this term before.

As the seconds passed, the dads grew louder, and panic set entirely in. The next-door neighbor raced home, only to find his power off also. Our house shook as the fathers continued to fiddle with the TV, jumping up and down and shouting. The mothers had retreated to the kitchen for safety. The power returned just as the Colts' place kicker, Steve Myhra, lined up for a field goal with the final seconds ticking down. The chaos escalated as everyone realized what was happening. I don't know whether they could hear the sounds from Baltimore in New York City, but I like to think the multitude of sound waves helped push that ball through the goalposts. Score!!!!

That's when confusion set in everywhere and certainly at Club Road. The score was 17 – 17, and no championship game had ever ended in a tie. OK, we didn't lose, but a tie? The screaming quickly evolved into a cascade of "Huh" and "What the ____." Adding to the confusion, the two teams and announcers did not know what would happen next. Some of the players even thought about heading into the locker room. We had been rescued from the jaws of defeat and delivered to the confusion of the unknown. The refs called team captains out onto the field, and it soon became apparent that this incredible game would add another chapter. As the dust settled, the refs dictated that there would be a "sudden death" period where the first team to score would be declared the winner. There was no precedent for this, and another round of beers was ordered. No one was sitting down and would not do so for the rest of the game.

The Giants got the ball first but failed to score. Next, Unitas began to drive the Colts down the field. Raymond Berry caught several passes on the drive as the Colts closed in on the goal line. The dads, now completely hoarse, continued to yell anyway. Then it happened again ... the TV picture blinked off, and the chaos returned. I thought one of the dads would smash the set, but it suddenly occurred to him that there was still power. The network was the culprit this time, and the game was halted while they fixed the problem. The picture suddenly returned, and Unitas soon handed the ball to fullback Alan Ameche, who dove across the goal line. We all went berserk with only one casualty: a rocking chair got in the way of the stomping and screaming; some glue would later reattach its arm. This chair would live another few years but would tragically die a horrible death at the hands of my brother Bill, who was watching a game that did not end as happily as this one.

This was the most surreal experience that this nine-year-old had encountered in his short life, but it was to get even more memorable. Poor Mom tried to get the family to sit for dinner, but this wouldn't happen. No one could sit, and with five Little Tavern hamburgers, twenty-two cookies, and three slices of cake under my belt, who wanted to face my mother's latest attempt to fix a meal? The celebration continued inside and out. Every neighbor felt it necessary to blast their car horn continually, and the 453 dogs that inhabited our neighborhood drowned out the car horns. Life was good ... until Mom decided her son needed to go to bed. Sleeping on Christmas Eve is impossible for a child, but this was far worse. I repeatedly re-played the last several minutes of the game, and the screaming was still erupting inside that young head. Sleep ... not happening!

That's when Dad did one of those fatherly things that bond a father and son and imprint on him for all time. Shaking his completely awake son, he said, "George, the Colts are flying back to Baltimore. Want to go to the airport?" I doubt I even took time to answer as I arose and dressed in seconds. My mother opposed this impulsive plan, especially since Friendship Airport (now BWI) was an hour away. However, there was no stopping either of us.

I sometimes feel I failed as a father, as I don't think I ever did something this impulsive with my sons. The hour-long ride to the airport lasted seconds as the excitement made me lose all concept of time. In the days before security, you could park outside the airport and walk out on the runway. We were not the only ones to have this idea. Thousands mobbed the grounds, so many that the Colts' plane needed to use another runway. Baltimore finally had its heroes, and all wanted to be a part of it. Dad knew when the plane was supposed to land and that time had passed. Not knowing the aircraft had landed on an alternate runway, the crowd grew apprehensive, but nothing diminished the continual cheering and singing. Everyone knew the Colts Fight Song, and as the all-volunteer Colts Band played away, everyone sang, even my father, who couldn't carry a tune. No one cared. As the crowd grew, Dad put me on his shoulders to protect me and give me a better view. I was a tall kid, and Dad must have suffered holding me up all that time. A bus came rolling down one of the airport roads, and it was clear that this contained our heroes. I don't remember recognizing even one player, but it didn't matter. I was there, and we were World Champions.

Years later, I no longer follow pro football. Those guys back in 1958 played for the love of the game, needing a second job since they were paid almost nothing. Today's players are paid millions and are insulated, often of necessity, from the public. As I write, the Baltimore Ravens are in the playoffs, and the public is exuberant ... that is, all except me. It is so different. I can't get excited, and I haven't watched a football game in several years; it's just not the same sport. In 1958, those were our guys out there ... our neighbors, store owners, and friends. I could even toss a ball with the players when I snuck into a practice. Not today! Most won't sign an autograph unless they're paid. I'm happy just to relive those glorious days. I do not think that the "good old days" were the best; I honestly believe that the best of my life lies ahead – I'll always feel that way. But this is one small aspect of my life where I choose to reminisce. My father has been gone for many years, but I'm sure he's watching and yelling if the games are televised in heaven ... barring a heavenly power outage. That day, however, we connected in the most special of ways. That was professional sports at its purest and a father at his absolute best.

THE HOUSE ON HAUNTED HILL

I had been lying in the old, musty bed for almost an hour now, alone on the third floor of a spacious old house. The dusty room was cluttered with boxes and old toys. The light from a candle in the hall created faint shadows that danced on the wall. Watching the flickering patterns, I saw anything my imagination would allow. The house always had an old basement odor and would easily pass as an antiquated museum: large portraits, massive, gilded mirrors, antiques, and enough old books to fill a small library. I made the mistake of going to see "The House on Haunted Hill" (1959) the day before with a friend, and now that it was dark, I was reliving the terrifying movie, scene by scene. But this house was not haunted, or was it? I had never been in a haunted house before. Whenever rational thought convinced me that I was safe, my imagination offered a counterargument. The steps creaked, but I knew no one was ascending the stairs. Suddenly, I heard the soft sound of organ music rising through the stairwell. Was this real or imaginary? Waiting for sleep to overtake me, I suddenly realized I was not alone.

As a child, I spent many nights in my grandparents' house, high atop a hill in northern Baltimore. The road passing in front of the house was a steep incline, and from there, forty-five steps led up to the house. My grandfather climbed these often, maybe part of why he lived to be ninety-seven. It was my job to shovel these steps after a snowstorm, and I readily did so for the reward of unlimited hot chocolate and candy bars. My grandparents lived here virtually their entire married life, and it was also my father's home as a child. If there had ever been a house that should have been haunted, this majestic structure would have been front and center. Vincent Price would have loved this dream house: dark, full of eerie sounds, and virtually a warehouse of unusual antiques.

I don't believe in ghosts. Strangely, ghosts usually appear only to those who believe in them. And why only at night? Our 360-year-old family home on the Eastern Shore has no ghost story attached to it. We've rented it out for ten years, and the only family reporting a ghost was the family who asked us before staying if the house had a ghost. My scientific mind can see no reason to believe a spirit could exist. After all, we're still waiting for Harry Houdini and Edgar Allen Poe to return. There's always a more straightforward explanation for unexplained phenomena, and one's imagination can outdo even the best Hollywood special effects.

My grandparents' house was a child's dream to visit. I could spend a week exploring all the rooms and never see everything. My first excursion into the house's immensity and unusual nature was when my father asked me to go to the "hat room" to retrieve a small trunk.

"The hat room?"

"It's up on the third floor beside the shoe room."

"The shoe room?"

"You'll know which it is, but you'll have to climb over a whole series of boxes and books on the stairway and landing going up to the third floor. You might want to take a flashlight because candles are the only lights up there."

Even this did not prepare me for what I found. The stairs and hallways were piled high with boxes, small furniture, books, and magazines, making this an obstacle course. My grandfather, a prolific reader, had more books than most small libraries—every history book he could get his hands on and possibly the most extensive collection of books and magazines on Christmas in the United States. My curiosity turned a quick errand into a half-day adventure. Of course, I had to stop and admire the naked statue of some Greek goddess; I couldn't believe my elderly grandparents had a nude figure. And it was anatomically correct, or at least that's what my naïve ten-year-old mind perceived. Other than a library, I had never seen so many books piled on the stairway such that only a narrow passageway remained. Upon reaching the third floor, I noticed the hallway was stacked with boxes. I could barely see that four doors led from the hallway. It was time to play *Let's Make a Deal* and choose the right door.

I climbed over a few boxes to get to one of the doors and opened it. The shoe room! My grandfather had never thrown out a shoe, as there was a three-foot-high mound of shoes in the center of the room—black, brown, and saddle shoes in varying states of wear. The room's perimeter was lined with stacks of magazines, and I soon forgot why I had been sent to the third floor. A voice calling me from below stopped me from wading through endless magazines, and I went out to try another door.

The next was undoubtedly the hat room, as a pile of hats equal to that in the shoe room dominated this room. Every imaginable type of hat was in there—top hats, bowlers, fedoras, and straw flat-top boaters. That menagerie of hats told the story of my grandfather's remarkable life. Of course, I had to try on many of them, settling on a top hat. I soon found the trunk and carried it back downstairs, returning later to explore these rooms. Time flew as I searched rooms and boxes, finding one treasure after another.

The downstairs was as cluttered as the other floors: tables piled high with books and trinkets, countless portraits, and massive, golden-gilded mirrors; I could have charged admission and given museum tours. One of the rooms must have been a living room at one time, but now it was full of furniture, portraits, lamps, and a unique musical instrument—a combination piano, organ, and chimes.

What characterized the house was the relative absence of light— dirty windows, partially blocked by piles of books, and no modern lamps. There were electric candles on the wall and candles everywhere. My grandparents were born in the nineteenth century, before the advent of electric lights, and were comfortable in a dimly lit house. To their grandchildren, however, the dark place evoked words such as "creepy," spooky," and "eerie." The only modern light stood over my grandfather's reading chair, surrounded by a wall of books and magazines. He was usually in that chair reading the latest book given to him, but often, he would play the piano; he had been self-taught and was quite good. My grandmother was also musically inclined and had composed several pieces.

The walls were adorned with massive portraits, and my grandfather could recite the complete history with the dates of each of those relatives. He loved to talk about his relatives from years ago, and the house's darkness provided a marvelous backdrop for those tales. None had lived in the house, so it was not likely they were returning for a nocturnal visit. Still, the stories transported me back in time and always put my life in the context of history: John McKim, who financed much of Baltimore's defense during the War of 1812; Grandmother Polly, who single-handedly took on a British ship during that war, Thomas Wilson who owned some of the early clipper ships that traveled the Atlantic Ocean.

When one stood on the road looking up at the house, it looked like the Hanging Gardens of Baltimore. There may have been a small lawn or garden at the base of the hill, but it was now overgrown with wildflowers and densely packed shrubs, which continued up the hill to the house. Shrubs and vines had also grown around the imposing structure, partially covering the ostentatious orange exterior. Many would stop and gaze when driving by the house, and the herbaceously

clad exterior matched the house interior perfectly. At least my grandfather had no lawn to mow.

The outdoors was a badly weathered memorial to an earlier time.
Slowed significantly by the march of time, my grandmother could no
longer garden, previously one of her passions. I reaped the benefits of
this neglect as she would often hire me to pick weeds. A crew of ten
could not have restored the gardens even in a week, so there was no
way I would put a dent in the project. Even more outrageous was that
my grandmother would contract to pay me by the weed. Now, these
weren't just ordinary weeds but ones thriving for years. It still was a
fantastic gig, and my friends would stand in line offering to help. I felt
like an archaeologist on a botanical dig—who knew what treasures
lurked beneath.

The inside of the house was the real treasure trove. On either side
of the first floor were two sun parlors, partially darkened by the numerous vines that had gradually engulfed most of the windows, but
this was the only retreat from the house's darkness. These parlors were
piled high with antiques, magazines, sculptures, and books, at least a
day's worth of exploring each. They were also the only place to eat
because every table in the house was buried under books, magazines,
letters, and mail, usually unopened.

In the winter, these rooms were chilly, and I would retreat into the
dining room, where my grandfather had a massive fireplace, always
with a roaring fire. This was his pride and joy; his fires had no rival.
Amazingly, he never burned the house down, although he came close
on several occasions. His fires were terrifying to a child, with flames
regularly licking the mantel, now blackened from years of fires. One
had to sit on the other side of the room to avoid suffering even minor
burns. He would throw garbage bags into the fire that would send
flames past the mantel, causing me to plan my escape from the soon-
to-be-burning house. My father remembered when a bag of golf balls
was accidentally thrown into the fireplace. These, upon exploding,

shot out into the room as burning projectiles. My father hid behind a table until the assault ended and helped put out the remaining small fires. The only thing more terrifying than this was their live Christmas tree decorated with numerous burning candles—no wonder the life expectancy of people years earlier was lower.

My grandmother's kitchen looked to be in the middle of a significant move—stocked cabinets with no hint of organization and counters so cluttered that there was no space to work. She was not known for her culinary skills, and her impressive organizational skills did not cross the threshold of the kitchen. Being invited to a two o'clock meal meant that you might, if lucky, sit down to eat by five. What I do remember were pies, chocolate, and Vienna Sausages. To this day, I don't know what a Vienna Sausage is other than it came in a can, and I probably consumed several pigs' worth in my visits to the house. Pie was the standard dessert fare, and one would always be given a whole pie to eat. I don't remember if I ever consumed an entire pie, but I always gave it a good try.

My grandmother loved chocolate and encouraged me to eat as much as I wanted; "You need your energy." This was the same logic she used on my horrified mother as she often presented my siblings and me with a one-pound chocolate bar each. They had once referred to my grandmother as the "Little Woman," and while she was a powerful woman and legendary swimmer, her chocolate consumption over the years reinforced the nickname. The house was where I was introduced to Hershey's Kisses. Not only were bags of them everywhere, but individual kisses littered every area of the house. She also used these tiny chocolate pyramids to make hot chocolate to die for. Oh, to be a mouse in that house!

I never did figure out how many bedrooms the house had. All the beds smelled like they had been through the Civil War (they probably did). In those early years, I never went into my grandparents' bedrooms on the second floor, and I never thought much about the fact that they had separate bedrooms. Years later, I wondered about the unusual housing situation. However, from the daily letters they wrote each other over the years, it was only too evident that both were devoted to each other. They were a most unusual couple, two remarkable individuals. My grandfather read constantly, and my grandmother sketched and painted; their rooms became their studios and retreats. My grandfather was often away in the Senate, and my grandmother made the best of things while he was away. They also kept unusual hours; I could hear at least one moving around whenever I awoke, no matter what the hour.

But it was the third floor that piqued my curiosity. For years, fear trumped curiosity, and the furniture piled on the landing above would have blocked my way even if I had been so bold as to venture upwards. The creaking of floors is second nature to an old house, but this house seemed to be alive, creaking as it inhaled and exhaled. The third floor was where most of the life of the house was, and with the passing years, my curiosity overcame my reservations. Then came that fateful day when Dad sent me to the third floor to retrieve a small trunk. Alfred Hitchcock should have used this part of the house.

Shortly after that first visit to that top floor, I was sent down to spend the night at that wonderful house. I was to sleep on the third floor, but in the bedroom, not the hat or shoe room.

This was my father's childhood bedroom, precisely as he had left it years before. I had entered a time machine as this was the first time anyone had been in the room for over twenty years. Toys, games, books, and *Boys Life* magazines littered the floor, covered with an impressive layer of dust, and my father's boyhood drum set sat in the center of the room. This was going to be a blast. I explored, finding one treasure after another. I was going to enjoy this overnight stay. That was ... until darkness set in.

Returning to the room after dinner, it was a different room. No longer a boy's room from years earlier, it was now a scene from *The*

House on Haunted Hill. The darkness heightened my other senses. The musty odor was overpowering now, and I heard every creak of the stairs and every moan as the wind slipped through those old window cracks. With my mind revisiting every scene from the horror movie, I tried to fall asleep; that was the only way to end the film playing out in my mind. That's when there was someone in the room with me. Unable to see anything, I hid under the covers with Fuzzie—no one ever bothers a boy with a teddy bear. I could hear footsteps as someone, or something, was moving around the room, but without any light. Terrified, I waited for a ghost to appear, a horrifying face to suddenly be spotlighted, or a skeleton to walk toward me. I shook so hard I had trouble keeping the covers over me. There was no way to call out as no one would hear me far below. As they say, minutes became hours; suddenly, it was morning. Had I just been dreaming? No dream, however, had ever seemed so real.

I couldn't imagine my elderly grandparents walking around that room at night, and I meant to ask them about it. An immense pile of pancakes made me forget. I had worried about what breakfast would be after hearing my father talk about having to drink a raw egg every morning as a child. I was spared that fate and, minutes later, launched into another day of exploring that marvelous museum. I could have made that night exhibit A in a case to prove that ghosts exist. As active as my imagination had been that night, I wouldn't have been surprised if I had seen a dancing hippo in the room. A child's imagination is so much more intense than an adult's. Children see tigers in their closets and monsters hiding under their beds. We laugh at them and try to bring them back to reality, but this imagination makes them so open to learning.

Many days and evenings were spent exploring that wonderful house, and fortunately, my wife Jackie was able to experience it years later, lest one think I imagined the shoe and hat rooms. I passed on the shoes, but I did acquire quite a collection of hats, including a couple of great top hats, to get me through high school and college. Sadly, my grandfather was mugged in Baltimore a couple of years later, and his hip was broken. More seriously, his spirit was broken as the thieves took the gold pocket watch he had won in the Penn Relays while at Johns Hopkins. Although Hopkins replaced the watch, his spirit never totally rebounded. My grandfather moved in with my parents, and we began cleaning out that unique museum.

Under any circumstances, this would have been a Herculean task, but adding to the project's immensity was my grandmother's propensity for hiding money. Everything had to be taken apart and checked. And I do mean everything! Bills were inserted in books and little boxes and taped to the back of pictures. She had even taken a box of Band-Aids, removed the bandage from each cellophane wrapper, and inserted dollar bills, returning the wrappers so that upon opening the box, it still looked like a box of Band-Aids. Our search motto was no stone left unturned, or, should I say, no Band-Aid left unwrapped. I wish we had had more time to go through things; I'm sure several treasures were lost. What I would give now to go back and search every square inch of that dusty museum.

I remember when my sister and I entered his bedroom for the first time, feeling like we were invading some intensely private retreat. All the presents the family had given him over the past ten years piled on his bureau, each gift still in its box loosely bound with the original wrapping paper. As typical young teens, we decided to wrap them back up and give them to him again for birthdays and Christmas. To this day, I feel guilty about what we did, but I honestly think he never realized it. Re-gifting the ten-year-old box of candy was crossing the line, and when he offered each of us a piece, we hesitatingly complied. Hard candy took on a new meaning.

It was sad to see the old house leave the family years ago. I've never seen another place quite like it. If any home could have had a ghost, it would have been this one. What visited me that evening in that house long ago probably only walked around in my mind, but the organ music was real. I spent several other nights there, but several years older, I enjoyed the darkness and mystery the house embodied. The house still stands, looming high above the road, and I often wish to revisit it. But before I talk myself into getting up the nerve to climb those steps again, I realize I would be disappointed; memories are best left unspoiled. I wish I had the imagination to create a good ghost story; that house would be the ideal setting. The house undoubtedly has modern lighting now and is probably quite elegant and different from the cluttered museum I remember. There would be no elderly gentleman reading, creating fireplace infernos, and playing the organ. There would be no grandmother painting in a darkened room or sifting through her mountains of treasures. To revisit the house would be to tarnish the memories seriously.

We often wish to revisit a time or place, but it rarely meets our expectations. Memories are just that, but they are real and very much alive. They are a part of who we are, and keeping them alive, while seemingly overly sentimental, is essential to our remaining whole. I still climb those dark stairs in my mind, and my grandparents are still a vital part of who I am. The benevolent ghost of that house still walks regularly through my mind, reminding me of a happy past and two wonderfully unique people. That kind of ghost I can believe in.

MOM'S ANNUAL VISIT TO HELL

My mother had weathered the birth of four children, shep-
herded them through all the common childhood diseases, sur-
vived several moves, and, for the first time in her married
life, was being rewarded with a family vacation—a break
from nonstop housework, maybe some time to bask in the
sun or read that book she could never make time for. She had
counted down the days, and finally, she and Dad had every-
one loaded in the family truckster. We were heading to the
Eastern Shore for a two-week vacation at Spocott, the fam-
ily's ancestral farm. As we drove down the long driveway,
Mom's mood quickly changed. Her children saw heaven; she
saw us headed in the other direction. As a good Catholic, she
believed in hell; she just never planned on vacationing there.

Our family was not poor. However, both of my sisters had significant medical issues, and much of Dad's salary found its way to
multiple doctors and hospitals. We were heading to Spocott for a vacation, though not the kind of vacation people speak of today. There
was no Disneyworld in the 1950s, and our family could not have
afforded it anyway. This was our econo-resort to which we escaped
from Baltimore in the 1950s and 1960s, but for Mom, Spocott was
anything but a resort.

My grandfather and his two brothers were born and lived most of
their lives at Spocott—he in a home on the other side of the property,
and they in the old family home. When one of the brothers died in

the early 1950s, half of the house became vacant, and this is where we were headed. Getting away for two weeks sounded like a dream to this kid—escaping the 100-degree heat. At the time, we had a gargantuan gray and white Plymouth station wagon with impressive fins rising above the taillights. It had a third seat facing the rear and, of course, no air conditioning. But then my room at home didn't even have a fan, so heat and I were well acquainted. My parents rode up front, Gussie and Bill rode in the second seat, and I took over the back seat with our beagle Nickie. The only window in the rear was the rear window, which stayed closed while riding. Nickie hated cars because these were the instruments of terror used to take her to the vet's office. She trembled for ten minutes, the time it took to go from home to the vet, and then relaxed when she realized this trip did not include a stop at her vision of hell. This was before interstate highways, and driving from Baltimore to Annapolis was one stop light after another. Nickie had climbed into my lap, adding to the intense heat, and although I was using a magazine to fan myself, it was only moving hot air. I scratched Nickie's back, and she looked at me with appreciation. That's when all the grease she had consumed earlier that day decided to reverse directions and exit.

Soon covered with vomit, I informed my parents of this blessed event, but there was no way to stop at this point. The heat in the back of the car started cooking what was now covering me. Nickie, relieved of her burden, rolled over and fell asleep. My mother passed back an emergency raincoat. I thought this gesture came about five minutes too late. With the driver in the car behind us smiling, I removed my clothes; the odor of vomit trumped modesty. Shoving the pungent garments onto the floor, I put on the raincoat. Worrying that I might be too cool in this 100-degree car, Nickie climbed back onto my lap.

We reached Cambridge, crossing the Choptank River Bridge, and looked for a place to eat since Spocott likely had no food. A restaurant across the bridge called "The Point" had the best hot dogs, my favorite food. I started to get out, remembering suddenly that I had no clothes. Hunger also trumped modesty, and I walked in wearing only my mother's translucent raincoat, perfect restaurant attire for a sunny 95° day. The hot dog removed all memories of vomit, heat, and nakedness. The vacation was on a roll now.

We pulled down the long Spocott lane, and I thought I was in heaven, not a row house in sight. Long rows of corn stretched out as far as the eye could see, a dream to a kid who could almost jump from one side of his yard to another in Baltimore. We pulled up to the house, surrounded almost entirely by screened-in porches, and I gazed at the vast yard. This was a child's paradise. Mom saw the house differently: it badly needed paint, several shutters were falling off, and the grass was two feet high.

I was helping my father unload the car when I heard a blood-curdling scream inside the house. Mom had entered the house a few minutes earlier, and we raced in to see what was happening. She stood in the center of the kitchen with tears rolling down her face. She was pointing at the kitchen sink, her lips quivering, but no words forthcoming. Part of the ceiling plaster was on the floor, and the walls had more bare spots than paint. There was a long snakeskin hanging from the ceiling light fixture, and in the sink lay the remains of a dead mouse. She finally forced out a few words, "George, I want to go home."

Mom retreated to bed for a nap, unable to do anything further. Her nightmare was beginning. We finished unloading the car and went to see my great-uncle Sewell at the north end of the house. Gussie, Bill, and I were assigned the bedroom upstairs in the old section of the house and then took off to explore the property: old barns, fields, and rows of corn to race through like a maze. Extending into the river was a dock my father told us to avoid because he wasn't sure it was safe. Darkness came soon, but we just wanted to run and play. I had never known this kind of freedom—no property line in sight. The sounds of nocturnal insects and a Great Horned Owl replaced the "bob-WHITE" calls of the abundant Bobwhites on the property. This was exciting for a child who only heard cars and sirens at night.

We were finally coaxed into the house to get ready for bed. This was Mom's department, and she couldn't get us to bed fast enough, even bypassing the usual nightly baths. This was the first time we had tasted non-chlorinated water, each drinking several glasses, thus ensuring my parents would get no sleep as we periodically marched downstairs to the only bathroom by their bedroom. On my second trip down, I remember hearing my mother say, "Who is it this time?" There was no way three young children would fall asleep, all piled into the same room, and we did talk long into the night, with sleep overtaking us finally one by one.

The house had not seen much attention over the last few years. It had been vacant since my Uncle Tom had died, and everyone was recruited to help with the cleaning. My mother volunteered to go to the store, probably as much to get away from the house as to get the much-needed food. The paint was peeling from the walls, and, as we had found the night before, the beds had a moldy odor from the fifty-year-old mattresses. We probably found enough dead flies to fill up a trash can. We discovered a new sport, swatting flies; every day was filled with competitions … one point for a housefly, two for a deerfly, and three for the large horsefly. Mom was not amused. With all the windows open, the fresh country air was bringing the house back to life. Nickie was in heaven, with rabbits for her to chase everywhere, and she was hoarse at the end of that first full day from hours of howling and barking. The rabbits could not have been safer, as speed is not the forte of a beagle. She turned in right after dinner … until she smelled the skunk. That began a long night, and, once again, Mom was to get no sleep.

My grandmother and grandfather spent much time on the other side of the property, called Windemere, and we visited them several times. The property was overrun with vegetation, a relic of the magnificent gardens that my grandmother had planted years earlier. Here, I was introduced to the official Dorchester County mascot, the mosquito. Windemere was ripe with those little blood-sucking pests. One had to sprint from the car to the house. My grandmother was a piece of work and not comfortable in the kitchen. The 2 p.m. dinner we were invited to finally appeared at 6 p.m., and it was frightening. My father said that if we were brave and attempted to eat it, he'd take everyone in for ice cream afterward. That was all the incentive we needed. However, no one ever explained to me what animal we consumed.

Ice cream was a highlight as we ventured into Dairy Queen in Cambridge several times. A vanilla milkshake washed away the residue of that mysterious dinner, and all was well with the world. Mom craved ice cream the way beagles like steak. This was the first time we had seen her smile, and Dad wisely said we would have to make numerous ice cream runs into town; he knew this was the only way to keep Mom from hijacking the car and driving back to Baltimore.

The joy of that summer at Spocott was the wide-open space. We could lay out a baseball field, a real contrast to trying to play on a narrow street in Baltimore. There was no pool, but we had a river to swim in. The bottom was muddy, and one had to wear old shoes because of the sharp oyster shells and even more treacherous barnacles. We had to share the river with one unpleasant animal, the Sea Nettle, second cousin to a Portuguese Man of War. These white jellyfish with long tentacles appeared in the latter part of the summer as the salinity increased in the river. They were starting to appear, and even though a sting could be painful, they didn't keep us out of the river. Unfortunately, I had a bad experience with one several years earlier at Sandy Point State Park, where one wrapped around my chest, sending me to the hospital. Right after that incident, that park installed massive nets to keep the Sea Nettles out; I always figured that I had suffered for the ultimate good of humanity.

Spocott had an old wooden rowboat we could use. We couldn't tie it up at the dock because it would probably sink in a few hours. It took everyone to get it in and out of the water. One would have to alternate between rowing and bailing, as the boat would sink slightly with each stroke. This superb vessel, with far more bare wood than paint, allowed this intrepid explorer to visit distant lands. I'd beach the boat and then explore some new territory. This was when I learned a difficult life lesson. I awoke one day to find opening my eyes impossible. I felt my way down to my mother's room, only to hear her scream. Her son's head was blown up like a basketball, with his eyes swelled shut. I had bushwhacked through the densest patch of poison ivy known to man the previous two days and was now treated to my first visit to Dorchester General Hospital ... although I never saw it. They treated me with something, and daylight finally found my retinas late that afternoon. To this day, I can spot that treacherous trifoliated plant from quite a long distance. That was one of Mom's three hospital trips on that vacation with her children. She reminded Dad that people are supposed to "relax" on vacations.

That summer, I discovered the best activity a child could ever partake of ... chicken necking. At the head of the Little Choptank River, Gary's Creek is a brackish section of the Chesapeake Bay and home to that world-renowned bottom-dwelling scavenger, the Blue Crab. They are not renowned for their intelligence, however. Chicken necks were plentiful, and one tied to a string and thrown off the dock would soon be in the grasp of a crab, who would try to run with it. The line would go taught, and one could pull it to the surface with the crab still hanging on. A simple scoop with a net would pull the beast in, and if one missed, the crab would soon be back on the line, allowing additional tries until it was finally caught. What a perfect activity for young kids. We spent hours on the dock hauling in crabs, keeping them alive by placing them in a submerged live box. This was fun for Mom as she got to sit in the 120-degree kitchen while the crabs steamed.

Dad had spent much of his childhood on the property, and the memories and stories flowed through him. Mom was a good sport and would spend most of the day cleaning, trying to steal a few minutes to read before she was expected to produce another meal. Her meals were simple, as a hot kitchen on a hot day was not the place to be. Although there was sometimes a breeze, those two weeks were hot, and Dad's first trip into town was to buy two fans, one for the kitchen and one for their bedroom. He sensed Mom's misery and did everything possible to keep her from declaring the vacation over.

The vacation ended too quickly for the children and not soon enough for my mother. I'd never seen anyone so happy to have reached the end of a vacation. The drive back from "The Farm" was quiet as we relived the wonderful memories: crabs, open space, swimming, boating, and listening to Nickie bark all night long at the new nighttime smells and sounds. Mom dreamed of Baltimore. It may have been the cheapest vacation a family ever took. The best part of this first return trip for me was not having to wear a raincoat home. Nickie was so exhausted from two weeks of barking and chasing rabbits that she quickly fell asleep in my lap. All was right with the world.

Ironically, she and Dad moved to the farm in their retirement. All her children lived there then, and family trumped mosquitoes and snakes. Dad was in heaven as he was always involved in some small work project on the property, and a pool was enough to coax Mom to make the move. However, Mom remained homesick for the city, where they would now head for "vacations."

As years have passed, I have come to respect what Mom endured for her family. In a weak moment, years later, she confided that she was often miserable at Spocott, but she never hinted at this when we were young. I already knew that. She was a city girl, and Spocott was all country. She knew how much Dad loved the property and must have enjoyed seeing her children enjoy the time spent there. There was never a less selfish person than her; her life was wholly devoted to her family. She would have gone to hell to be with Dad, and for her, the property was only a couple of notches above that incendiary place. She tried to like the place, but there was always a surprise right around the corner—pouring a bowl of cereal and having a live mouse roll into the bowl, seeing a giant black snake in the toilet as she was about to sit down, hosing down a child who had fallen into an outhouse pit, and treating one of her children sprayed by a skunk. For her, Spocott was one nightmare after another. However, she was with the family; that was all that mattered.

The houses are fixed up and air-conditioned now. The barns are still there to explore, and the crabs are less plentiful but catchable. The substantial underwater grass beds in which they shed years ago are mostly gone, and life is a little more dangerous for a vulnerable soft-shelled crab (about eight hours from molting until a new hard shell was formed). The sounds and smells are the same; the marsh odor dominates on the hottest days, and the Bobwhites still sing, although they are much less common. Rising sea levels will eventually reclaim the land for the Bay, but it is still a place of peace, hard work, and stories. I am the only surviving family member of that early vacation, and the property still evokes memories of my early family and those wonderful hot summer days. Nickie is long gone, but beagles still rule the property. Maizie, the latest barking hound, is now chasing a Bald Eagle across the yard. The bird is about five feet above the ground, carrying a fish, and Maizie isn't bright enough to realize that what she is chasing could almost carry her away. The Great Blue Heron is standing guard by the shore as it did over fifty years ago.

If there is a heaven somewhere, Mom has a place of honor. She paid her dues for years as a part-time resident of hell on our farm. Heaven for her would be a place devoid of the mice, snakes, flies, and mosquitoes she endured for years, but even if those were part of the all-expenses-paid residence in heaven, she would endure it for the family; there was never a more selfless person than her.

ITALIAN FOOD IMMERSION

It was almost 11 p.m. that cold Friday evening in Baltimore, but, as in most cities, life was bustling as many individuals were celebrating the end of another work week. Unnoticed by most were a father and son walking through a dark alley in Little Italy. Carrying a flashlight, the father had been told where to go. Finding what he was looking for, he stopped and lifted his son, giving him the flashlight. The son lifted the lid, and the odor hit him like a freight train. He hesitated briefly, and gathering his courage, he jumped into the dumpster.

I still like Italian food, but I shouldn't. Spaghetti was a staple of my early childhood, but sadly, it came out of a can. Franco-American spaghetti made an easy meal for my mom. This and Dinty Moore beef stew were the core of Mom's arsenal of meals in a can. The stuff later came out as SpaghettiOs, as if making the pasta into little Os would make it more edible. Only in America would we try to improve a product in every way except taste. The Os were easier to get on a spoon than strands of spaghetti, but it was still largely tasteless and far less fun to eat. Tasting this, any Italian would have disavowed that spaghetti was their dish.

Never in contention for a "Best Chef" award, Mom loved meals found in a can. Five minutes of preparation time suited her well as she could wait until the last possible moment; *open a can, dump it into a pan, and heat it until warm* was her kind of meal. Only later did I realize that spaghetti had any taste.

Temporary salvation would come periodically as my father would take the family out to dinner. We frequently visited Jimmy Wu's Chinese restaurant since my father claimed to know Jimmy. Jimmy never remembered him, but we always enjoyed dining with our "old friend." The challenge was trying to eat with chopsticks. My father would attempt to show us how, much to everyone's entertainment, but finally, his good friend Jimmy would come over to instruct. Until he first demonstrated the technique, I thought chopsticks were a joke the Chinese played on clueless Americans. After making the Americans look stupid, they probably returned to the kitchen and got their forks and spoons. Can one eat a pea with chopsticks? (They can, but the only way I could eat a pea without a fork was to use my fingers.)

Our favorite place to go was the Oriole Cafeteria on York Rd. It was simple and cheap. My grandfather was often the one who took us out, and he loved this place. He was unsteady on his feet as he was approaching ninety, but he fought his way through the simple buffet, refusing to let anyone help. He perfected the art of the never-ending plate as he navigated the line, accidentally clearing his plate every time he bent over for the next item. He'd reach the end of the line, perplexed that most of what he put on his plate was no longer there, and would head back to the beginning to start over. His plate ended up with a tiny portion of everything in the buffet melded together in one amorphous blob. He would devour it, saying it was the best meal he ever had.

Then, one evening, Dad decided to take us down to Little Italy in Baltimore for an authentic Italian meal. In the early years, Dad worked long hours, and having the family go out for dinner didn't fit with the early bedtimes of young children. However, this one evening, Dad came home early, and we soon headed to Velleggia's Restaurant in downtown Baltimore. He was a brave soul to want to take us all out to a fancy restaurant since none of us were experts in acceptable restaurant etiquette. We all dressed up, got the standard "How to Behave" lecture, which went in one ear and out the other, and piled into the family wagon, or with apologies to Clark Griswold, the family truck-ster. This was to be a meal to remember … or, I should say, to forget.

The restaurant was an adventure for a kid who thought the Oriole Cafeteria was gourmet dining. Spaghetti didn't come out of a can here, and since that was the only word I recognized on the menu, it was what I ordered. The background music, candle in a wine bottle on the table, and fancy menu told me we were in a different world. Filling up on bread while we waited, I was shocked to realize that bread had taste. We quickly grew impatient; cafeteria dining had not prepared us for the wait, but our patience was rewarded when the food came out. This was not Franco-American spaghetti!

At that time, I was wearing a removable brace or retainer for my teeth, and I was supposed to carry a little cylindrical container to hold it. I, of course, had left the container home and would have left the retainer home if Mom hadn't reminded me. The retainer is a medieval torture device inflicted on young children—also a way to shut them up since it made speaking awkward and painful when tightened. Pe-riodically, the orthodontist would scold me for not wearing it enough, and for several weeks after, Mom would be on me to wear it. I would conveniently "forget" to wear it when going out, but this evening, Mom insisted. That evening, I took it out and wrapped it in a nap-kin. Mom, seeing this, appropriately scolded me for not bringing the container. "Don't do that, George. You'll forget it, and that cost us a lot of money." Realizing that there was no other option, she relented, and I dove into the spaghetti, shocked that it tasted nothing like the substance that came out of a can … pasta that tasted like something other than wallpaper paste. Real tomato sauce! And giant meatballs; one needed a microscope to find meat in our usual canned fare.

The meal rolled on with all of us taking in the ambiance, lis-tening to Dad's stories, and trying to stuff a giant meatball into our mouths at one time. My sister Gussie would try to get my brother Bill laughing when his mouth was full of spaghetti, and the numerous red splatters on the tablecloth were a testament to her success. This was a real treat to a family inexperienced at stepping out into the real world. My sister Kim was not with us. Diagnosed as mentally retarded, she was at home with a babysitter. Kim's explosive temper tantrums had worn my mother down, and she could not have enjoyed this dinner out with Kim screaming and trying to race around the restaurant. I missed her because Kim made every occasion an exciting free-for-all. The meal finally drew to a close, and we headed out to try to find the car. Parking spots were hard to find in this city area, and we had parked about five blocks from the restaurant. Gussie got Bill giggling again, and Mom's patience had faded quite a bit earlier. We finally made it to the car and began the fifteen-minute drive home.

Bill and Gussie fed off each other, and I delighted in their antics. Gussie could get a corpse to laugh, and Bill had learned from her. Their constant banter and teasing worked on Mom's nerves. They completely ignored her warnings, pushing the silliness to a higher level. My father patiently drove on, wholly focused on the Baltimore traffic. He was winding us through the city, which he knew like the back of his hand. I knew we were close to home as we passed John Hopkins University. That's when Mom asked the question ... THE QUESTION! "George, you do have your brace, don't you?"

We have many moments when fear turns to panic, and one cannot speak, quickly rewinding the previous hour. Hoping against hope for a miracle, I realized the worst-case scenario was playing out. It wasn't in my mouth, and a quick feel of my pockets found these empty. This happened once before, and after letting me sweat for several seconds, Mom had produced it with a smile. I exhaled as I realized that this could be repeating. Parents love to use brief torture to make a point—an effective deterrent ... sometimes. I waited for her to turn and produce the napkin-enshrouded retainer, but this didn't happen. My silence had answered the question for her as she screamed, "George, stop the car!"

I waited for the inevitable "George, I warned you!" Even that, however, did not need to be spoken. Instead, "George, take me and the children home, and then you'll have to return to the restaurant with young George." The next few minutes were painful, as no word was uttered. Even Gussie and Bill were quiet except for my sister's predictable comment, "Mom, are you going to kill George if they can't find it?" There was no answer, and I considered opening the door and leaping out.

The ride back to the restaurant was quite different since Dad's philosophy was to change the subject, knowing I was already suffering enough. While we talked about the Orioles, my thoughts were on the retainer. I knew the table would have been cleared by now. Would they have found the retainer? But then why would a server bother to check every napkin? It would be in a trash can, and all I had to do was figure out what can it had been thrown into. I still hoped it had been found, but … I was expecting the worst. How much did the retainer cost since I would have to fork over the dough for a new one? My quarter allowance meant I would be coughing it up for years.

Entering the restaurant, we saw our table now occupied by a small group, obviously well into their meal. We asked to see the head waiter, hoping the waiter had found the retainer. He knew nothing of it, and my heart sank. He did say that he would find our waiter because lost items often did not make it to him right away. There was still hope. The server soon approached us but did not find anything when he cleared the table. However, he did say that he knew in which trash can he had placed the debris from the table. We followed him into the kitchen and waited while he talked to the kitchen personnel. When he returned, I could see from his facial expression that lousy news was heading our way.

"I'm sorry, but they carried that trash can to the dumpster."

I felt the growing hole in my pocket through which my allowance would fall for the next twenty years, but Dad, the eternal optimist, said, "If they just emptied that can, then it must be right on top of the restaurant garbage." *Was he serious? Were we going to sort through the garbage ... in an Italian restaurant?*

The employee led us out the back door and pointed to the dumpster. With no hesitation, Dad said, "OK, I'll lift you," and into the dumpster I went. At this point, my memory fails me, the result of a pasta/tomato sauce overdose. I have no idea how long I was in there. The flashlight was useless as all was now the same color, and my sense of touch was my only tool. My sense of smell has always been sub-par, and I attribute this to that olfactory tornado that night. I realize no one would ever do this today, but this was a different time, and we were not the Vanderbilts. Feeling each napkin, I eventually grabbed one, which revealed the object of our search. My joy in recovering the retainer temporarily took my mind off how gross I felt. Climbing out of the dumpster, Dad's laughter told me all I needed to know about my appearance. I looked like the victim of an 80-mph head-on collision.

The walk back to the car was long as each step made me increasingly aware that I was now the world's largest meatball. There was no way Dad would let me crawl into the car looking and smelling like this. He always kept an emergency raincoat in the car, which I had worn twice before when our beagle had unloaded her breakfast on me at the start of a family road trip. Fortunately, no police officer drove by as I stripped beside our car and donned the coat. I had quickly gone from being an upstanding youth to a potential flasher in downtown Baltimore, but it was great getting rid of the "spaghetti outfit." I didn't realize I still reeked of spaghetti sauce until Mom met us at the door. She might have been relieved that the retainer had been located, but I only remember her screaming to me to head immediately to the shower without touching anything.

Amazingly, I still like Italian food, although I must admit, I wasn't eager for an Italian meal the following evening. The spaghetti odor overload dulled my senses, but the rest of the world could locate me by smell for quite a while. Swimming in spaghetti must be the equivalent of being sprayed by a skunk. No bath could possibly get rid of the scent. At least with skunk spray, tomato juice is supposed to lessen the odor. More than a couple of people noticed the smell in school the next day. "What happened, Radcliffe? Did you take a spaghetti bath?" Actually … yes! Two nights later, my parents had to attend a social function. Mom told me she had left dinner on the kitchen table; would I fix it for the four of us? Hungry, I ran down to the kitchen, and there it was … a large can of Franco-American spaghetti.

CHRISTMAS MAGIC

It was Christmas morning in the Radcliffe household. Gussie was the first to awake, quickly getting her siblings to join her as they charged into their parents' bedroom. Mom moaned, pulling the covers over her head while Dad gazed at the clock … 5:15 a.m. The children climbed onto the bed, causing Mom to hide under the covers. Dad's comment about how another hour of sleep would be an excellent idea was not heard amid the shrieks of the children, and he soon rolled out of bed. No one was going back to sleep. He had to add the dreaded question, "I wonder if Santa Claus has come yet?" After all, it was still dark. Gussie's engines were fully revved, and there was no stopping her. Once she shifted into gear, she would be downstairs before anyone else took the first step. The problem was that Mom and Dad had only been in bed for five minutes.

Life can often seem out of control; it certainly is unpredictable. Traditions and routines provide the stability needed in our lives. Although our family was shaken by the medical issues of my two sisters, Mom's bouts of depression, and ultimately unexpected deaths, traditions kept us grounded. The holiday season brought us back to Earth; no matter how wacky the year had become, holiday traditions allowed us to find that normalcy again and reflect on all that had transpired the previous year. For us, it was also magical as the patriarch of our family was Father Christmas, also known as George L. Radcliffe, my grandfather.

My paternal grandfather was deeply rooted in history and tradition and a student of Christmas, possessing one of the country's largest private collections of Christmas books. He studied Christmas as an academic subject and could elaborate for hours on the different holiday customs in other countries and throughout history. He made sure that our family had deeply rooted holiday routines. For him, growing up on the Eastern Shore, the whole year revolved around Christmas, with preparations for his holiday beginning on December 26th. The entire Spocott community was involved in raising the game for the feast, the extensive baking, making the elaborate decorations, hand-making their Christmas cards, and researching the history and traditions of the holiday. As a child, he even grew popcorn to string his tree. It became my grandfather's passion, and he involved succeeding generations in the elaborate traditions.

My father was the assistant to Father Christmas and had been well trained in the Christmas traditions and routines. Christmas was the ultimate marathon for him, and he orchestrated forty-eight hours that would surpass any child's dreams. While other children may have gotten more presents, we were the beneficiaries of Mom and Dad's tireless efforts, creating as magical a holiday as any child could wish. My grandfather insisted we have an Eastern Shore Christmas, but we lived in Baltimore. No problem ... he simply moved the Eastern Shore to Baltimore for the day.

The nonstop excitement began early Christmas Eve as the Eastern Shore came to our house. Spocott farmer and honorary family member Hamp Asplen arrived with a truck loaded with ... the Eastern Shore—cedar trees, holly, pine, and bayberry, oysters, pies, and mistletoe, all from the family Spocott property near Cambridge. Instantaneously, our house became an olfactory buffet.

Tradition dictated we put up the tree but not decorate it. Santa Claus did that job. Not only did the old guy have to visit every house on the planet, but he had to trim all those trees. I was always solving math problems, and at a young age, I worried that the jolly old elf might find it challenging to complete all that decorating. Sitting down with a pad and pencil, I calculated the time he would need to trim every tree. If he worked quickly, he could decorate twelve trees an hour, but this would net him less than 300 in twenty-four hours. Baltimore alone had over 100,000 households. Santa seemed to be defying the reality that math dictated. Mom was wonderful in relaying details of the Santa routine, but she wasn't prepared to enter a mathematical discussion of his evening. She managed to distract me from this intellectual pursuit but would have to reveal the truth the following year. What a joy to finally figure out that my parents did all the work because then I, the oldest, could help once my younger siblings had settled in.

The aroma of the greens in the house is so much a part of my Christmas memories. The bayberry was less impressive than the holly until the warmth of the home opened the plant's pores, making it the main olfactory attraction. Bayberry was an essential part of Christmas for my grandfather as he always made Christmas candles and soap out of the waxy coating of the berries. Or so he claims. One Christmas, he and I gathered a mountain of berries, which, after being boiled in water, produced enough wax to make a candle that would have been appropriate for a birthday cake. We both decided that this was just perfect.

Christmas Eve excitement gained momentum with the traditional lunch out. Getting four young children to a restaurant was no easy task, but this event started the Christmas countdown. Money was an issue, but finances were not going to cause any change in routine. The Oriole Cafeteria on York Road provided an economical option and suited a group of kids with no patience. We turned on Christmas music as soon as we arrived home, and Dad began putting up Christmas decorations all over the house. Nothing would go up before Christmas Eve, even though my parents could have used the extra time that day. We helped, oohing and aahing as we unwrapped each angel, snowman, and reindeer. My mother disappeared into her room, a common occurrence anyway, but this day, I suspect it was to finish wrapping presents. Since Santa brought us all our gifts, this must happen in secrecy.

The music was a large part of the season. Unlike today, when Christmas shows and sales begin in July, no Christmas music was played in our house until Christmas Eve. There was no gradual build-up that left one half bored by the time Christmas finally arrived. At our home, it exploded out of nothing twenty-four hours in advance. The Christmas carols were so welcome, as we had not heard them for 364 days. No modern Christmas songs were played in our house. The only exceptions were Nat King Cole singing "The Christmas Song" and Irving Berlin's "White Christmas," my father's sentimental favorite.

The next part of the Christmas Eve ritual involved my grandfather's chauffeur, Swain Foxwell. He was the next "Santa Claus" to show up. As colorful a figure as I ever knew, Swain, a semi-educated waterman, had chauffeured my grandfather for years, and their relationship had developed into a beautiful friendship. Slaughtering the King's English with every sentence, his grin spoke volumes and he was family to all. He came by to exchange presents during the afternoon, my father doing the purchasing, unknown to us. I was always amazed that Swain knew what we wanted. As he left, we gathered around a TV to watch Dickens' *A Christmas Carol* with Alistair Sim. While most of us didn't have the attention span for the visits of the three ghosts, it was the joyous Christmas Day finale we waited for.

Next came the day's highlight: the arrival of Santa Claus in Baltimore. My mother's college, Notre Dame of Maryland, held a special Christmas event involving a couple of carols followed by the arrival of the Big Man himself. The anticipation of Santa running down the auditorium aisle drove us into a frenzy. Every child stood and stretched to get a first look at him as he appeared in the back. I always left the building worrying that this little side trip might put a severe crimp in his schedule, the result being that I could never be 100% sure he would make it to our house. I suggested canceling the event to increase the probability that he would make all his rounds, but once he started bounding down the aisle, all worry dissipated quickly.

The next big event was that evening as the entire neighborhood gathered for a party and caroling. We lived on a small one-way street lined with row houses, and every family on the street made it to the party. The snacks passed as our dinner, but we were all too excited to eat. When the time came for caroling, all assembled in the street and lit candles. Humorously, with the whole neighborhood doing the caroling, no one was left to sing to, just the infants with their sitters and the few seniors on the street. This never seemed to matter. Reflecting, I realize how unusual it was to see an entire neighborhood interacting. It was the only time we all got together, and no one was ever missing. The carols just pushed the excitement of the children to a different level. My little sister Kim could never accompany us, and it was always fun singing for her.

Upon returning home, it was time to hang stockings and put out the milk and cookies for Santa. I remember thinking that the Big Guy must be tired of milk after a million or more houses. And after several billion cookies, it was no wonder he was a candidate for a fat farm. My efforts to provide a substitute were voted down; tradition ruled. Truth be told, if we left Santa an alternate snack, I could have eaten the cookies.

This officially ended an incredible day. I am astounded now to reflect on how much had been crammed into a day. My father's plan was genius: keep us so busy that we wouldn't drive him crazy with questions and worry. However, one aspect of his plan failed; he hoped we would be so tired that we would fall asleep because his work could not begin until four children began sawing wood.

Then came the only dreaded part of the day: a bath. But since

Santa avoided houses with dirty children, I quickly succumbed. Getting in bed was a far cry from going to sleep. And if falling asleep with your eyes wide open wasn't hard enough, I had to listen for Santa's sleigh. Being on the top floor of a row house, I figured I was in the best position to hear. Straining to hear while I lay in bed, I was unaware that my father made countless trips to the attic and back, carrying mountains of boxes down the steps. His night was always long, assembling the presents and decorating a tree. As I lay awake, every creak of the house suddenly became the reindeer's hooves, and every time a throat was cleared downstairs, that jolly elf had to be doing his thing. How I ever fell asleep those nights still boggles the mind, but exhaustion ultimately won out.

The following morning, all raced down to my parents' room, but getting them to move quickly was difficult. Of course, we didn't realize that their Santa Claus routine meant they had just gotten in bed. We couldn't go downstairs until Mom was up, but Gussie sped this process up by throwing off the covers and physically dragging her mother out of bed. Dad had to prolong the suspense by seeing if Santa had come. Those were the longest few seconds as all mulled over the possibility that the Big Guy had not made it. I'm convinced Dad intentionally stalled to torment his kids. Finally, he would call us down, but Gussie was downstairs before he got halfway through his sentence. Turning the corner into the living room took my breath away. A few hours earlier, the room had been bare, with a naked tree sitting in the corner. Now, it was a wonderland of lights, presents, candles, decorations, and a tree glistening with lights, ornaments, and tinsel. I sat in awe; Bill and Gussie attacked.

More paper and debris wouldn't have flown around if someone had set off a bomb. Gussie had all her presents opened before I opened my first. Being the oldest, I had to be cool and proceed slowly. I relished having a pile of presents left while the others were done. There were the ritual dud presents: underwear, socks, and some piece of clothing that my mother alone wanted us to wear. "George, you'll look so handsome in that yellow sweater."

"But, Mom, it won't stay yellow after the next neighborhood football game."

But Santa was good to us. Finally came opening the stocking, all too predictable. I could imagine my mother getting to Christmas Eve and suddenly realizing that there were no gifts small enough to go in the stocking. Out came the old standbys: oranges, apples, soap, toothpaste, toothbrush, more underwear, and a small package of tissue. To her credit, she wrapped each item; after all, ripping open the paper was half the fun. My father always built a fire, trying to burn the paper as fast as we opened it. My mother salvaged whatever paper she could to reuse the following year. This proved to be her downfall as one Christmas, I noticed old tags, including a couple that read "To Mom from ...." She tried to explain how Santa somehow retrieved our paper from the year before, but the more she tried to explain, the worse the story got.

Next came giving our presents, usually something we had made in school or purchased at the local drugstore for ten cents. My parents always said this was the most wonderful gift they had ever received, but we knew better. Mom would say my drawing was the most precious present ever, followed by the obvious question, "What is it?" Still, we were excited to be on the giving end, if even in a small way. Then we dove into playing with our toys, awaiting the arrival of Father Christmas. He and my grandmother would arrive late in the morning, and my poor father, already severely sleep-deprived, worked overtime again. Since neither of my grandparents drove, my father became a chauffeur. He had to make multiple trips up and down a flight of forty-five steps, escorting them and carrying bags of presents. Always with a smile, he pulled off the significant logistical move.

These grandparents' presents were always unique. As if we hadn't been spoiled enough, they would go way overboard: bicycles, wagons, and a fire engine one could peddle. No clothes here. My grandmother became my Christmas hero, starting a bear tradition with me. Each year, she would give me a teddy bear larger than the one the year before. The practice had to end at age seven when I received a bear considerably taller than I was, and I was tall for my age. Being a remarkably creative child, I named it "Big Bear." And everything was wrapped, from Big Bear to a bicycle. How in the world does one wrap a bike? The bear tradition had to end as an even larger bear would not have fit through the doorway to the house. My grandfather would always give us a nice check, which was initially disappointing to a young child. We would immediately pass it over to my father to deposit in our savings account, a challenging concept for a young child to grasp. But knowing this, my grandfather would always present us with a crisp ten-dollar bill. The money was always spent by December 26th.

Next came the large family party with all four grandparents, aunts, uncles, and cousins. Confusion quickly turned to chaos. The laughter and merriment, fueled heavily by my Uncle Teddy's delightfully inappropriate jokes, made for a lively meal. The menu was always the same: turkey, mashed potatoes, beans, sauerkraut that almost no one ate, and pie for dessert. In later years, my mother hired someone to help with the cooking, which was hardly her forte, but in those early years, with my father's help, she managed to pull it off. I figured this was why her cooking was so bad—she needed 364 days to rest.

As the day flew by, I saw my parents fading. Mom retreated to the bedroom after dinner, and Dad made a valiant effort to keep up with us. Each Christmas ended with the best tradition for a child. There was no bedtime; we could stay up all night. Dad knew we'd eventually crash, with the adrenalin rush of the last two days finally taking its toll. We tackled the night with the most elaborate scheme for an all-nighter but inevitably crashed well before midnight. Dad would stroll in to remove the assembled bodies from the living room floor and carry us to our beds.

One Christmas, that excellent plan went to Hades. Unannounced, two of my parents' close friends arrived with all twelve children. Yes, that's not a typo—TWELVE. My parents, dreaming of impending sleep, somehow rallied and invited them in. Sixteen hyper children, with parents too tired to intervene, dismantled the house quickly. The four of us could trash a home in an hour, but sixteen children in three hours could cause complete and total devastation. With a baseball game in the second-floor hallway, tag team wrestling in the basement, and objects raining down the staircase, the situation was ripe for disaster. I remember we were generally well-behaved, but adrenalin and the sheer numbers created havoc. My mother bravely offered everyone dinner, and out came peanut butter, jelly, and several loaves of bread. As I went upstairs later that night, I remember seeing one PB&J sandwich ground into the Oriental rug and another stuck to the wall on the stairway. It would take my father the next two days to salvage the house.

Each Christmas had its unique moments: the year we all vomited our way through the whole two days, the Christmas Eve my parents locked all the presents in a closet only to realize they had no key, or the one where frozen pipes flooded our entire basement with a foot of water. However, none of these catastrophes touched the magic of the season. Christmas became the event that marked the passing of another year. Regardless of what was transpiring each year, Christmas was the constant. As the lives of the children evolved, Christmas remained the same, and it was so comforting to have something stay unchanged. I'll remember forever a little gift my brother made for my parents. He made a tiny sleigh led by eight reindeer, each constructed from a peanut and pipe cleaners. That silly sleigh would be placed in a prominent spot on the mantle each year. Even after my brothers' death, the peanut reindeer appeared yearly until decomposition finally claimed them several years ago. Life constantly changes, as it must, but Christmas traditions persist. Christmas becomes the rock we retreat to each year to see that nothing significant has changed.

Reflecting on these special days, I realize what my parents endured to provide us with such magnificent holidays. These days were absolute jewels, carefully planned and orchestrated. Our military forces should have been so well organized. Even when my mother began suffering from depression, she would always rise to the occasion for the Christmas marathon. The bar was set high for me when it came time for Jackie and me to orchestrate our version of Christmas, but we paled in comparison. Our Santa could not even decorate a tree; the family did this. Our boys had some of the same Christmas experiences, but equaling with my father's epic production would have been difficult.

What is sad is knowing so many didn't have the same experiences as I did. Today, the emphasis is on gifts, but for us, the memories were the real gift. Traditions were necessary; they gave us something to look forward to. And the countdown to Christmas began the day before, not months ahead. This was before the excessive commercialization, with Christmas appearing in stores three months in advance and Christmas specials in July. Everything was about family and friends.

We were less than a generation removed from World War II, and both my father and uncle shared Christmas experiences from that war. The combination of fear and loneliness in a wartime situation is something most of us can't imagine. My father recounted a moment while stationed on Kwajalein Island in the South Pacific. While the troops made every effort possible to create a Christmas spirit, the unspoken sadness of separation pervaded all. He was in a rec hall when "White Christmas" started playing. He said there was not a dry eye anywhere. "Dreaming" was sadly all that one could do under those circumstances. Dad played that song repeatedly for us and ensured we understood the significance.

Christmas takes on a different meaning as family members pass on; for many, it becomes cloaked in a veil of sadness as deceased loved ones are remembered. With my original family all departed now, Christmas Day is always a rush of memories but not sadness for me. I'll see Gussie ripping open her presents, Bill giggling as he plays with a new toy, Kim racing around the room while Mom tries to catch her, and both she and Dad directing the magical show. And, of course, Father Christmas will be overseeing the whole event, smiling as he sees his traditions living on in successive generations. If you see a tear rolling down my cheek that day, it won't be sadness you see, just warm memories enveloping me as I keep all alive in me. On Christmas, we all become a child again; it is a cleansing event as we rejuvenate and reconnect.

And I did hear Santa and his reindeer on the roof that night many years ago.

Yes, There Really Are Angels

I grabbed my suitcase, throwing in a change of clothes, a good book, and, of course, as many teddy bears as the suitcase would hold. Descending from my room on the third floor, I quietly opened the front door and began the five-block trek. I was running away from home again. My parents were not worried; they knew exactly where I was headed.

I am a skeptic and need concrete evidence before I believe something. The purported eyewitness stories won't convince me that ghosts haunt houses or aliens are visiting Earth; please show me the physical proof. Tell me the latest rumor, and I'll ignore it. Want the latest gossip; sorry, not here. Religion and I have rarely seen eye-to-eye. How wonderful it would be if there were a heaven, but I'll create my heaven on earth, thank you! But there are angels; I knew one—a genuine guardian angel. Everyone should have one, and I'm not sure I would have survived childhood without her.

Augusta Heiskell Boggs was my maternal grandmother, small in stature but enormous in importance. She married William Aloysius Boggs, and they had four remarkable daughters. "Ma," as I called her, ran from attention. Years later, we had difficulty finding photos of her as she either hid from the camera or stood behind much taller subjects. I was her oldest grandchild, and her home was my refuge. Many weekends, I packed a suitcase and walked down to her house for relief from the stress of my life.

Adults always feel they need to advise a child, but Ma knew that was not her role. She listened, never commenting or passing judgment. She comforted and let one know they mattered through her actions, not words. I might have had a stressful week of school and home life, but after a weekend at this safe house, I was calm and ready to face another week. Some weekends, there would be limited talking, just those simple, reassuring smiles and hugs. And if I had to vent, she would listen patiently, letting me do all the talking, changing the subject when she felt my venting was no longer productive.

This was never more obvious than when she was with either of my sisters. Kim, of course, never could talk and was prone to epic temper tantrums. Ma patiently waited for the storm to pass and Kim to climb back into her arms. When Gussie hit her teens and was drowning in physical and psychological problems, Ma was always there. Gussie would be lashing out at the world, and Ma would listen patiently with a smile. Consequently, at Ma's house, Gussie found a degree of peace. She was a different person there. It wasn't that my parents weren't patient; Dad had his work, and fireworks would often fly when the four of us were thrown together. Gussie could evoke a reaction from even the calmest individuals, but I never saw Ma lose her temper. Her understanding of Gussie may have been partly due to having a mentally ill mother herself, but it was also not her nature to judge. She made every one of her eighteen grandchildren feel important.

Ma was also the empress of my bear world. She introduced me to and frequently read *Winnie the Pooh* and similar stories. Years later, in school, she rescued me by finding me *Winnie Ille Pooh* when my Latin teacher assigned us the task of reading and reporting on a book written in Latin. My parents tolerated my obsession with bears, but Ma encouraged it, often becoming a willing participant. Fuzzie and the others were royalty in her home, accorded a place at the dinner table, and always included in bedtime stories.

I learned so many practical skills in that home. Ma taught Gussie and me how to cook. My mother was not a memorable cook, at least not for the right reason. Birthday cakes were always store-bought, and Christmas cookies were only present if someone gave us some. One December, my sister and I trekked to her house to learn how to bake cookies. We baked all day and returned home with our first-ever Christmas cookies, although we had remarkably little to show for all our efforts. Instead, we had stomach aches of monumental proportions.

I have one potent memory of her, as vivid as the day it occurred. While I was certainly happy at home, I would not use the word peaceful to describe it. I remember one evening at her house when I was worried about something, although the subject escapes me now. I was in a small room, drifting in and out of sleep, fitful at best. An oscillating fan was on, and Ma was sitting quietly in the corner, waiting patiently for me to fall asleep. I was always aware of her presence as I drifted in and out. She never moved or said a word as she waited with the patience of Job. Whatever I was fighting with internally would drift away whenever I realized she was still sitting in the room. To this day, the sound of an electric fan is the most soothing in the world, and I vividly remember the peace I felt that night in the room. That memory is indelibly carved into my memories; I can see, hear, and feel it now. Ma became a rock in my life, a safe place to retreat as I battled the awkward growing-up process.

I often find it interesting that I loved to play ball and roughhouse with the best of them at my house, but when at her house, I was content with a much greater range of activities. Unlike at home, I was allowed to explore and play in the kitchen. Here, I discovered the joyous mess of mixing baking soda and vinegar, created unimaginable concoctions, and occasionally made something edible. Her breakfasts were epic, although her four girls remember her as an average cook. She did have an absent-minded streak, and the day she left home with six eggs boiling on the stove was classic. The house, fortunately, didn't burn down, but a complete fumigation was required.

I was allowed to play with her sewing machine and once made a suit out of … newspaper. Not surprisingly, I did not choose the fashion industry as a career. She would read all day to us if we wanted, and the house was loaded with books of every description. I never remember being bored; she was always quietly in the background, supporting whatever we did. I don't remember her scolding me or getting upset, but somehow, I always knew my limits. And on nice days, there was a wonderful yard and neighborhood to explore.

She had a remarkable sense of humor but never told a joke. Her humor was subtle, often aimed at herself; she was not one to take herself too seriously. Toward the end of her life, when several thought she might be failing mentally, she was still sharp. One evening, after dinner with us, she was getting ready to drive home. My father insisted he drive her, and we would return her car to her the next day. She stubbornly refused and left. Mom was angry that Dad had given in and worried that her mother might have an accident on the way home, especially since it was an unusually dark night. They insisted she call once she got home, a five-minute drive.

Twenty minutes passed, and Dad was about to head to her house to check on her. The phone rang, and he answered, "Hello."

He heard a deep voice on the other end of the line. "This is Sgt. Schwartz at the 41st Street police station. Do you know an Augusta Boggs?"

Starting to panic, Dad said, "Yes, that's my mother-in-law. Is she all right?"

"Yes, sir, she's fine, but somebody may want to come get her. She drove down a sidewalk, toppling bushes, and finally knocked over a mailbox."

"I'll come get her. Where is she again?"

"Sir, I'll warn you that she's confused and disoriented."

Before Dad could respond, laughter broke out on the other end. Changing her voice back to normal, Ma said, "So you all thought I couldn't make it home, and ... thanks for a wonderful dinner." A first-class lawyer, Dad was not one to be taken in easily by a joke, but that soft-spoken woman certainly took him out that night.

It has been over forty years since Ma died. At the time, I was so busy raising three young children that I did not have enough time to reflect on her passing and impact on my life. As the years have passed, I miss her more, not less. It seems like it shouldn't be that way, but she is so much a part of who I am. That small, quiet woman with the gray hair saved me in many ways.

To this day, I can honestly say that I never encountered another person like her. My memories don't match what her children remembered; it's much easier to be a grandparent than a parent. For starters, it's a part-time job. The support that she gave Gussie and me was so desperately needed. While I feel the need to provide advice for some ridiculous reason, I learned from her that support was far more critical. I don't think I ever told her how critically important she was to me, and I will always regret that. She probably knew it to some extent anyway; she was that wise. She was the master of selfless, unconditional love. I know I was important to her, and I'm sure the time I spent with her was also essential to her. But her impact on my life was beyond measure.

People always talk of the carefree days of childhood when one is unencumbered by the responsibilities of adult life. Yes, there are lovely, carefree moments, but growing up is hard work and stressful: learning, adapting, and finding one's place in the world. As adults, we sometimes forget how difficult childhood can be; some days, it is as much survival as enjoyment. The role of a grandparent is sometimes underestimated; we all need additional adult guidance, especially the wisdom that comes with age. Many grandparents today have a more limited role because families are more mobile. Grandparents often live far away, or the family's schedule makes little time for them. What a loss. Years ago, grandparents were a critical part of the nuclear family. A child needs multiple adult viewpoints because their parents only present one way to approach the world. If one is a Christmas tree, one's parents fashion the trunk and branches, but grandparents put on many of the ornaments. Ma not only added many ornaments but also stabilized a somewhat shaky tree. I was one of the lucky ones, living within five blocks of all my grandparents. I learned from all of them, but Ma was so much more than that. She was my angel, watching over and supporting my every mood. I never saw her wings, but I know she had them.

NOVEMBER 22, 1963

Every generation has days that are indelibly inscribed in their memories, events that change the way we view the world. For my parents, it was December 7, 1941, the attack on Pearl Harbor; for my children, it was likely September 11, 2001, the attacks on the Pentagon and World Trade Center. For me and many of my generation, that day was November 22, 1963, when President Kennedy was assassinated. Everything changed that day: my view of the world and the innocence with which I viewed life.

I was in sixth grade in 1960 when Kennedy was elected President over Vice President Richard Nixon. I came from a very Democratic family, and even with a minimal understanding of the politics involved, it was easy to be a Kennedy supporter. I did not understand the details of the issues, but I liked Kennedy because he was young and a dynamic speaker; Nixon always seemed tired and frequently angry. With a grandfather who had been a United States senator and a close friend of two US presidents, politics should have been in my blood. My father was even asked at one point to run for mayor of Baltimore, but as a shy kid with a minor stuttering issue at that point, a political career was never in my plans. However, the two of them took seriously to the campaign, and I was soon loading up on posters, brochures, bumper stickers, and campaign buttons, most of which I still have today.

Only two in my class supported Kennedy over Nixon, marking the first time I showed any interest in politics. I watched all the presidential debates, televised for the first time. Kennedy was a fresh face in Washington, young for the position at age forty-three. He had a charming wife and two children. His family was like our families. The election was projected as a toss-up, and I was determined to watch the election results. My mother had purchased a tiny television (an impressive nine-inch screen) that could be moved from room to room, and nobody noticed when I carried that set up to the third floor on election night. I was allowed to watch results in my parents' room, staying up past my regular 9 p.m. bedtime. By 10 p.m., nothing had been resolved, and I headed up to my room.

Turning on the small set with the volume turned down, I continued to watch. If anyone had come up to check on me, I had time to turn off and hide the set once they started up the stairs. I was adding up the electoral votes as the evening progressed, and after midnight, things looked bleak as many of the Republican states were reporting. My parents' door opened once, and I had to turn the set off until I heard their door close again—likely Mom going down for a bowl of ice cream or one of her tasteless diet sodas. The next thing I knew, I was waking up. Looking at my clock, I saw that it was 5 a.m. The television was still on, and I soon heard that the race was still undecided. That seemed good news, as Nixon had a lead when I dozed. Tired from minimal sleep, I continued watching. California soon went for Kennedy, and those electoral votes gave him the presidency.

When I went for breakfast, I pretended to be ignorant of the results and looked surprised when Dad announced the news. Even though I suffered from only a few hours of sleep, the positive results gave me the energy to get through a school day. I wore my most prominent "Kennedy/Johnson" button that day. My friends would have been obnoxiously gloating if Nixon had one, but the other Kennedy supporter and I kept our cool. The election results said it all.

I watched his inauguration from my grandmother's house because snow had canceled school that day. We watched Kennedy, without a hat, brave the cold and utter those unforgettable words, "And so, my fellow Americans: ask not what your country can do for you—ask what you can do for your country." It was a glorious day.

With World War II well in the rearview mirror, the Korean War over, and economic prosperity taking hold, Kennedy's initial years as President were deemed "Camelot," a time of innocence against the backdrop of the Cold War. Several blunders, including the Bay of Pigs, tarnished his armor, but it was an excellent time to follow the news and politics. Many opposed Kennedy because he was Catholic. I had partially rejected my Catholic roots, but I still found this surprising, a testament to my naïve nature. I was aware of antisemitism and racist views, but I had never realized how widespread hatred could be.

I was in ninth grade on that fateful November day in 1963. I was daydreaming in study hall when another student turned around and asked if I had heard that Kennedy had been shot. I remember being stunned and then furious as some students joked about how we would finally be rid of him. I'm sure they regretted those comments before the day was over. Gilman was an all-male school, and I doubt that would have happened in a coeducational institution. The teacher interrupted work a few minutes later to confirm the news and tell us that Kennedy was dead. As with so many traumatic moments, it took a while for the info to sink in. I remember students immediately beginning to speculate on who had done it. If this had happened today, school would have been dismissed. But in 1963, the school day continued,

Ironically, this Friday was the day of the big football game with our arch-rival, McDonough. And in a decision I'm sure later regretted, officials of both schools decided to go ahead with the game. That led to one of my life's most bizarre and eerie experiences. What usually would have been a thrilling afternoon became just a blur. I doubt that anyone who attended the game can remember who won. The stadium was hushed, with most conversation about the assassination. Since none of us had seen any news, most of the discussion was hearsay. The dominant talk centered on how something like this could have happened. We knew assassinations had happened historically, most notably Lincoln's, but this was happening now. I remember one team scoring a touchdown and hearing a handful of fans cheer, but most of us were oblivious since we didn't even know who had the ball. Sports are essential to a fourteen-year-old kid, but not that day.

Upon arriving home, we discovered that all the TV networks were running continuous coverage with no commercials. Our whole family sat in front of the TV and followed every lead and story. Lee Harvey Oswald, the assassin, had been traced to a movie theatre in Dallas and been shot, but no one could understand why he had fired the bullet. Oswald's Cuban and Russian connection fueled speculation, but the act still seemed inconceivable. All plans for the weekend were canceled. Saturday began with breakfast in front of the TV, a first for our family. There had never been this kind of TV coverage of an event. Unlike today, when all-day news covers everything in excruciating detail, there was usually minimal coverage of events. With limited satellites, rarely was anything covered in real-time. With no computers and little live TV, this was the first time we had been thrust into the middle of a news story. The entire country became engrossed in the events: the assassin, the reaction of citizens, and speculation on motives. It was a surreal day; usually, I would have been outside playing football in late November, but no one moved from the TV that day.

Sunday morning, it was time for church. We didn't want to go, but Mom was insistent. Missing church was never an option for her. That morning, the officials planned on moving Oswald, and we didn't want to miss any coverage. As we left the service, someone ran up with the news that nightclub owner Jack Ruby had shot Oswald, and millions had watched this on TV. We raced home to resume our weekend in front of the TV. My father, the non-Catholic then, had seen the whole thing.

By lunchtime Sunday, Kennedy's casket had been put in the Capitol Rotunda for viewing, and people were lining up by the thousands to file by and view it. Since we were only an hour away, I talked my father into taking the family to DC to view the casket. We got to Washington about 2 p.m. and realized that the line was blocks long. After finally finding where the line ended and getting a parking place, we joined the queue. The line moved slowly, and as kids, we were somewhat impatient. However, there was no discussion of abandoning our place in line. It was a moving experience. A shared understanding and emotions joined thousands of strangers, everyone sharing their feelings, speculations, and experiences. People cried and shared memories with strangers. We felt a bond with all around us, no matter how different they were. The line moved ever so slowly, and we never seemed to be getting any closer to the Capitol.

The temperature plummeted as the sun dropped below the buildings, and the late fall wind picked up, funneling between the buildings. None had come adequately dressed, expecting to be in and out in the afternoon. People huddled together, shared coats, and clustered in doorways when one was passed. Darkness fell, and this was probably the coldest I had ever been up to that point in my life. As we passed six and seven o'clock, hunger added to the discomfort. Finally, we approached the Capitol and slowly filed up the steps. I was cold and tired and barely remembered passing the casket in the Rotunda. We'd been in line for over six hours, an afternoon I will never forget. Few words were spoken in the car ride home as we reflected on what we had just been through—one of the rare moments Gussie was speechless. We were moved and changed forever.

The next day, all schools were closed for the State funeral, a fourth day in front of the TV. The casket was pulled through the streets of

Washington by horses, and Kennedy was buried in Arlington Cemetery. There was no dry eye in the country as Kennedy's young son, John Jr., saluted his father's casket as it passed. Those four emotionally draining days changed the country forever. It was a defining moment in growing up, separating the uncomplicated and uninvolved period of childhood from adulthood. From then on, being an uninformed child was not acceptable. The world was more complex than we had thought, and evil was out there. The Oz of my childhood crumbled more that weekend than at any other time. It was the end of an age of innocence for me. I had never met Kennedy or understood his policies until now, but we had lost a leader and friend. All who remember that day carry a scar.

So much has happened since that November day, and this country has never regained its innocence. It never will, but it is a resilient country now as it was then. Undoubtedly, there will be more tragedies in the future, but it is still possible to be optimistic. Tragedy unravels many countries, but ironically, it seems to strengthen ours. For one brief period sixty years ago, Camelot existed. One bullet brought it all down.

SABOTAGE

It was fourth-period class, and I had just returned from lunch. I felt slightly nauseous, but my thoughts were on the impending history quiz; I was paying little attention to my classmates. The final bell rang, and I looked up. Mr. Stigman was absent, which was unusual, and only a handful of students were in the class. Little did I know that the rest of the school day would be one wild ride.

In the mid-1960s, I was fighting my way through high school. The school had lost its excitement for me, and any diversion improved the usually dull days. The school was an excellent preparatory school, and I was comfortable there, although shyness and stuttering made me a less-than-exciting classmate. I don't remember what year it was, but I remember the month—November. It was a Friday, with the usual weekly football game later that day, and talk of the game against a rival school provided the buzz throughout the morning. As on most days, I just dreamed about lunch; I was a typical young teen.

Lunch at school in those days was an adventure. We were served a hot meal each day; at least, it must have been hot at some point in the preparation. We all sat at long tables with a teacher at the head of the table. The teachers would rotate weekly, and we always looked forward to the "fun" teachers finally making it to our table. Students rotated as waiters, bringing platters of food to the table. This trumped the PB&J sandwich my mother had always packed in elementary school, but if the meals were often less than desirable, they were memorable. The usual stories circulated about a cook's finger being cut off, slicing hot dogs for the franks and beans, or a student finding the glass from a light bulb in the chocolate pudding. Someone swore they found a band-aid in a baked potato, and we believed it. Youth equals gullible.

The students in every school serving meals must have their collection of school meal horrors. Things have improved considerably since then, but it was often difficult to know what we were eating, not that hungry teenagers cared. Occasionally, we would be served what we called "mystery meat;" there was a rumor that these were veal cutlets, but the jury is still out. They were often well-cooked, and I remember a friend snapping a metal knife in half trying to cut one. The fried chicken was also a "favorite," although we decided chickens couldn't be that small. A sparrow seemed a more likely source: one bite of a drumstick, and one would have to wait for seconds. The cooking staff was also creative with leftovers, as a previous entrée would often reappear later in the week in a different form. Jell-O was a frequent dessert, and several days later, the Jell-O would reappear fluffed up by repeating blending, increasing its volume by 1000%. The stuff was so light that it would evaporate in our mouths before we could even swallow it. But this day, we had the dreaded creamed ham and noodles and were in for a big surprise.

We left the lunchroom after this gourmet meal and went outside for some exercise. It was only about five minutes before we sensed something was wrong. A friend I was throwing a football with suddenly dropped the ball and sprinted for the building, followed by another person. It was a spectacular fall day, and class would not start for another ten minutes. Why were people going inside? Soon after, several more ran in. Was there something great inside that I was missing? My stomach soon answered the question. Nausea began to build, and I suddenly lost interest in football. I went inside, and there was a line by the bathroom. This was highly unusual, but the sounds emanating from the bathroom indicated what activity was occurring there. For me, vomiting was not imminent, so I waited.

The bell rang for the next class, and I grabbed my books and headed upstairs for class. Upon entering the room, I got out my notes and reviewed them for the upcoming quiz. The second bell rang, signaling the beginning of class, and many of the students and the teacher were missing. Students staggered in one by one, looking as bad as I'm sure they felt. Suddenly, the day's hot topic was not the upcoming football game. We were in one of the better classes, Mr. Stigman's history class. He may not have been the best teacher but was beloved, infusing humor into his lectures. But he was nowhere to be seen.

Suddenly, the two hot topics of the day merged into one. It was clear at this point that the food was suspect, the dreaded ham and noodles being the consensus culprit. But this was no accident; we had been POISONED! Obviously, the rival school we would play later that day had orchestrated the poisoning, desperately trying to throw the upcoming game in their favor. Intense nausea pushed us to that conclusion in a matter of minutes. It seemed logical to the teenage mind since we knew we had a much better football team. Speculation quickly became outrage, as several more students had to exit the room quickly. Still no Mr. Stigman.

Finally, Mr. Stigman entered the room, explaining how difficult it had been to find a vacant toilet. He was making light of the matter but was not his usual color. He organized his notes, picked up a piece of chalk, cleared his throat, and then ... quickly sprinted from the room. My digestive malfunction had escalated several levels, and I decided this was a good time to exit. Walking promptly turned to running as matters deteriorated; my digestive system went to code red as reverse peristalsis was imminent.

I don't know how to deal with this subject diplomatically, so I'll resort to math. There were about 450 students in that building and only twenty toilets. This was not a good day to wait in line. Unless you were one of the precious few to get hold of a toilet or sink, the outdoors was the only other option. If we hadn't felt so bad, this would have been hysterical as outdoor bushes and the nearby woods were quickly fertilized. Students quickly discovered that trash cans were not a good option as one was still stuck with the odiferous contents. To make matters worse, many students were beginning to fire out both ends of their digestive system. Any thought of anyone getting an education that afternoon quickly disintegrated.

There is a point where things get so bad that humor necessarily returns, and by the end of that first class after lunch, we crossed that threshold. Poor Mr. Stigman was never heard from again that day, and I don't even remember if anyone went to the next class. I remember looking through a window and seeing the biology teacher lecturing to the only two students in the classroom. We had already decided he was an alien and would thus have been immune to the poisoning. Ironically, we were studying the digestive system at that point, so that must have been one fun class, complete with graphic demonstrations. Students were milling around between runs to a bathroom or private place of their choosing and discussing how this other school could have pulled off the mass poisoning. Was one of the Gilman cooks in on the conspiracy? Had a parent of one of the rival schools' students worked for the company that supplied the infamous ham? Theories abounded as groups of students came up with competing conspiracy theories. However, there was no question in our minds that the poisoning was intentional.

The vomiting seemed to be a one-time event, but things seemed to be moving to the lower part of the digestive system, creating some embarrassing moments for some students. The nurse had already used up her emergency clothing supply, and these were primarily for the elementary students anyway. It's funny how, years later, I've blocked out all the horror of the day and only remember the humor of the experience. I don't remember much of the rest of the day. I did get to a toilet once, a significant victory, but I had to vacate quickly for the angry mob lined up in the bathroom. My only memory of the football game later that day was that our coach must have used up all his allotted timeouts early as players streamed off the field regularly. I wonder if the other team knew what was happening; if not, they must have been puzzled beyond belief. I assume one of the teams won the game that day, but that fact was forgotten amidst the many comical memories. Mr. Stigman did return the next week and summed it all up in his usual witty style. We always believed that our football team was sabotaged that day; that's the way teens reason such events. I pity the poor custodial staff that day. They had the worst day of all.

That following Thursday, we arrived at lunch, and all talk of the Mass Poisoning Conspiracy had died with no apparent resolution. There was now a new controversy to focus on. It was another typical day until the infamous creamed ham and noodles suddenly appeared on the table again. They always say you should get back on when you fall off a horse, but it was too soon to see this horse again. Each teacher at the head of the table got no takers when they tried to serve the entrée. Mr. Stigman was at our table that week, and when the vomit-to-be appeared, it was the only time I ever heard a teacher use profanity. Every student would have come to his defense if he had gotten in trouble. A couple of students even left the dining room at the sight of it; the memories were still too fresh. But when the fluffed-up Jell-O appeared for dessert, we sent back to the kitchen for seconds and thirds. I wonder if anyone even remembers who won the football game that year. I doubt anyone even cared!

THE SWEATER

Peering off the back of the large boat, I watched the wake roll away from the stern while gulls fished for food scraps thrown overboard. Suddenly, I saw a white sweater flying off the stern, descending to the water below. Turning to see who had just lost a sweater, I noticed everyone staring at me. Why? It wasn't my sweater, but it would significantly alter my life, adding to a downhill spiral I would not recover from for years.

My mother wanted her children to be raised Catholic, as she and her sisters had been, but surprisingly, married a non-Catholic. Dad supported her wishes, and we were all baptized Catholic. I bought into the religion because Mom and the nuns in my parochial school drilled the details into me; I decided hell was not a place I wanted to visit, and I was told being Catholic put one at the front of the line to get into heaven. At first, I was enamored with the stained-glass windows, organ music, and burning incense. By age twelve, church was losing its appeal, and my mother suggested I become an altar boy. It did puzzle me that there seemed to be no place for my sister in Catholicism except as a nun, but I didn't think the religion was ready for that; conformity and Gussie were not well acquainted.

I could have refused, but since I had to go to church anyway, why not get behind the scenes since altar boys had certain privileges and access to the mysterious inner sanctum of the immense cathedral we attended. Memorizing the mass in Latin was a blast, like learning the coded language of a secret society. I can still rattle off "per omnia saecula saeculorum," even though I never knew what it meant—like learning the password and secret handshake for a private club. It was the ultimate behind-the-scenes tour in the world of Catholicism. We might as well have been speaking gibberish. Lighting candles, ringing bells, and assisting with communion got me noticed, and I could stand a little attention. It also beat sitting in a pew, watching the second hand on my watch move slower and slower.

My social life was not exactly filled to the brim at that point. Childhood was fading into the distance, but I was clinging to aspects of it, unprepared to face the world of teens. Hopelessly naïve, life was still a somewhat simplistic journey at that point. My circle of friends was changing dramatically, starting with a move to a different neighborhood four years earlier and now from the changes my new friends were going through, for which I was not yet ready. I enjoyed the sense of belonging as an altar boy, but it was clear that I was not planning to ascend the ladder to become a future pope. I hadn't developed any close friends in this new group, but I still felt a part of it. After all, I knew the secret password!

As a reward for our services, the parish priests organized a day trip to Tolchester Beach, an amusement park across the Bay. I have no idea why I went on the trip since I hardly knew any of the group; likely, Mom accepted for me. I can't recall even one name from that group. Many of the altar boys went to the church school, and an entire older class from the school joined us on the trip. I do remember the priest who was on the excursion with us. He and the other priests at the church had always made me feel welcome, and they were part of why I continued being an altar boy. They were friendly and down to Earth, and my serving allowed me to get to know them all in a non-religious capacity.

What should have been a fun outing took an ugly twist and sabotaged my remaining self-esteem. I remember nothing of the park. Knowing no one, I likely camped out at the food pavilion. However, the trip home was significant. The weather was spectacular that day, and I remember standing at the back of the boat, watching the wake as Tolchester faded in the distance. Years later, I would have been watching for birds, but my natural history genes had not been activated at that point. I was alone, watching the churning water behind the large boat, feeling the breeze on my face, and reflecting on the day. A group of kids came up behind me. They were clowning around, and I remember them teasing one of the girls. If I had been listening more carefully, I might have been aware of what they were plotting. I was looking to the side of the boat with my left arm hanging over the back of the ship. I suddenly felt something touch my forearm, and I jumped. Turning in that direction, I saw a sweater dropping off the stern into the water. A girl was visibly upset, and I correctly assumed the sweater belonged to her. She ran off, I thought, to tell someone she had lost a sweater.

I was soon asked to report to the priest, who seemed upset, asking why I had thrown the girl's sweater off the boat. I was shocked and confused, and it suddenly occurred to me that the sweater had been placed on my arm and then fallen overboard when I jumped. I explained my side of the story to him, countered by a couple of older boys refuting it, saying they had seen me intentionally throw the sweater overboard. I explained again that I had never seen the sweater but had only felt it when it was placed on my arm, causing me to jump. I tried to explain what happened again to no avail. I reasoned that people knew I was a good and honest kid, but this didn't matter. The priest told me how disappointed he was in me, and a couple of the girl's friends severely admonished me. I returned to the stern alone, remaining there the rest of the trip. Why wouldn't people believe me? But then the guys who had put the sweater on my arm must have been happy to have me take the fall. The girl in question gave me evil stares, and I could hear everyone talking about me in a derogatory fashion for the remainder of the trip. I said nothing.

When I returned home, I told my father what had happened, but he had already been called and filled in on the day's events. I went through what happened and suddenly realized he did not believe my story either. This had never happened before; my parents had always believed me. Why would anyone think I would do such a thing? Next, the upset father of the girl called. I could hear my father's side of the conversation as he apologized for his son's actions. But I had not done anything ... at least not intentionally. It was a long night. Fortunately, I didn't go to school with any of the kids, but a week later, in church, I overheard a mother pointing me out as the boy who had thrown the sweater off the boat. I remember the look on her face as I walked by. I immediately dropped out of the altar boy program, assuming I would likely be kicked out anyway. I don't remember much after that point. My parents paid for the sweater and shielded me from interactions with any of the adults involved, but I knew they were disappointed in their son.

Strangely, that silly incident became one of the defining moments in my early life, as I blew the incident way out of proportion. The innocence of childhood died for me that day, but I was utterly unprepared to enter the adult world. I had told simple lies before, getting caught often, as my father was a crackerjack trial attorney. No one thought me a saint, but there had never been a time when I had been falsely accused and not believed. True, the sweater had touched me last before going overboard; I did not hesitate to admit that, but all assumed that I had acted intentionally. My already small social circle shrank, and my stuttering increased in frequency and severity. The lack of friends increased the stuttering, which made me pull back even more socially, a vicious circle that sent me spiraling downward. My naïve view of the world was shattered that day.

Why can small events have a far more significant impact than they should? Many kids have survived far worse traumas than what I experienced that day. The human mind is mysterious, as we dwell on isolated events, often failing to see the whole picture accurately. The expanding thirteen-year-old mind can blow events far out of proportion. I taught students that age for many years, always remembering that incident. Students can be cruel, but they can also quickly become damaged goods. It is such a fragile period, and how events play out at this age can make such a massive difference in the path that a child chooses to follow. Children can exaggerate incidents in their minds, and adults frequently fail to see how fragile these young adults are.

I had seen the cruelty of kids before, but losing the trust and support of my father and other adults was the lasting hurt. I had always thought I was a good kid but began to doubt myself for the first time. I was entering the dark period of my life, and it would be several years before I would finally climb out of it. I wish I could have cornered my thirteen-year-old self and helped put the incident in proper perspective, and I remember that whenever I was dealing with a troubled student. Give them adult guidance, then drop down on their level and empathize with their feelings. That's a difficult bridge for most adults to cross; we assume that adult advice will right the ship, but without the accompanying empathy, the advice falls short. I needed both that day, but my usually wonderful parents were dealing with more significant problems then. The sweater incident was so trivial compared to my sisters' issues. My innocence was gone, and I crossed over to the dark side.

Somewhere out there are a couple of guys who probably don't even remember what they did that day, and I doubt if the now-nameless girl remembers losing her sweater. But it changed my teen years and sent me into a shell for several years. I laugh at it all now, but I can still feel the doubt and rejection I felt that day. I'm sure we all have those events which have become exaggerated in importance. I hear people frequently yearn for the happy days of high school or, more usually, college, but I never hear anyone wanting to be thirteen again. Once again, this is why I chose to work with children this age. For most of us, it was a difficult part of our life. While the problems are not the severe ones we experience years later, the emotional impact of even minor events can be traumatic. While so many adults lament the behavior of students this age, I was always so proud of the many who survived it to become remarkable adults. It is when we all discover the meaning of courage and learn for the first time how to navigate the complexities of adulthood. How many times I wished I could have gone back and kept that sweater from falling off my arm, but like so many of the stepping stones in life, it became an essential part of determining who I was to become. I never returned to Tolchester or served as an altar boy, but I can still see that white sweater floating gradually down to the water to be swallowed up by the boat's wake.

THE ROCKING CHAIR

In a house filled with family antiques, there was one piece of furniture no one would ever throw away. An old rocking chair sat in a prominent place yet looked so disreputable we couldn't have paid someone to take it. Taped and glued back together many times, no one could sit in it, but it was a priceless treasure to our family.

My paternal grandparents collected family furniture; their house was a veritable museum with everything from Grandfather John's crib from Ireland to Grandma Travers' grandfather clock. My father, as an only child, inherited all the family furniture. His godmother had no family, and her furniture headed our way when she passed. With this fantastic collection of furniture, any one of several historic pieces could have been the family treasure. However, that title went to a sad-looking rocking chair with no historical or monetary value. The unremarkable piece was glued together in eleven places, and even the dog was smart enough not to sit in it. The material was worn with tape covering three holes, the arms were chipped, and no one ever found it comfortable. Multiple tubes of glue kept it alive over the years. Still, this was the most prized item we owned, and it was displayed prominently. No one dared sell or dispose of it. It wasn't always so disreputable looking, as my siblings and I were rocked to sleep in this chair many evenings as infants. Then, one day, it met its fate at my brother's hands.

Bill was as passionate a baseball fan as there ever was, and the Baltimore Orioles were the only team for him. To him, an Oriole game was more profound than a church service, and he attended this church religiously. Growing up a few short blocks from Memorial Stadium, we spent many afternoons and evenings there. We especially enjoyed the occasional Sunday doubleheader when we got two games for the price of one ... a whole day at the ballpark. Fifty cents got you a seat in the bleachers, and by the second game, we could move to a better seat as many departed early. The bleachers were where the real fans sat ... colorful Baltimoreans who slew the English language, but no more dedicated students of baseball ever existed. With an extra quarter or two to buy a soda, hot dog, and popcorn, what else could one need for a spectacular summer outing?

Of course, the away games meant at least one radio playing the game in our house. Often, multiple radios blasted away so that none of us even missed one play as we moved around the house. Even when we finally got a television, we turned down its sound and turned on the radio to get better play-by-play coverage. 1966 had been a memorable season as the Orioles won the World Series for the first time, slaying Sandy Koufax and the mighty Dodgers in four straight games. We entered 1967 with high hopes, as most of the championship team had returned: Brooks Robinson, Frank Robinson, Jim Palmer, and Boog Powell, to name a few. By mid-May, however, things were not going according to plan. The week of May 8th began poorly, with the Orioles losing two at home to the Chicago White Sox, including a 13-1 drubbing, which left the Orioles five games under .500 and now heading into Yankee Stadium for a weekend series against the Bronx Bombers. Bill was in a foul mood. With my graduation less than a month away, I was somewhat preoccupied. The Orioles won the first two games of the series, and all thought this was the point when a lousy season turned around.

On Sunday, May 14, Bill watched the game in my parents' bedroom, the location of the only family TV, as away games were often televised locally. A steady stream of exclamations emanated from the room that afternoon.

"Come on, just get the ball over the plate!"

"Steve [Barber], you're killing me!"

"Don't walk him!"

"No, no, no! Get the bum out of there!"

And an "oh my God" when Brooks Robinson, the human vacuum, made an uncharacteristic error at third base.

A few comments, I prefer not to quote.

The Yankees scored three runs in the bottom of the first inning. No one was concerned as the previous day's game began the same way, with the Orioles scoring four runs a couple of innings later to take a lead they would not relinquish. And the Miracle O's repeated this feat, scoring four runs in the top of the sixth. Even if I hadn't been listening to the game, I would have known what happened as the house shook from Bill's screams and victory dance. It appeared that 1966 was no fluke; the Orioles were on a roll. The dancing, however, was cut short by a Joe Pepitone home run, which put the Yankees back in the lead. There was plenty of time for an Oriole comeback, and all remained calm in the Radcliffe household.

That's when Oriole's nemesis, Mickey Mantle, came to bat and quickly deposited a Stu Miller pitch deep into the right field seats. I didn't hear the crack of the bat, but no one could have missed the ensuing explosion downstairs. That and Bill's screams sent me running down from the third floor. I'm not sure what I expected to find. Through the years, my siblings and I had smashed a TV and collapsed a bed or two, but Bill now stood beside an unrecognizable pile of rubble. There was one less piece of furniture, and only after a closer inspection did I identify the remains of the rocking chair. Bill was too upset to utter words, and I decided I needed to head back upstairs.

Dad's toolkit contained an array of glues, and over the next week, he amazingly reconstructed the chair, gluing ten of the breaks back together and installing one metal brace at a critical point. A child of the Great Depression, he was never one to throw anything away. Again, it looked like a chair, but even a superficial look would convince one to find another place to sit. The chair survived two family relocations and another forty years but, sadly, outlived Bill. Dad finally threw in the towel on it after the fourth collapse. It was a sad day when the beloved rocking chair found its way into a dumpster.

❖ ❖ ❖

The following conversation occurred in 1981 when I was married with three wonderful sons. There was a knock on our front door, and upon opening it, I found Bill standing there, visibly shaken and almost in tears.

'I couldn't sleep. I just had to come by to stop you."

"Stop me? From what? Bill, what's going on? Quick, come in."

"Don't you realize what's going to happen?"

"Bill, what the heck are we talking about?" Maybe I had missed some horrific news story. I was worried.

"I couldn't stay away any longer. This is just awful."

"For Pete's sake, what are we talking about?"

Jackie joined us at this point and invited Bill into our family room. "Is something wrong, Bill?"

"He hasn't told me what's up yet."

Bill sat down but was visibly shaken, on the verge of tears. He seemed to gather some composure. "It's Andy [our second son]. You've got to do something."

"Andy is fine, Bill. He's upstairs playing right now."

"But you must stop this. He's going to suffer severe psychological damage. I can't keep silent about it anymore."

"There's nothing wrong with Andy. I don't understand what you're talking about."

"But he's a Yankee fan. You have to stop that. I'm so worried about him if he keeps rooting for the Yankees. Think of what it might do to him."

Our son Andy remained a Yankee fan for the rest of his life, and doctors never detected any psychological damage. Bill never got over it.

❖ ❖ ❖

As in many families, baseball was more than a sport. My brother Bill only briefly played baseball but did become a marvelous tennis player, taking up the sport after a year of little league baseball as a ten-year-old, in which the coach never once played him in a game. I played little league baseball for two years, and Andy played for several years before switching to tennis like his uncle. My only claim to fame was winning a trophy for being the best infielder on a winless baseball team. Andy could claim that he hit a home run off a pitcher who struck out Barry Bonds in a Major League game; he and the pitcher played little league baseball together. However, baseball was the language we all spoke.

I was five when the Orioles came to Baltimore in 1954. Summer and early fall became a walk from one Orioles game to another. My grandfather, dressed as Lord Baltimore, even led the parade to the stadium in 1954 for the inaugural game. When not at a game, the radio was on, and in the 1950s, Dad even bought a rare-for-its-time battery-operated radio so that we would never miss a game. I remember riding in a car, holding the radio outside the window for better reception so no play would be missed. Car radios later solved that problem.

However, the fundamental importance of the game to our family was that it provided a thread that connected my father, brother, and me. My father was not one to talk often on a personal level; he was a constant fountain of commentary on politics, current events, and

SPORTS. He would have gotten a superficial response if he had tried to delve deeply into my hopes and fears. But baseball was our family's language. It engaged us, connected us, changed the topic of discussion when needed, and showed us he cared. We suffered through those early years when wins were rare, and we celebrated together when the Orioles found the recipe for winning. So many memorable family memories revolved around Orioles highlights and the frequent magic moments:

- Laughing hysterically as the slowest Oriole of the day, catcher Gus Triandos, legged an inside-the-park home run as Hall-of-Famer Ted Williams lumbered after the ball in the outfield.

- Attending all three games of a 1964 series with the mighty Yankees when the Orioles came from behind to win each game.

- Sitting in Memorial Stadium and watching the final game of the first World Series win for the O's in 1966, sweeping the Dodgers in four games, beating both Koufax and Drysdale.

- Watching the incredible Brooks Robinson show in the 1970 World Series against the Cincinnati Big Red Machine.

- Listening to a come-from-behind Orioles win in the 1971 World Series to tie the Series at 3-3 while on military duty and watching an officer break all protocol by screaming out word of the victory to the pilots using a semi-secure radio.

- Enjoying Earl Weaver's classic manager tirades, thoroughly enjoyable, while maybe not modeling exemplary behavior.

Baseball is unique in the way that it is played. There is time between each pitch and play, and Dad, Bill, and I analyzed every piece of the action. While some say this makes the sport too slow, the slower pace provides a chance to escape the rat race of life … to stop and smell the grass. The slower pace allows the fan to take the position of manager or coach, guessing strategy and pitches. Timed sports elicit emotions and exclamations; baseball facilitates conversation. Because baseball is a sport of statistics, a true fan has the data to second-guess every move. It is also a sport with no clock. While there is no question that a clock makes for an exciting end of a football or basketball game, the lack of a clock in a baseball game means that any game can be won by a trailing team, regardless of the score. You can still win if you are behind by ten runs with two out in the bottom of the ninth inning. I remember listening to a game as a young child with my father when the Orioles blew an eight-run lead in the ninth inning to Ted Williams and the Red Sox; that was not a happy summer day for a young kid. A football team does not come back from a large deficit with two minutes to go in a game. How often did I see people file out of Memorial Stadium only to have the Orioles rally in the ninth? We never left early!

Bill became a local reporter, covering human interest stories, but he always managed to sneak in an article on the Orioles. In a newspaper editorial after the Orioles lost to the Pirates in the 1979 World Series, his eternal optimism radiated,

> There's a cliché that ricochets through the city that loses a World Series. "Wait 'til next year," the old saying goes. To most people, the "wait 'til next year" cliché is strictly reserved for losers. This year, the phrase has a new meaning in Baltimore.
>
> In 1979, the Orioles captured the city of Baltimore and, in the process of doing so, saved the franchise. By drawing 1.6 million people to Memorial Stadium and giving Baltimore "Oriole Fever," the 1979 Orioles gave Baltimore a "next year" to look forward to.

His nephew's love of the Yankees rocked Bill, but he put family over baseball. Tragically, Bill died in an automobile accident in 1982, and baseball took on a different meaning for all of us. The Orioles made it to the World Series the following year, winning in five games, but there was little joy this time. Although Dad and I watched and cheered, there was no Bill to question managerial decisions and argue umpire rulings. We watched the last game together, sharing the moment. Knowing how much he would have enjoyed the games, I often thought of Bill. I couldn't rejoice with the win the way I should have. I could hear the comments he would have made and his exclamations when things went wrong. Sitting in the room was an old rocking chair, still glued together but nearly crumbling. Dad and I looked at the chair often, but neither could express our thoughts. The victory felt good, but somebody should have been sitting in that chair.

THE WINTER MAGICIAN

My father was not a talker; he was never one to sit and have a heart-to-heart talk with his children. Always caring, he was far more likely to talk politics, share the latest exploits of the Colts or Orioles, or relay a funny story. He was a man of action. He kept his family busy even when some might want to sit around. 1963 was a pivotal year for our family, and the mounting troubles could have torn us apart. In his inimitable style, Dad chose to act. In a surprise move, he orchestrated one of the more memorable events in my childhood, which caught us all by surprise and temporarily defused the building tension.

My father always had some plan, some way to break the monotony and keep our family fresh. When I was a young child, he always took me places: the harbor to watch ships unloading, Penn Station to watch trains coming and going, and the airport to watch planes taking off and landing. Most of these adventures, as were our frequent trips to Memorial Stadium to see the Orioles, were impromptu. Saturdays often held a surprise, and over breakfast, he would announce some grand plan for the day: a day trip, a significant clean-up project, and, at least once a year, what he called the Big Move—everyone in the family would switch bedrooms. My parents and sisters would always get first choice, and Bill and I were usually left with a third-floor room or a cold but private room in the back of the house. Though less comfortable, that latter room had access to the back staircase and the kitchen, fantastic for late-night food runs. The moves involved a day of moving furniture and possessions, but it was always a fresh beginning.

In 1963, he caught us all by surprise. The magic that had been our family was fading. I was thirteen years old, some days going on sixteen and others eight. No one ever remembers age thirteen as the high point of their life, and it certainly wasn't for me. Kim's removal from the home almost two years earlier took some of the life out of the family. Many of my friends had drifted in other directions, and my grades and love of school were declining. Gussie's physical problems were worsening, and several friends had deserted her. She had run away from home a few months earlier, and Mom showed more significant signs of depression. Bill, always good-natured, seemed to be the only one weathering the family storm. As winter set in, everyone's mood lowered a few notches. In many ways, we were a family in trouble. Dad remained upbeat with his stories and daily news updates, but even he sensed trouble.

Snow is a big deal for a kid: a chance to get a day off school, an oasis in the middle of the boredom and drudgery of winter, and an opportunity to act like a child: snowball battles, building a snow fort to protect you from snowball-wielding comrades, and making the obligatory snowman. Throwing snowballs at cars is not a practice I would condone, but when I was young, it was permitted on our narrow one-way street, where cars navigated uphill slower than one could crawl. All neighbors except the two resident grouches understood that semi-icy projectiles would rain down on their vehicles as they moved up the hill. We had a Baltimore City policeman who lived on the street, but he just fired snowballs back at us. The abundant neighborhood children would be stationed along the road, and no vehicle escaped the expected barrage. But alas, we moved to a larger neighborhood with houses farther apart, and snowballing cars became taboo. Winters seemed to last forever, and the infrequent snowstorms were hardly enough to amuse a kid. In addition, I went to a school that prided itself on only closing eight times in its sixty or so years of existence. Winters became just waiting for spring.

In March 1963, it snowed, switched to freezing rain, and finally changed to cold rain. School was in session, and the ice eliminated any potential fun. But then it grew cold … very cold. We had school that day and came home to a bitter cold with no snow. This was not the weather event that a thirteen-year-old dreamed of. My father had cascaded us with countless stories of his childhood adventures. He and his army of buddies had lived the kind of childhood they make movies of; as a scout and sometimes under-supervised child, he had camped, explored, and re-enacted adventure after adventure with the proper blend of mischief and creativity. He was the counterbalance to my mother's overprotective nature, as he always encouraged us to build or invent something, even though we lacked the skills or tools. That afternoon, as we sat inside feeling sorry for ourselves, he told us to go out and explore the ice in our yard. Braving the cold, we bundled up and ventured out to investigate the "ice patch." It was getting dark and … cold. Mom soon called us in for dinner, which sounded great, even with her cooking.

During our tuna fish dinner, Dad tried to strike up a conversation, but other than an occasional token response, all were silent; we were a family in trouble. We went to our rooms to do homework or at least pretend to do so. I heard my father go out and assumed he was heading to a meeting, but the door repeatedly opened and closed. Paying it no mind, I stared at a textbook, reading and rereading the same passage. My brain was far away. I was making little progress by eight, and it was time for a snack.

From the kitchen, I could see lights coming from the side yard. I had no clue what Dad was up to. He soon came in the back door shouting, "Everyone come downstairs."

"But Dad, we have homework."

"Forget homework. Everyone, go get bundled up and get your ice skates."

We all had ice skates that were used infrequently at a local rink. "Ice skates? But it's late. The rink won't even be open."

He simply said, "Look outside."

I opened the back door and saw that our entire side yard was lit with lanterns and several spotlights.

"But Dad, there are just several small patches of ice."

"Not anymore."

And he was right. Unbeknownst to us, Dad had turned the hose loose in the side yard, and with the assistance of a little more freezing rain, it was now one large sheet of ice. Completely startled, we stared at the yard. The ordinarily dark area was lit with several flood lights, and the yard was now completely covered with ice, reflecting enough of the lights upward that it seemed like daylight. The branches of nearby trees glistened with a thin layer of ice and looked like Christmas trees covered with tinsel. Gussie let out a yell and went searching for her skates. After minimal deliberation, I decided homework could wait and ran off to uncover mine.

With skates on, we soon forgot the cold. Then came surprise number two. Music started blaring from the side porch. Dad had moved a radio out there, and we were now skating to Mitch Miller and the Gang singing "Roll Out the Barrel." Within a few minutes, we were skating in small circles, none particularly adept at ice skating.

We were joined by a family of children from next door, each toting skates. I was never the greatest fan of ice skating; my poor balance made it an adventure and often humorous spectacle for an observer. However, this evening was different. It was a school night, we skipped homework, and no one mentioned the dreaded word "bedtime." Although it was bitter cold that night, the lights somehow added warmth to the setting. We skated, shrieked, laughed when we crashed, and had the time of our lives. We stayed out until 9:30, coming in only when the other family left. As I lay in bed that night, I felt like a child on Christmas evening … on top of the world, happily exhausted, hoping this was a sneak preview of life. My father was the hero; he had turned a bleak winter day into a memory for a lifetime. If the story ended here, it would still rank among my top ten childhood memories, but this story was just beginning.

It was hard getting up the following day. Math homework was incomplete, and my father was willing to write me an excuse. Sadly, however, this was far from the first time, and I knew the drill. I was too proud to resort to a "my dog ate my homework" excuse; any student with that lack of imagination deserved to have to repeat a grade, although Dixie did chew up an assignment once. As we reviewed the assignment, I could finish the work in class, eventually turning in a "complete" paper. Math was my best subject, and the teacher probably knew what I was doing. I could fake it one more time. The whole day, I could only think about the night before, a badly needed oasis in the desert of being thirteen. My father came home early that evening again, sending us right up to do homework. "We're having dinner early tonight." Figuring that he planned one of his frequent evening meetings, this didn't seem unusual. But once again, he had big plans!

We heard laughter from the side yard before we had even finished dinner. Puzzled, I ran to the window and gazed out into the yard. There was even more ice tonight; my father had continued to water those imaginary plants. The lights were on, and several kids from the neighborhood were skating back and forth across the small lot. We raced for our skates and quickly joined them. The floodlights soon came on; this time, Dad had set up his massive speakers on the side porch, and we were soon skating to the big band sound of Benny Goodman—hardly rock and roll, but I had to admit that this swinging big band sound was more than acceptable. Dad cranked up the speakers and was probably violating every city noise ordinance. The music was great, but no child in his right mind would ever admit to liking their parent's music; this was automatic banishment from teen-dom. Soon, other kids started to appear, and then more ... finally, our yard was overrun with every child from several blocks around. The parents sat around drinking coffee and more adult-like beverages, and several moms kept a nonstop pipeline of hot chocolate heading out to the side yard. I never knew how the word got out; I suspect Dad was primarily behind it, but then, between the lights and music, how could one not know what was happening?

Then it suddenly hit me. Our yard was "party central," THE place to be. When you're a shy kid who stutters, the world does not revolve around you but seems more like a train racing by you at neck-break-ing speed. But tonight, I was a star; our yard was where everyone wanted to be. We skated and laughed; neighborhood rivalries and jealousies evaporated. This was an actual community event, and our house was the community capital. For one evening, I forgot that I could count my friends on one hand, that I stuttered uncontrollably much of the time, and that I would easily place last in the Coolest Kid Competition. That night, I was a king and accepted. We all skated well into the evening, and no one noticed the cold.

The temperature warmed the next day, and although a few ven-tured out onto the ice the next afternoon, it was clear that the Rad-cliffe Skating Rink had passed its heyday. Years later, it remains one of my most vivid childhood memories. No one is left from my family from that period of my life, and my father has been gone for years. I never thanked him for that special evening. I wish I could return and see what motivated his engineering the whole experience. To what extent was he aware of how desperately I needed a life during those difficult days, and how much of it was fueled by his desire to create a unique social event? Like so many parents, he undoubtedly expected no thank you. Our laughter and enthusiasm were probably all the thank you he needed and expected. But I wonder if he knew how desperately that thirteen-year-old boy required a boost. In this technological age, how many parents would tear their brood away from the TV and computer screens to go outside on a bitterly cold night?

I'm hardly at the end of my life, but I am entering the period of life reflection where we look back at the hills and valleys of our journey. We all have many impromptu special moments where we briefly rose above the daily grind. They form the stepping stones through the tangle of childhood. That was an extraordinary forty-eight-hour period that made the grind bearable. I emerged from my teen years relatively unscathed despite many dark days. I like to think that Dad sensed my pain, and that was behind his actions. But he was always looking for a chance to provide memorable experiences for his family. The following winter, he would take his whole family to see the Beatles in Baltimore. He would have preferred to see Benny Goodman, but he knew what we needed. Time after time, he threw out that life ring to his children. He, better than almost anyone I ever knew, truly knew what family was about. With two daughters having major medical issues and my mother often suffering from depression, he bravely and unselfishly kept the family afloat through thick and thin. We all rose above the monotonous routines for two winter days and experienced something unique. Thanks for the memories, Dad!

WITH APOLOGIES
TO ALEXANDER

The phone continued to ring while I initially pretended not to hear it. Finally picking up the phone to stop the ringing, I heard:

"Hello, may I speak to Maggie Radcliffe, please?"

Responding, I said, "She's not here."

"Is there a better time when I could reach her?"

"No."

"This is about her car warranty. Can you give her a message?"

"That would be quite difficult."

"Is there a better number with which to reach her?"

"No; first of all, Maggie never had a car."

"Oh, I see."

"In fact, she never had a driver's license."

"Really?"

"Also, Maggie is deceased."

"I'm sorry to hear that."

"Oh, and by the way, Maggie was our dog."

Sorry Alexander, but I don't like telephones. I despise them for a good reason. My wife Jackie marvels that I suddenly develop a hearing deficit when the phone rings. She makes fun of me but understands the basis for my avoidance. And most importantly, please don't call me when I am in the shower!

I always carry a cell phone, but I don't have to like it. My life has seen us move from big, clunky metal objects with a rotary dial and party lines to cell phones and beyond. This writing will soon be outdated since phones evolve into something dramatically new each year. Someday, the phone will probably be a computer chip installed in us so that we can communicate with anyone anywhere in the world by simply saying or thinking of their name or number. That allows for a frightening scenario where someone could hack into you. Or maybe since our thoughts will all be interconnected, telecommunications will be replaced by telepathy. All will be technologically connected into one large organism just as the body's cells are interlinked—a science fiction nightmare. We think privacy is an issue now; just wait! Maybe all this technological evolution is progress, and I love progress. It's wonderful that I can call my wife from my car in an emergency; that aspect simplifies life. However, every advancement has a negative side effect.

Few alive today remember the atrocity of the party line, several phones sharing a line so that you could hear another party's conversation. While waiting to make an important call, one might have to wait for Margaret to finish telling Ethel every detail of her gall bladder surgery—or suddenly realize that another person is breathing on the line while you are talking. We worry about losing privacy today; try a party line. Our house in Baltimore had its own line, but I remember encountering these dreaded party lines elsewhere, a different way to get to know one's neighbors.

In the 1950s, there may not have been scam calls or salespeople trying to sell you an extended warranty on a car you traded in five years ago, but children loved to make prank calls. My sister Gussie was the master of many of these.

"Hello, is your refrigerator running?

"Yes."

"Then you better hurry up and catch it before it gets away."

Or to a store owner:

"Do you have Prince Albert [cigar brand] in a box?"

"Yes."

"Then you better let him out."

We also discovered a number we could call to make our phone ring, which was a great way to torment our parents. Children have always been mischievous—ask the ancient Greeks and Romans.

One could also use a phone to get the exact time. When you dialed the appropriate number, you got:

"At the tone, the time will be three forty and ten seconds. *Ping*.

"At the tone, the time will be three forty and twenty seconds. *Ping*.

"At the tone, the time will be three forty and thirty seconds. *Ping*.

I always felt sorry for the poor woman who had that job. That would have been one long eight-hour work shift.

Phones in the 1950s would be considered antiques today. Heavy enough to be used as a boat anchor, they all employed a rotary dial to input the number. For each number dialed, you'd insert your finger into the correct number and rotate, then wait for the rotary dial to circle back. You got the wrong number if you didn't turn the dial far enough. The dial seemed to freeze in an emergency while resetting for the following number. But this was better than having Mabel dial the number for you, which is what my grandparents grew up with. That made Mabel the town gossip queen if she was so inclined. In the 1950s, there was no such thing as an answering machine, and a long-distance call could bankrupt you quickly. People today misplace cell phones all the time. There was no misplacing your phone then; it would be easier to lose your bathtub. However, when we saw the old phones from earlier in the century, even we thought we were using advanced technology. You could hold the receiver rather than stand beside the wall on which the old contraption was mounted.

One never sees a pay phone anymore. This was our answer to to-day's cell phones; if you needed to make a call, there was usually a pay phone within walking distance. Of course, one required the change to make the call. I wore penny loafers in my teens; these had a leather slot where one could insert a coin. Mine carried a dime, so I always had the money for a pay phone call. As kids, we always checked every change return slot for those nickels or dimes a previous caller failed to get. Making a long-distance call, however, posed risks. One could be at a critical point in a conversation when the operator would inter-rupt you to have you add another dime that you often did not have.

Person # 1: "Have you heard the news about Uncle Fred?"

Person #2: "No, what's up?"

Person #1: "It's awful, he ...."

Operator: "Your time is up. Please add another dime."

After a frantic search, Person #2, "I don't have any more change. Can I ...?"

Operator: "Thank you. Have a nice day."

Then came the next advancement: plastic. I must bite my lip when I use the word "advancement" here. Plastic made things cheap-er, but it created many problems with its disposal. Everything is plas-tic now, and the planet is just figuring out what many have known for years—plastic is an environmental nightmare. Metal deteriorates; plastic lives forever. No one objected, however, to cost savings. Then came the push buttons on a regular phone; no more taking a minute to rotate the dial for each digit. Now, one could punch in a number quickly, making it possible to now receive three times as many wrong number calls as before. Mobile phones appeared soon, and now one could talk anywhere in the house, even on the toilet. That would un-doubtedly add excellent sound effects to a rather mundane phone call. And then came the cell phone, which I swore I would never own, just as I said I would never own a color TV set.

Cell phones and economical phone plans make phone calling very cheap compared to years past. I remember friends in college running up monthly long-distance bills well over $300, enough to buy a cheap used car then. The ability to make free phone calls has made robocalls possible, where a computer can dial thousands of households playing a recorded message. Now, I can have every company, charity, and scam operator call me as I sit down to dinner. I've perfected my strategy with these calls. I can now hang up before the third word is spoken, and with a little more practice, I'll hang up after the first word. And when you call me, don't pause before you speak, or you'll be talking to the dial tone.

But why do I hate telephones? Simple—I am a stutterer. There's nothing more fun than trying to answer a phone when one's stuttering makes it impossible to begin a sentence with the word "hello." I got smart after a couple of years of running whenever the phone rang, realizing I could start with "Radcliffe's Residence." I might have sounded like a butler, but it got me through to the following sentence. Invariably, there was a question asked me, which elicited a monstrous pause. I can answer a phone with "hello" now; the anticipation brought on the stuttering years ago. However, I still run when the phone rings or, in the case of my phone, quacks. It's no wonder that many people thought I had only been dealt half a deck.

However, the real reason for hating phones is that sometimes bad news travels over phone lines. The night of March 7, 1982, did me in forever. I was in the shower after a day of working outside. The phone rang in the next room, and I assumed Jackie would answer it. This was before an answering machine would pick up the call so that the phone could ring endlessly. And this night, it did. So, dripping water and soap, I stumbled out of the shower, grabbed a towel, and fumbled for a while with the doorknob, finally making it to the phone.

The man on the other end of the phone was incomprehensible, and I thought some drunk had gotten the wrong number. I didn't hang up for some reason, and I realized the caller was sobbing and gasping for breath. However, I still couldn't understand a word he was saying. I finally interrupted and asked who it was. On his fourth attempt to give me his name, I deduced that it was my sister's father-in-law. He continued rambling, and I finally picked out the words, "he's gone." Something must have happened to my brother-in-law; my sister would be devastated. But why was he calling me? That was my sister's job. I told him how sorry I was. He stopped and said, "No, Gussie." Was my sister dead? A cold chill started to run through me, helped considerably by the fact that I was standing in a cold room, dripping wet. I finally asked him to slow down and repeat what he was trying to say. He replied, "They're both gone!"

Oh my God! My sister and her husband were both dead. Then, for the first time, he calmed down somewhat and said, "Bill and Gussie; they're both gone!" My sister and brother had both been killed in a car accident. At that point, I ceased to feel anything, and I have no memory of the rest of the phone call.

Why do I narrate this bit in this essay? It's been over forty years since that fateful night, but chills run through me if the phone rings when I shower. I'm immediately carried back to that horrible night, and I go into a sort of trance. Since that night, I have never gotten out of the shower to answer a phone, and I pray I won't hear Jackie calling me to the phone. That call was over half a lifetime ago, and I reconciled with their passing years ago. However, the phone ringing while in the shower immediately returns me to that horrific evening.

I do not miss the inconvenience of phone calling in years past, but I worry about what cell phones have done for us. I watch kids in restaurants texting friends and downloading videos instead of talking with their families, or even more ridiculous, texting someone sitting at the same table. I see many kids unable to amuse themselves, feeling lost if there is no phone to play with. I see people calling others multiple times a day and texting everything from what they had for dinner to what a friend wore that day. While staying in close touch with someone is terrific, constant communication borders on pathological dependency. I always carry my phone with me, but I only text the people who have stopped answering calls. My life isn't so exciting that others must have my thoughts streaming into their phone. But it is excellent in an emergency.

Sorry, Alexander, but I don't call people to chat. I probably should do that more than I do. Many must think I'm anti-social; I'm just anti-phone. I like to see who I'm talking with and read their body language. It's so much easier for people to lie without visual contact, and lying becomes too easy when texting is involved. But if you're lying to my face, I'll know it. The other day, I went into the store to confront the salesperson rather than call to find out why an order had not come in. He told me he'd been trying to call me for a week but made minimal eye contact. I said, "No, you didn't." His body language confirmed my suspicion as he squirmed uncomfortably under my gaze. Then he went into an elaborate litany of excuses. I finally told him it was OK that he had forgotten, but spare me the excuses.

Progress is still a net positive if people don't skimp on the values of the past. Today's cell phones will be in antique stores in a few years, and we'll live in a different world. Humans will always need to connect, and any device that enhances this will be a positive. We need to retain our independence and identity, and I can see us becoming one giant amorphous blob if technology goes too far. You're welcome to call, but don't hold your breath waiting for me to call. And if I don't answer, I'm probably in the shower!

IS THERE AN EXORCIST
IN THE HOUSE?

Gussie was jumping up and down, screaming at the top of her lungs. Tears flowed down my sister's face as she seemed to have completely lost control. She was holding my arm, squeezing so hard that she was restricting my blood flow; I had never seen her like this before. Mom was terrified and worried. She knew her daughter had emotional issues, but Gussie had never exhibited this level of hysteria before. Mom thought her daughter must be possessed, and as a good Catholic, she believed in the existence of Satan. Would we need an exorcist? Gussie, however, was not alone as everyone around us screamed so loud that my ears hurt. The Beatles had come to town.

The Catholic Church had a history of doing exorcisms, and they would come back in vogue in the mid-twentieth century with the publication of William Peter Blatty's *The Exorcist* and, a couple of years later, the movie of the same name. Gussie's head neither spun around nor did she vomit pea soup; however, that day, she was entirely out of control. If she was possessed, so was a sizeable portion of the teenage female population. The Beatles were having that effect as they toured the United States for the first time in 1964.

February 9, 1964, was one of those "Do you remember where

you were?" days. Our family regularly watched the Ed Sullivan Show on Sunday evenings, which aired on CBS from eight to nine. It was preceded by other family shows (*Lassie*, *Bonanza*), and sitting around the TV for these became a family ritual. The Beatles made their first of three appearances on the show, and music for my generation was changed forever. Elvis had appeared on the show several years earlier, but the Beatles' appearance made national news.

This was their first US visit, preceded by talk about their long hair, collarless suits, and singing ... which was different. Newspaper stories referred to their singing as sounding like a "pipe organ." (I never entirely understood that analysis.) I suspect a sizeable portion of the US population was watching that night. Neither my sister nor I had any of their songs; their album in this country had been prematurely released just before the show, and Gussie and I were just getting into "popular" music. My sister had Peter, Paul, and Mary's first album, which we thought was radical. I had been too young for the Elvis mania several years earlier and was hardly a big fan, although I had Dad purchase "You Ain't Nothin' but a Hound Dog," as beagles ruled my world.

The show was broadcast live, as was virtually everything back then. Ed Sullivan was about as exciting as mud but did have a knack for booking interesting acts: singers, comedians, and bizarre acts such as Topo Gigio, the dancing mouse puppet. He had signed the Beatles for three shows for $10,000, a monstrous sum back then. When he announced them on the show, showing enthusiasm for a change, we suddenly realized that we had the volume turned up too high. The audience was filled with young girls screaming, crying, and almost pulling out their hair. My parents sat dumbfounded while Gussie, age thirteen, scrambled to get closer to the TV. I remember two of their songs from the show: "I Want to Hold Your Hand" and "All My Loving." Nothing was radical about the music; even my father admitted it was "decent." My mother said nothing, her jaw halfway to the floor;

she only noticed their long hair and never got over this.

Gussie immediately became Beatles-obsessed; that was the understatement of the century. She purchased the album and played it continuously for the next several months. And I do mean CONTINUALLY. My parents often had to turn off the album in the middle of the night. While I enjoyed the music, I had to be a "cool" fourteen-year-old guy and only admit a casual interest. Suddenly, every musical group in the world looked like clones of the Beatles in musical style, dress, and hair length. Some were quite good, and some were nauseous. My sister purchased a Herman's Hermits album and discovered that if she played "Mrs. Brown, You've Got a Lovely Daughter," she could send me running for cover. She finally had found a way to get her older brother away from her room without getting into trouble.

I found a way to fight back. My favorite musical groups were the Motown artists, a mix of soul and popular music: Smokey Robinson and the Miracles, the Temptations, Stevie Wonder, and the Supremes. As Gussie would turn up one of her albums, I would crank up my record player: the Dave Clark Five vs. Marvin Gaye or the Beatles vs. the Four Tops. I did like the early Rolling Stones, the bad boys of rock that Gussie abhorred. There were no CDs or tapes back then, just vinyl records: 33-rpm albums and 45-rpm singles. One had to change the turntable speed, depending on which was playing. Gussie would play her albums non-stop, and I would sneak into her room and change the speed. We both enjoyed our musical warfare, and I had to admit a year later that I liked the Beatles.

1964 was indeed the year of the Beatles, including the release of their first movie, *A Hard Day's Night*, which was artistically excellent and innovative, but to a fourteen-year-old, it was just more Beatles. Then, Dad pulled off one of the most extraordinary moves ever orchestrated by a parent. One morning, over breakfast, he slipped an envelope to Gussie. She casually opened it, suddenly shot out of her chair, knocking it over, and then raced around the kitchen screaming.

At first, I thought something horrible had happened, but I soon realized these were screams of joy. Grabbing the envelope, I stared at … tickets to the Beatles' concert in Baltimore. Mom wasn't smiling. She could only remind us that all four of the Beatles needed haircuts.

This launched the next round of Gussie's nonstop Beatles music marathon, leading up to the concert in September. There was one positive. I had to wake my sister for school each day—raising Lazarus would have been much more manageable. But now, before I was even downstairs, I would hear "I Saw Her Standing There" blasting from her room. The build-up to the concert was an event with Gussie counting down the days and then the hours. A new school year had started, but the talk was about the Beatles coming to Baltimore. The day finally arrived, September 13, 1964. There were two concerts, I believe, but we had tickets for the evening concert—$3.75 for the best seat in the house; ours had to have been much cheaper.

We had trouble getting to the Civic Center since every young female on the planet was camped around the Holiday Inn nearby, hoping to see the boys from Liverpool. They would surround and search each passing car, hoping to glimpse the Fab Four. Our seats were in the balcony in the rear of the Civic Center. We should have had binoculars to see the stage. I had been to a few concerts before, but nothing that would even be classified as contemporary music. There were several opening acts, none of which most of us remembered. The thousands of young girls packing the Center would scream every time one of the stagehands walked out to adjust something before realizing they could not be John, Paul, George, or Ringo. My sister and the friend who came with her were remarkably reserved, considering their pre-concert behavior. I was simply curious.

Finally, the Beatles were announced. Those were the last words I heard for the next thirty minutes as the audience exploded into a din my ears were unprepared for. We were too far away to see clearly, but we could read "The Beatles" on Ringo's drum set. At this point, they were recognizable only by their position on stage. The only two songs that I could detect enough to identify were "All My Loving" and "She Loves You." I waited for the screaming girls to catch their breath, but the intensity never subsided. Gussie's reserve lasted two notes into the first song, and she and her friend leaped out of their seats, erupting immediately into one continuous scream. My mother was horrified, worrying that my sister would fall off the balcony as she jumped up and down. At one point, Paul McCartney spoke, and Gussie's screaming increased several decibels. She grabbed the closest thing, my arm, squeezing it with the same intensity as her scream. I had only begun to regain feeling in my arm as we reached the car after the concert.

The half-hour set ended quickly, and we began the long walk out of the Center to our car. The screaming erupted periodically as someone walked out onto the stage, but my ears still pulsed with the residue of lingering screams. I wonder if my current hearing loss began that evening. I had been through the experience of a lifetime … and lived to tell the story. My sister announced the following day over breakfast that she was dropping out of school to marry Paul. My father smiled while my mother's horrified expression from the night rose to a higher level. "How can they stand that awful hair? They look like girls." Mom never did get over the long hair. Several years later, when picking me up at college, she refused to let me in the car because of my longer hair. By then, styles had changed dramatically, but my hair was still shorter than most. I had to walk the mile and a half down the hill into town for a haircut while she waited, crying all the while.

Music changed forever that year, making the 1960s the most fantastic decade of musical innovation. The Beatles had been the advanced guard of a wave of British Rock that legitimized much of what had already taken root in this country. Groups like the Beatles, Rolling Stones, Dave Clark Five, Yardbirds, and Spencer Davis

Group took their origins in popular American rhythm and blues acts like Chuck Berry, Little Richard, and Fats Domino and spawned several musicians that went on to take popular music to a higher level: Eric Clapton, Jimmy Page, Jeff Beck, Jimi Hendrix, and Steve Winwood. It was an extraordinary period of musical experimentation and change, starkly contrasting with the Vietnam War and assassinations that plagued that decade. The music energized a generation tired of war and desperately seeking change. While preferring the Motown Sound, I had to admit the Beatles were unique. While Motown helped combat the racial prejudice that was still rampant, it never affected the worldwide change that John, Paul, George, and Ringo did. The Beatles' sound evolved considerably during their short tenure, something few groups can claim, and their songs have endured some sixty years now, popularized by so many that followed them. I will never forget that February night when popular music changed forever. I even found my mother humming one of their songs years later; miracles never cease. However, she never got over the long hair.

Perfecting the Art
of Procrastination

"Never put off till tomorrow what may be done day after to-morrow just as well."

– Mark Twain

It was 8 p.m. on a cold February evening in 1966, and my term paper was due the next day. I had researched Stonehenge for my junior year project, beginning the previous September, and now, twelve hours before the project was due, I had twenty-six plus pages yet to type. My mother had insisted that lights be out by 11 p.m., and I regretted leaving a typing class out of my studies. My two-finger hunt-and-peck technique wouldn't get me close to completion, and I had passed panic mode several hours ago. There was a ten-point penalty for each day the project was late, and this project was a significant part of our grade. I needed to wake up from this bad dream.

There was a partial excuse for the quagmire I was mired in. I had completed all my research a month earlier, but by amazing and unfortunate coincidence, a significant book on Stonehenge had just been released. While scholars previously considered the impressive assemblage of stones an ancient Druid temple, Gerald Hawkins' *Stonehenge Decoded* theorized Stonehenge to have been an astronomical observatory. My semester-long research project was already outdated and incorrect. I finally purchased the book, which finally arrived two weeks before the project was due. Hawkins' research forced me to revise most of my paper. Even without this turn of events, I probably would have been sitting in my room that February evening in a similar predicament. Procrastination was my new middle name.

I began to type, one letter at a time. I was not my father's secretary, who could type well over 100 words a minute; I'm not sure my brain can process that fast. By 10:30 p.m., I was starting page four of the twenty-six pages plus contents and footnotes; I had naturally been slowed down by several trips to the kitchen, more to escape the thought of my impending doom than to eat. And, of course, I had to see what was on TV that had my brother and sister laughing so hard. I remember calculating that at this rate, even with no sleep, I would be done by late the next day. Maybe I could come down with a sudden illness; I had pulled that stunt a couple of times years earlier, but we had been told that illness was not an acceptable excuse for a project of this duration. "If you're sick, have a parent bring it in that day." Giving up seemed to be the only reasonable plan of action, but that would put me in the same predicament one night later, with a now twenty-point penalty overshadowing my efforts. Maybe I would wake up and find this was all a dream. Ironically, I still have this recurring dream today, and what a relief to finally awake.

None of this would happen today. Computers, word processors, spell and grammar checks, and the internet would make this experience more pleasant. Artificial intelligence could research and write the paper now. But this was 1966 when a significant mistake meant rolling the sheet off the typewriter, crumbling it into a ball, and tossing it across the room. White-out had just been invented, but it took time to apply, and if one took the paper out of the typewriter roller, it was challenging to return to the same line spacing. By 10:30, an impressive wastepaper pile sat in the corner of my room. I continued typing, hoping my mother would forget the 11 p.m. curfew. By 11:45,

I had managed to begin the seventh page, but doing the math still left me short of a timely completion. I heard my father's door open, and he called up the steps to have me turn my lights out. I was doomed!

Then I had a brainstorm or, more correctly, a brain trickle. I could type under my covers with a flashlight. The blankets would muffle the sound, and I could get enough done to have a chance of completing it the next night. This was a manual typewriter, which slowed my progress, but at least I didn't have to worry about an electric cord under the covers. I wouldn't want my obituary to read "death while typing." I found a flashlight in my room and constructed a stand for it in my tent. It was stifling, and I had to come up for air periodically, just long enough to lose my place. I was working from a rough draft, so I only had to type. This began the longest night of my life. I had even calculated and constructed a timetable, pacing myself to finish it in time. Hours and pages drifted by, and I seemed to be closing the gap. At one point, I contemplated taking a thirty-minute nap but wisely passed on what would have been a sure-fire disaster. As we grow tired, our cerebral processing deteriorates, and we can soon convince ourselves of anything.

At 5 a.m., I finally went to the kitchen for a snack. I woke our beagle Dixie and put her outside. The cold air woke me up, which only made me more aware of my nausea. Dixie and I returned to the third floor. My parents had heard me, but getting up early was not a sin. Out of the covers now, I attacked the keys with furious abandon, as much as two fingers would permit. The minutes ticked away, and I realized that there was a chance I could succeed. I suddenly realized I had missed a footnote and would have to retype several pages. Forget the required margin: I would violate the rule once since that retyping would have been the kiss of death.

School began at 8:30 a.m., an hour away, but it was also a one-mile walk away. I still had a page or two to type when my mother saved the day, telling me she would drive us to school. I rolled the last page off at 8:15, as she called for the second time that we needed to go. After a quick ride to school, I entered class just as the bell rang. What a night! For the record, I got an 88 on that paper, with two points removed for an improper margin.

That's what procrastination hath wroth! I wish I could say that I learned my lesson, but my life includes a couple more near disasters, although fortunately not as memorable. I know I'm not the only person who has ever delayed a project until the last minute. Life has taught me many lessons, most of which I learned the hard way. I hate to say it, but sometimes this is the best way to learn ... a message with an exclamation point. I rarely put off a task now and have found that procrastination sometimes has a good side to it.

It would be too easy to say that this stalling behavior was just a function of laziness, but I know I am not generally lazy. Indecision can play a factor, but I often work well under pressure. Although not usually the case, some of my most creative moments have occurred under pressure when I was forced to use a drastically different approach. If a decision that needs to be made is clear, albeit challenging, I can make it, but sometimes, additional time puts matters in a different light. And sometimes things need to be procrastinated. A full plate forces us to prioritize, and some things don't get done. Often, these were things that I had worried about but didn't need to get done. I'd have to live to be 150 to complete half the items on my "to-do" list.

Procrastination can frequently make a problem worse, especially in the medical arena. Stalling contacting a doctor when cancer is involved can be a death sentence. We don't want to run to the emergency room every time we sneeze, cough, or have a headache, but when does reasonable caution evolve into procrastination? The cost of medical care further clouds good decision-making, while the overuse of medicine, in our climate of perceived liability, applies pressure from the opposite direction. I realize many males think an ignored problem will disappear, and sometimes it does. Is this procrastination, ego, or stubbornness?

It is an avoidance of the inevitable, which is the real issue. How often does an apology get put off? My favorite thing to put off these days is a phone call. This may be a throwback to earlier years when I stuttered considerably. It is certainly not the reason today. We all have our procrastination top ten lists: putting off starting a diet, delaying necessary surgery, tax avoidance, and putting off required work for a course. Speaking of the latter, I am reminded of a college friend, Sid, in the procrastination graduate program. He delayed all work in his four courses until two weeks before exams. He would then pull out his texts and typewriter and begin his semi-annual marathon, averaging less than two hours of sleep per night throughout the period and even less during exam week ... and the sleep he got was not quality sleep. One day, he fell asleep sweeping a floor in our kitchen, sleeping soundly until someone rudely kicked the broom out from under him. He then slept in the center of the room before someone finally tripped over him.

Sid had survived several semesters doing this, but he had reached new heights or depths this one semester. He became dysfunctional about a week into the marathon and soon became the mental equivalent of a celery stalk. The night before his English exam, he was reading a required novel for the first time and planned on completing that and a ten-page paper on it by morning. He asked us to ensure he made it to the 8 a.m. exam on time. He somehow succeeded, at least to a limited extent, and unwisely decided to lie down briefly at 7 a.m. Someone fortunately remembered his request and went into his room to see if he was OK. He returned quickly, saying, "I think Sid might be dead. I can't wake him up." Racing into his room, we found him fortunately alive but unresponsive. We dragged him into the shower to wake him up, and although we got his eyes open, he could not stand. At this point, it was 7:40 a.m., and the dorm was at least ten minutes away from the exam location. Three of us half dragged, half carried Sid to the exam room. We sat him down, put a pencil in his hand, and kept him awake until the professor began to hand out materials. As I was later told, he was snoring away about halfway into the exam. I never heard from Sid after college and often wondered what became of him, but he did graduate.

My brother Bill also had the family procrastination gene, which manifested yearly around Christmas. We would all meet for Christmas Eve dinner, after which Bill would begin his Christmas shopping. This was before the days of Wal-Mart and stores that would stay open around the clock. The only store open was a pharmacy, and these weren't like pharmacies today, where you can buy everything from a loaf of bread to a TV set. His presents were unique. If we were lucky, we would get a box of candy, but usually, the gifts would be far more memorable. I particularly remember the shaving cream before I started shaving—the following year, hair tonic that I never use. We treasured this Christmas tradition and would have been disappointed with anything else. Truth be told, that first year, I did start shaving!

To procrastinate or not, that is the question. Whether 'tis nobler in the mind to put off the inevitable … ay, there's the rub. I ran into one fellow who had an interesting solution to the problem. Since, to him, the world could end tomorrow, why hurry? Just enjoy today. I often wonder if he wakes up disappointed that we're all still here. But then, possibly he's right; maybe God is just procrastinating pulling the plug on the world.

Tenth Place Ribbons

I was sitting at the starting line, waiting for the horn to begin the race. I was seriously overmatched and expecting to finish last. However, I was not discouraged—quite the opposite. No one expected me to win, and I didn't care. I was determined to enjoy this marathon canoe race. My crew and I had our paddles in the air, ready to dig in. To complicate matters, the wind had picked up, and we would now be fighting the wind and significant waves over the seven-mile course. The horn sounded, and with a battle cry, we took off. We did not win, not even coming close. This was not Hollywood. But I learned something far more important that day than winning a trophy.

OK, I never won a tenth-place ribbon. I grew up in an era when kids were allowed to endure the life-altering trauma of losing and having nothing to show for it. Everybody is a winner today, or at least we tell them that. If they don't get a ribbon, we award them a certificate of participation. I have no problems with recognizing the value of everyone, but losing is a part of maturing. While the winning aspect of competition can undoubtedly be overblown, life is about neither winning nor losing; it's about growing, and sometimes losing facilitates growth better than winning. Winning feels good, but it is a short-term high. How good can it feel to receive an "Achievement Ribbon" when one knows they came in last place? And how satisfying is it to gaze upon that treasured tenth-place ribbon hanging on your wall? In my twelve years of school, I never won a blue ribbon ... ever. My granddaughter has no wall space left with all the ribbons she has won from her horse shows. That's wonderful, and I am so proud of her. But should she feel less proud of herself if those walls were bare?

I did win the first Draft Lottery in 1970, placing me first in line for an all-expenses paid tour of duty in beautiful, rainy Vietnam. I never made it to Nam, and I'm guessing this keeps my winless streak intact. All that "failure" must make me a candidate for lifelong psychotherapy. I probably set a record in school that will never be broken—thirteen years of school play days and competitions, and I never once won any ribbon. And to think, I never became a deranged criminal or had to endure years of psychotherapy because of it.

I'm not a huge fan of competition among children, but it is a part of our existence. I applaud our focus on participation as the key element, but tenth-place ribbons don't build self-esteem. I did lack self-esteem when it came to sports because I always lost; I was not built to win gold medals either. In fifth grade, my lacrosse coach pulled my father aside and asked him to talk me into dropping off the team so he wouldn't have to play me the mandatory minimum time as the league required. I understand that sports, almost by definition, must be competitive, but too many children are sloughed off to allow a focus on the cream. This is better today than when I was growing up, but there is no need to make every child feel like a star. Participation and the joy of the game should be the focus, but not at the expense of good, healthy competition. Competition should motivate us to move to a higher level. I couldn't play lacrosse, so I should have been gently pushed in another direction. There were better activities for me that I could have found successful. The key is not to give every child a ribbon but to fit them with the activity best suited for them. There are so many avenues where one can find success.

Society's obsession with certain sports is another issue; there is a "sport" in which every child can find success. After sitting on the bench for every minute of every little league baseball game, never once taking the field in a game, my brother Bill wisely quit and happily discovered tennis, soon whipping the snot out of his older brother. My son Scott found and excelled at horseback riding. I later discovered hiking. Today, I work with students in the world of competitive birding; lest you think this is not competitive or athletic, try going twenty-four hours nonstop in an activity involving much walking and even some running. A competition, yes, but the emphasis is on teamwork, learning, and just having fun.

My parents should have known early on that I was headed for athletic mediocrity. I participated in two Easter egg hunts as a toddler, never finding even one egg. My father coached me after the first hunt to be more aggressive, but his coaching was to no avail. I didn't have the Easter egg killer instinct, and other kids would push me aside, going for the egg I had spotted. Some kind woman did take an egg from her son's basket and gave it to me. I was still traumatized. My sister Gussie was the aggressive one. Eighteen months younger than me, she always had a basket overflowing with eggs.

I was packed off to Hyde Bay Camp for the summer at twelve. The camp had an excellent attitude where fun was paramount to winning. Now, you can't tell kids that winning is unimportant because they will find a way; it seems ingrained in us to an extent. Survival of the fittest means "win" to a preteen. The end of the summer would find the campers competing in a series of specific events, and once again, ribbons ran in the other direction when I showed up. Expectations are low when one has never won a ribbon, and I honestly got into the fun side of the competition. They don't award ribbons for having the most fun. They should! My wall would be dripping with ribbons.

In my fourth summer at the camp, I won my only ribbon. Knowing I could never engage in any activities requiring agility or speed, I signed up for a canoe race. This was not a typical canoe race but a seven-mile race from one end of Late Otsego, in Upper New York State, to the other. I signed up for a chance to canoe the lake, not to win anything. The more competitive and athletic campers chose equally talented partners. I was built like a strand of spaghetti with a big butt. No one looking to win would have chosen me. I was OK with that. In an activity where two captains choose teammates, I was always among the last two or three chosen. By age fifteen, I accepted that fate; I had nothing to lose because no one ever expected much.

For the race, I had to choose my two crew members. I would take the stern, both powering the canoe and keeping us heading straight, and they would power us from the bow and middle. I surprised everyone by choosing two younger students as my crew. While other canoe captains chose size and power, I was looking for serious, hard-working campers who would also be good company for the long race. We looked utterly outclassed when the six canoes lined up at the starting line. Anyone can be dangerous, however, if they have nothing to lose.

It was a beautiful day with a strong north wind. Problem # 1: We would be racing into a strong wind and waves the entire way. Problem # 2: Seven miles is a long way, and with the wind at times blowing canoes from side to side, this was a much longer race than seven miles. Problem # 3: Our canoe seriously leaked!

The other five canoes shot out of Cooperstown at the south end of the lake, but the steady wind and waves quickly slowed the pace down. If the canoe was pointed directly into the wind, one could make headway, albeit slowly. Once one veered even a few degrees from straight into the wind, the wind would quickly push the bow off course, and the crew would have to fight to get the canoe back into the wind. We were comfortably in last place, with no thought of winning; we were enjoying the challenge of paddling. The wind intensified, and one of the canoes pulled into shore. We were now in fifth place. We dug in and gradually closed the gap. By the time we were two miles into the race, we had moved up to third place. Slow and steady was working, and we were soon just a little behind the two lead canoes.

Halfway up the lake, all were exhausted. There were no breaks, as we had to keep up the momentum. The slightest pause would have seen the canoe blown off course. Soon, another canoe behind us pulled into shore. The camp boat rode by, asking if we wanted to quit. A quick look at my canoe mates told me we were in for the long haul. The fourth-place canoe had fallen far behind and was now hugging the shore to avoid some of the wind. By this point, we could no longer feel our arms. Winning was never a goal, but finishing was. We got in a rhythm, knowing that the only way to finish was to not stop for even the smallest of breaks. As the canoe bounced through the giant waves, it was easy to think we were making progress, but a glance at the shoreline showed us that we were virtually standing still. Our middle person paddled and baled as each wave sent a bucket of water into the canoe. The camp boat drove by again to see if we were all right, suggesting that it might be a good idea if all abandoned the race at this point. We just smiled and dug those paddles in deeper. We were in a rhythm that kept the canoe moving, even if at a snail's pace. As they say, minutes became hours.

Finally, we rounded Peggs' Point to head the short distance into the camp. The fourth-place canoe had disappeared behind us, and the two canoes ahead of us had a comfortable, commanding lead. Both had an extremely athletic crew, clearly much more substantial than us, but we had kept pace with them the whole way. We crossed the finish line, ceremoniously flipping the canoe. Every muscle in my body ached, but a remarkably contented feeling swept over me. We lay in the shallow water, unable to move, legs cramped, and arms reduced to non-functioning dead weight. There was no thought of which place we finished in, just that we finished when others, better than we, hadn't. I honestly think that third-place ribbon was the only ribbon I ever won, but to me, it was the Super Bowl Trophy of Kiddom.

Today, we think we can manufacture self-esteem with ribbons and constant assertions that "every child is a star." You could have called me a star every time I walked onto a lacrosse field, but I knew others were better than me. Self-esteem comes from hard work and gradually ascending the mountain of success; there is no elevator to the top. And the reality is that we cannot be a star at everything we do. Recognizing that is part of learning who we are. When we look back on our lives, gratification will not come from the awards but from knowing we played the best game with the hand we were dealt. How sad to see a past sports or entertainment star spending the rest of their lives reliving their few glory years. Ultimately, the awards are forgotten, and our character is our legacy.

Back to the canoe race. The third place ribbon I won did nothing to boost my self-esteem, but the fact that we persevered and finished after a grueling afternoon of paddling did. No one told me how great we were, and no one was paying attention in the award ceremony when they got to awarding the third-place ribbon for that event. But I knew I had accomplished something that had nothing to do with the race. I must have thought about quitting 100 times that afternoon, and my two crewmates often did. I kept us going and smiling. In a movie, we would have come from behind at the last minute and won first place against all odds. I'll take that third-place ribbon and what it represented. Self-esteem comes from hard work and accomplishment, independent of winning and losing. It comes from overcoming personal obstacles. But the race and the competition that day were key. If it had been just a leisurely paddle, there would have been no incentive to perform at the highest level; giving up would have been much easier. Hard work changes you and makes you a more robust and better person; ribbons collect dust. Achievement is about substance, not fluff, and building genuine self-esteem takes time and sweat. Many today understand that, but all too many are looking for the shortcut to the top; it doesn't exist.

I saw the best example of the good side of sports and competition while in Air Force Basic Training at Lackland Air Force Base in the summer of 1971. To complete basic, we had to surmount several obstacles, one being a one-mile run. While this distance is hardly a challenge for individuals that age, two factors made it more complicated: I was never built for speed, and the temperature in San Antonio was 110 degrees that day. Yes, you read that correctly—110. Throughout the six weeks of training, we ran the mile many times. I was hardly a speed demon, but I could qualify. We had two in our dorm group who were so fast that they lapped much of the dorm in each run. They would race each other, and on the qualifying day, all wondered who would win the "race." There was also an individual who never even came close to finishing in the eight minutes allotted. Sadly, it looked like he might have to repeat basic training.

Each individual had to cross the finish line in under eight minutes to pass the test. The two speed demons took off when the starting whistle blew and stayed neck and neck throughout the race. I plodded along, and our slower member fell hopelessly behind the rest of the group. The two speed merchants stopped ten feet short of the finish line. Running backward, they ran back to the slow member of the group. Each grabbed an arm and took off, almost carrying him at times. With well over a lap to go, they raced as our drill sergeant counted down the time, and with ten seconds left to spare, they crossed the line. Our sergeant said, "All crossed the finish line in under eight minutes. Everyone passes."

None of us knew they would do this, and we were all amazed. To this day, that is one of the most impressive things I have ever seen. The two barely knew the other fellow but took teamwork to a level I rarely saw. Each wanted to "win," but helping their dormmate to pass was more important. They knew it was the only way he would pass. We expected our sergeant to negate the run, but he said nothing. I suspect he was secretly pleased.

My treasured third-place ribbon has long since gone to the trash heap, and the annals of Maryland sports will never include my name in any capacity. I thought about inventing a sport and automatically making myself a world champion, but that's only one notch better than someone trying to get into the Guinness Book of World Records for making the world's largest meatball. I'll settle for being me.

SUNDAY NIGHT MAGIC

God rested on the seventh day. That was ample justification for procrastinating doing the homework I had put off until Sunday. Friday afternoon, my mother shipped me off to dance class, part of her dream that I learn the required skills for qualifying for life in Baltimore society. I failed. Saturday was ... well, Saturday; no one does homework on Saturday. Then came Sunday, which unhappily began with church and Sunday school. I would have gladly sacrificed both to stay home and do homework. Sunday afternoon was all about sports—the Orioles and the Colts. Every weekend, I had the best intentions—to do my homework after dinner on Sunday. If my brain had been even partly working, I would have known this plan would fail because Sunday evening was magic in our household.

Television was still a new phenomenon in the 1950s and early 1960s since the sets were becoming affordable for middle-class families; it was beginning to replace many family activities from the previous generation—radio, table games, and reading. Initially, many questioned its intellectual value, with TV acquiring nicknames such as the "boob tube" and "cultural wasteland." Programming was dominated by family situation sitcoms, which projected a stereotypical view of white middle-class society, westerns where the "good guy" cowboys always won out over the "bad guy" Indians, and mindless children's programming with no educational value, serving only to get children to buy the latest sugar-laden cereal.

The family sitcoms served up a hefty dose of fluff, showcasing what some considered the ideal white middle-class family with the successful father, obedient homemaker mother, and sometimes mindless children being just disobedient enough to make for thirty minutes of family drama. As children, we thought these to be projections of reality, not realizing that real families had more severe problems and that many minority and lower-class families could not identify with any of this. *Father Knows Best, The Donna Reed Show,* and *The Adventures of Ozzie and Harriet,* in many ways, promoted conformity to this unrealistic model of American life. Even worse but more entertaining were shows like *My Favorite Martian* and *I Dream of Jeannie,* about a man who marries a witch. At least *Mr. Ed,* a show about a man with a talking horse, would never be confused with reality.

It was impossible to turn on a television during that period and not see a group of cowboys galloping across the plains with guns blazing as they chased a band of Indians. These shows were the stereotypical good vs. bad guy, starkly contrasting with the real world of complex, marginal characters. After World War II, America was not ready to face reality. *The Lone Ranger, Hopalong Cassidy,* and *The Cisco Kid* became role models for millions of American kids. Sadly, these reinforced the stereotype of Native Americans as savages, not the remarkable people they are. As a result of these shows, every boy ran around with his metal toy pistols, killing "Indians." I always marveled at how every bullet and arrow missed the show's hero. My sister Gussie, one to be different, took up the Native American cause, always leading a group of braves to rebuff the hordes of cowboys.

Children's programming was limited to cartoons and shows such as *Howdy Doody*. Buffalo Bob would enter our living rooms on Saturday morning, asking the Peanut Gallery, "Hey, kids, what time is it?" Then, all would launch into the "It's Howdy Doody Time" song.

Clarabell, with his seltzer bottle, would join the fray, but he could not speak since that would require exceeding the show's meager budget. Then Howdy Doody would enter, a ridiculous-looking puppet with a freckle for each of the forty-eight states in the union. I never figured out what they did when Alaska became the forty-ninth state in 1959. Early Saturday morning, parents slept in while kids huddled around the TV in their pajamas, armed with teddy bears, dolls, and blankets, while Bugs Bunny outsmarted Elmer Fudd and Mighty Mouse was "here to save the day." Cereal advertisers quickly realized that they had a captive audience. Between cartoons, we saw children telling the "silly rabbit" that "Trix are for kids" and Tony the Tiger informing all that Sugar Frosted Flakes were "gr-r-eat!" Thus began our generation's obsession with sucrose. To make matters worse, manufacturers often hid a small prize at the bottom of the cereal box, so a child would have to overdose on the product to finally reach the prize, which never matched the lucrative picture on the box,

Because most could only afford one television set, families often watched shows together, except on school nights when children were supposed to do homework. I say "supposed" because once my bedroom door closed, Mom and Dad couldn't see the tower I was building or the comic book that suddenly materialized. No one in the 1950s seriously thought television had educational value, but it did bring families together when watching a show. There may have been limited communication while watching, but there was emotional bonding, communal laughter, or joint "oohs" and "ahs" as the Lone Ranger outsmarted the bank robber. Nowhere was this truer than on Sunday evenings.

At 6:30 Sunday evening, our family had a date in front of our television set, usually beginning with *The Wonderful World of Disney* with part of a Disney movie. The set was in my parents' bedroom, and we piled on their bed. Over the years, the line-up varied, but *Lassie*, *Perry Mason*, and *Bonanza* followed. However, everyone waited for 8 p.m. when The Ed Sullivan Show came on. The shows were only part of the family treat because this was the day Dad spared us Mom's cooking and brought in dinner.

This was before fast food, but fantastic take-out options still existed. Baltimore had the Harley's Sub Shop, which opened a branch a few blocks from our house. This was a family favorite and my first introduction to subs. Dad also picked up our meal at Jimmy Wu's China Inn, our introduction to Chinese cuisine. Little Tavern Hamburgers was the third piece of the Sunday night trifecta of meal choices. One could buy a burger for ten cents; several were needed to satisfy one's appetite. Dad could bring home a large bag of beef and buns at that price. These were a treat except when Dixie, the world's fattest beagle, made off with the whole bag, resulting in one very sick dog—has any other dog eaten fifty-four hamburgers at one time? The Little Tavern burgers also made a good movie snack; buy four or five to eat throughout the movie. Soon, a new meal solution, TV dinners, could be pulled out of the freezer to save us from Mom's cooking.

The success of the Baltimore Colts in winning the World Championship in 1958 and 1959 introduced Baltimore to fast food as several Colt stars opened restaurant chains. Alan Ameche, the fullback, opened his franchise, and the Ameche's Powerhouse, a precursor to the Big Mac, became a delectable Sunday night option. Then Gino Marchetti, the Colts' defensive end, opened Baltimore's first legitimate fast-food franchise, and Gino's became a Little Tavern alternative. We looked forward to the food and the shows, but the real prize was family fun and sharing as we all ate, watched, laughed, and joked. Dixie added another element of comic relief as she ran around the room, trying to steal everyone's food. Lord help you if you turned away from your meal for even a second.

The evening always culminated with the Ed Sullivan Show, with Ed beginning each variety hour by announcing that it would be "a really big shu." We endured Topo Gigio, the talking and singing mouse puppet, juggling acts, ballet, and singer Ethel Merman to see an up-and-coming stand-up comedian and the latest music group. The show introduced performers like Elvis Presley, the Beatles, the Rolling Stones, and the Supremes to the world.

In later years, *Perry Mason* occupied a Sunday evening time slot, solving every mystery, no matter how complex, in the one-hour time slot. Just as the cowboys never lost a fight, Raymond Burr, as Mason, never lost a case. As I got older, I watched Sunday night movies, exposing myself to some remarkable old films and ensuring that no homework would get done.

The shows were generally good shows and undoubtedly entertaining. Still, they lacked any relevant social content, allowing many children of that time to grow up ignorant of so many social realities: poverty, discrimination, injustice, and the true horrors of war. But this was a time in this country when many were unprepared to deal with reality. Our fathers had risked their lives in World War II, and that generation had endured the Great Depression. This was a time when all wanted to relish the freedom we had fought to preserve, but the 1960s brought us back to reality. The televising of the Vietnam War on the evening news every night marched the real world into our homes, and Martin Luther King and others thankfully brought the issues of segregation and discrimination to the forefront.

However unrealistic, the Sunday night television lineup brought families together. Indeed, no poor or minority family identified with *Cinderella* or *Leave It to Beaver*, but for us, life slowed down, and all gathered and enjoyed being a family. Problems disappeared, school was forgotten, and time stood still. It was the best of times—unfortunately, Monday morning with no homework done always followed.

The Monster Lives

I could not believe I had followed Frank down into that dark basement. We should never have been down there. Even though the house was supposed to be deserted, we tried to be as silent as possible. I was almost afraid to breathe, and I heard every heartbeat. That's when we bumped into it. I tried to identify what lay before me, using only my hands to see. Frank was the first to recognize it. "George, you're not going to like what this is." Continuing to run my hands over the object, I suddenly stopped in terror. We had to get out of there and fast!

Stories become embellished over time; nothing can work this magic better than a young child's imagination. Often, the story evolves into something that bears little resemblance to the original, but even in these cases, the story retains a tiny morsel of truth. Such is the story of William, a monster who roamed central New York State. The legend dates to the early twentieth century, and elements of it are likely wholly fabricated, but I am witness to the fact that there is some truth to it. In 1965, I was a participant in part of the legend. I have told the story many times, and while I enjoy embellishing aspects, at least part is genuine. Does the monster exist? You be the judge. My participation in it may be the most ignorant thing I have ever done.

The story's first part is a legend passed down in the annals of Hyde

Bay Camp, where I spent eight summers. Like all new campers, I was told the horrifying story in my first summer at the camp. I lay in bed in our tent that summer evening while my counselor told us the story. Initially skeptical, I knew he was trying to scare us, but as the story unfolded, I grew increasingly uneasy.

William was the son of a prominent local family. It was soon apparent that he was a bad seed, and when he murdered someone, much of the family wanted to wash their hands of him. He was tried, convicted, and sentenced to be hung. His father could not bear to lose his son and paid a doctor to fit a harness so the hanging would not break his neck. The doctor could then take the body down from the gallows, falsely pronounce him dead, and carry him back to the family property for burial. An empty coffin would be put in the ground, and William could escape the area.

All proceeded as planned, and his body and coffin were returned to the family estate. The family discovered that something had gone wrong, and William's neck and vocal cords were damaged. He also seemed to be brain-damaged and had turned violent. He was placed in the wine cellar, where he lived for years. Over time, his body became more deformed. His head swelled to where he seemed to have no neck, and his eyes became as black as coal.

Legend said that he escaped from the wine cellar and roamed the countryside. Our camp was right across the lake from where he supposedly lived. A gentleman who lived beside the camp was hunting nearby and walked into a covered bridge over a stream that fed the lake. Resting there, he suddenly heard moaning and what sounded like forced breathing. He had never heard an animal quite like this and approached the sound. Suddenly, a figure who had been up in the rafters pounced on him, and they fought. At first, the man thought it was an animal but soon realized that this creature walked on two legs. The figure, however, had no neck, seemed almost too hairy to be a human, and had eyes so dark they appeared missing. The man escaped but had his eye torn out in the scuffle. He wore a patch on his eye for the rest of his life.

A couple of years later, an incident occurred at a nearby girls' camp. One evening, one of the cabins heard something moving through the brush outside. Thinking it was an animal passing nearby, all ignored it. The rustling continued, and soon, they heard a moaning sound and what sounded like forced breathing. Thinking that maybe this was a fellow camper needing help, several went out to investigate. A five-minute search turned up nothing, and they returned to their cabin when they noticed that one girl was missing. A search turned up the girl's mangled body. No wild animals in that area could have done this, and the camp was permanently closed.

We were getting very quiet at this point in the story; there was now enough believable detail in the account to worry us. The counselor continued with several other minor sightings but warned us to be careful if we heard something in the woods, especially if we heard that forced breathing. He paused briefly, and I heard something walking through the woods near our tent. Suddenly, I heard forced breathing, and someone reached through the side of the tent and grabbed me. That's one of the rare moments in my life when I screamed. However, it was simply another counselor who had been waiting outside for this point in the story. Our tent was supposed to be quiet at that point in the evening, but I'm sure we woke up the entire camp.

Twelve-year-old kids have more than enough imagination, and we were not about to sleep. After the story, we all had to go to the bathroom, but no one was brave enough to leave the tent since we had to walk through a dark section of woods to get to the bathroom. We would have to hold it until morning. All but the youngest campers were told that story, and over the summer, many reported hearing this deep, forced breathing at night.

I soon got over it, writing it off as an excellent story for scaring the bejeezies out of young kids. That was... until I met the man who owned the property beside our camp. He was supposed to be the one who had been attacked on the covered bridge, and he did have a patch over his right eye. One, bolder than I, asked him what had happened; he just turned quite pale and said he would rather not talk about it. I began to worry. Later, we were on a small hike along a local stream near the camp two weeks later and came upon a covered bridge. So, there was a covered bridge. A friend entered the bridge and soon came out screaming, "There's someone in there." Asking no questions, we all took off running, and that hike ended quickly. My friend swore that he heard heavy breathing, but then he also claimed earlier that the ghost of George Washington came to visit him one night.

I still thought the story was a fabrication, but I was uncomfortable with small parts of it seeming genuine. That's when I found a girls' camp nearby that had been forced to shut down—another true component of the story. The camping season ended soon after, and I left the camp and William behind, returning to Baltimore.

I returned the next two summers to watch new cadres of campers subjected to the legend, and, of course, William was often heard walking the woods around the tent area. He was now an integral part of the camp experience, and the story grew more comical as I aged. William would be old by now, and rational analysis was relegating William to the same drawer as Big Foot and the Loch Ness Monster. That was until the summer of 1965.

I returned for another summer with more responsibilities, and I was now sharing the legend of William with younger campers. I couldn't tell the tale as well as others, though I could at least get the details correct. A friend was a remarkable storyteller, and he shared it masterfully. On a bet, he once terrified a group of teenagers with a rendition of *Goldilocks and the Three Bears*. I couldn't even tell a joke. I told the story to one group of campers with some success, and the next day, one camper said he had heard deep breathing in the woods near the outdoor bathroom. That got the attention of several other campers, and soon, there were reports of this forced breathing and a creature running through the woods at night. Chuckling, I assured them all were safe. That was ... until I heard it myself. I wondered if another counselor was behind this, but everyone seemed to have an alibi. The reports continued. The campers' imaginations soon had William regularly patrolling the nearby woods for a fresh victim.

Near this time, several other counselors and I led a trip up the mountain behind the camp. We hiked through a cow pasture, hoping the cows would be too busy munching away to notice. We were horrified to find two cows mauled and partially eaten. That night, the campers started putting pieces of the legend together on the mountain around the campfire. William must have attacked the cows for food. After embellishing the story, they retreated to their tents, a little more uncomfortable than usual.

I laughed it off, although the dead cows did seem odd. Everything soon became more serious one evening. Several of us were sitting down by a campfire near the lake. The campers were all in bed and quiet, and it was an excellent time for the counselors to relax and chat. A full moon that night seemed to light up the lake, and we could see clearly as our eyes adjusted to the dark. One staff member was sharing a story when a scream shattered the quiet. This was not the cry of a camper—much too loud. Before I could process this, the riding counselor screamed, "Oh my God, it's the horses!"

He charged up a trail from the camp to where the horses were kept, and the rest of us followed behind him. It was tricky without a flashlight, but we knew the trail well. Reaching the pasture, we saw the horses racing in every direction, emitting sounds more like screams than the usual neighs. I wasn't a horse person, but something was terrorizing them. We could see the horses running away from the center of the pasture, and a two-legged figure was racing across the field away from us. That was no human! Whatever it was—approached and cleared a five-foot fence with ease.

That incident was the talk of the camp the next day, and that evening, Frank and I sat around the campfire, speculating on what we had seen.

Frank said, "That was no human. Did you see the way it jumped over the fence?"

"Frank, I agree it wasn't a person, but there are bobcats and bears in the area."

"Did you ever see a bear run like that or clear a fence that high?"

"Are you telling me you think that was William? Come on; he would be an older man now. It's a great story, but ...."

"Then how else can you explain all the strange things happening this summer?"

"I don't know, but I doubt a sixty-year-old deformed man is running around in our woods."

"Well, I haven't told anyone else this, but I think I found where he lives now."

"What!"

"Yeah, we were hiking back from Shadow Brook and found this old, deserted building. We started exploring it, and it has a basement."

He waited for me to respond, but he had my attention now.

"If you remember the legend, that's where they put the coffin."

"Frank, that was forty years ago."

"But it wasn't far from the covered bridge where that guy was attacked. It all adds up."

"Well, did you look in the basement?"

"Couldn't do it; we had a group of kids with us." After a pause, "But we should have. After last night, I'm convinced William is still alive."

I tried to change the subject, but the more we talked, the more my imagination took off. While I still thought the story a wonderful collection of unrelated facts, too many strange occurrences needed to be explained.

Frank suddenly jumped up. "I've got it. Let's go back to the house and check out the basement. The house is obviously deserted."

"Frank, I've got another camping trip tomorrow."

"I don't mean tomorrow… NOW!"

"Have you lost your mind? It's 11 o'clock, and I need to get some sleep. And I'm not hiking over there in the dark. How would we even know how to get there at night?"

"Come on. There's still enough light from the full moon, and we can take a canoe. I know a spot on Shadow Brook not far from the house."

"No. That's too crazy."

"Well then, I'll go over there alone. And you'll see—you'll miss all the fun."

I didn't want to go; I was afraid to go, but I didn't want him to go alone. I tried to talk him out of his plan, but we soon slid a canoe into the water.

Neither of us spoke as we paddled across a section of the lake. With no wind and enough moonlight, we could see trees reflected on the lake's surface. All was silent, and we soon left the lake and paddled up the broad stream. It was much darker in the forest, but we could see the turns and obstacles. We had to portage around one fallen log and soon reached a point Frank indicated was near the house. Climbing onto the bank and securing the canoe, we walked through the woods. Realizing that neither of us had been bright enough to bring a flashlight, I contemplated turning around, but Frank was already crashing through the underbrush.

And there it was. This was the first time I had known there was a small house near the stream. It was in a small clearing, well camouflaged by vegetation, and the moonlight filtered by the trees gave the house a sinister appearance. We approached the house, and Frank explained that since the door was locked, we would have to climb through a basement window.

"But Frank, we don't have a flashlight."

Frank ignored or never heard my comment as he raised a small ground-level window. Before I could say anything, he slithered through the window and dropped.

"Come on. The coffin's got to be down here."

To this day, I have no idea why I climbed through that window. I was usually a timid person, but Frank was so persuasive. I soon found myself standing on a concrete floor. The house even smelled old—the aroma of mold and dirt overwhelmed me as I tried to get my bearings. I couldn't see a thing and soon felt along a wall, trying to find the door Frank had just entered.

"George, there's something over here."

That got my attention. I had been so absorbed in the walk and feeling my way around a pitch-black room that I had forgotten the target of our quest.

"Over here. Just walk toward my voice." Then, "This is it! The coffin!"

When we talked by the campfire, I had doubted the existence of a coffin … or any part of the story. Frank was known to exaggerate. I reached the so-called coffin and began to feel along it. Undoubtedly, this was some long chest. But it was the right size and had fancy handles on the side. "Oh my gosh—this is a coffin."

"I told you so. Now, who's going to open it?"

"Frank, we can't see anything, and this is getting way too creepy for me."

Frank again was not listening, and I soon heard the creaking as he lifted the lid. "I opened it; now you stick your hand in to see what's in there."

That was enough. For the first time, I was terrified. The thrill of the quest was long gone, and my mind replayed every horror movie I had ever seen. I wanted to run, but I was frozen. "I'm not sticking my hand in there."

"Hey, we've come this far. Let's find some evidence that William uses this coffin."

"But what if HE'S IN THERE?"

"OK, at the count of three, we'll both stick our hand in."

"One." I waited for two, but two never came as a door opened at the top of the staircase. I was terrified already, and neither of us spoke. We saw no light but soon heard a footstep as someone started down the stairs. That did it! We ran even though neither of us could remember where the doorway was. After bouncing off a wall several times, I somehow found the door and could see the window with faint light streaming through. Frank was already through the window, and I was not far behind. I kept expecting something to grab me, but I followed Frank into the woods once through the window. There was enough light to at least see the trees, but we were tripping over logs and continually getting tangled in brush. By pure chance, we found the stream and located the canoe. We soon were paddling so fast that we probably left a wake. There was no enjoying the night air as we were too frightened to utter a word.

The campfire was still burning, and we beached the canoe and stumbled out. We looked at each other, but no words came out. We laughed—not because this was humorous, but because we were still alive. Sometimes, when emotions are extreme, the opposite reaction surfaces. After putting the canoe on the rack, we sat again by the campfire.

After a long silence, he said, "Did you feel anything in the coffin?"

"Are you nuts? I wasn't going to put my hands in there. And I thought you said the house was deserted."

"It was. That was William. I told you he lived there."

I was almost ready to believe this. We never shared the details of that late-night canoe trip, and as time eroded the memory of that night, I wondered if it had happened at all. The skeptic in me doesn't believe in ghosts, Bigfoot, or alien space visitation. My scientific mind recognizes the power of suggestion and imagination and that complicated phenomena often have mundane explanations, but ....

How Not to Interview
for College

I was terrified, sitting in the admission director's office for my first college interview. I had rehearsed in school earlier and repeatedly reviewed possible questions, but this was not how I had envisioned it playing out. While waiting for the first question, I looked down at my clothes. My T-shirt was stained with a hole in each armpit. My jeans were covered with paint and dry mud, partially camouflaging the numerous holes. My tennis shoes were well-worn, with a hole in one of the toes. I hadn't taken a shower in two days and had not shaved in a week. And I wasn't even at the right college! Was this a bad dream?

"So, George, why are you interested in attending Hamilton College?"

Junior year of high school can be a nightmare as subjects become more serious, students start paying attention to their cumulative averages, and the word "college" pops up daily. Being the most naïve student on the planet, I thought of colleges well beyond what my B-C average should have warranted: Princeton (expected since my father went there), Cornell, and UVA, for starters. We perused college guides as if we even had a clue what was a good match for us, took

SATs until we finally got the scores up to an acceptable level, and were groomed on how to impress in an interview. I had one strike against me as I had an enormous discrepancy between math and verbal SAT scores. My math score was 730 (out of 800): mild applause. My verbal was around 500: trouble – Princeton would not be impressed. Any interview would not win me any points since I was a stutterer. The interviewer would undoubtedly ask some questions that required an answer with a word I would get hung up on. If I had an ounce of common sense (and I was about an ounce short), I would have given up any thought of college and begun planning for a life of poverty. However, I still planned on touring colleges that following summer.

In the summer of 1966, I was sixteen and a counselor at Hyde Bay Camp in Cooperstown, New York. My junior year in high school had been unremarkable, but then everything about me academically was commonplace. I was well into my five-year academic slide, which had seen me drop from a top student to a struggling one. I disliked school and was the poster child for a teen social misfit. This was my fifth summer at the camp, and I was now a junior counselor. The camp had become my escape from reality, although, in hindsight, it was probably far closer to reality than my life in Baltimore. Also, several classmates were at the camp, but the atmosphere was completely different from school. I was different from many, but the camp encouraged individuality and creativity. Saying I fit in would be an overstatement, but the camp's less inhibited atmosphere was missing the social rules that defined school and my life in Baltimore.

That summer, I was responsible for the youngest kids, ages seven and eight, too young to be separated from their parents for an extended period. The job was challenging as I dealt with homesickness, bedwetting, and a myriad of behavioral issues. However, I loved working with children, and the summer flew by. School never crossed my mind as my body relaxed for the first time in ages. As the last of the kids left in mid-August, we started dismantling the camp: pulling up the long dock, taking down the large army tents we had slept in all summer, and securing buildings, boats, and supplies. On the last day, I helped pull up the dock and painted one of the sailboats, and by the time my parents arrived for my ride home, I was wearing more mud and paint than clothing. My parents were hurrying to hit the road, so I threw my gear into the car. My mother was appalled at my appearance, but I assured her I could shower and change in the motel. Reluctantly, my parents allowed me in the car.

We planned to check out some upper New York State colleges as we headed home. Colgate and Cornell were on my list, and Colgate was close, in Hamilton, New York. I'm unsure where the communication breakdown was, but when I awoke, we were driving up a steep hill; was this Colgate?

"We're at Hamilton, George. We've got time to drive around the campus before we head for a motel."

Never having seen Colgate before, I had no idea what it looked like. I only knew it had the same name as the toothpaste I used. It seemed much smaller than expected, and something told me I wasn't where I thought I was. A short conversation ensued, which ended with Mom saying. "This isn't Colgate; it's Hamilton College."

Completely confused, my father said that we might as well look around. It would give us a college to compare others to. We passed in front of the Admission Office, and my mother insisted I go in and get a catalog. Looking at my condition, I thought this a less-than-brilliant idea, but when Mom insisted, I gave in, too tired to argue. Then she had another idea: why not schedule an interview for the following day? I assured her that I had no intention of attending Hamilton College. Still, she presented a good argument for an interview: practice before interviewing at the other two colleges. Reluctantly, I trekked up the steps of the building.

It was a small building, with only one person visible when I entered. I asked for a catalog, which the gentleman quickly produced.

Usually, being grubby would not have bothered me, but talking to a well-dressed gentleman when I was wearing enough dirt to plant a garden made me want to exit hurriedly. However, I asked if I could schedule an interview for the following day. He immediately got up, saying, "Let's do one right now. I've got some free time."

Stunned, I looked down at my muddy shoes, mud and paint-covered blue jeans that were no longer blue, and a t-shirt that looked like a slice of Swiss cheese. All that I could muster was a prolonged "uhhhh." Laughing, he said, "Don't worry about it. I'll pretend you're clean and wearing a nice suit." He introduced himself as the chief admissions officer. I swallowed hard when I realized who he was, but I wasn't attending Hamilton College. What the heck!

Maybe it was the physical exhaustion or lack of sleep, but this ordinarily cautious soul threw caution to the wind and followed him into his office. He soon asked the obvious question, "Where the heck have you been? I've never seen anyone that dirty." I launched into a discussion of dismantling the camp, followed by a brief synopsis of my summer experience. I remember noticing that I was adding an unpleasant aroma to his small office, but we talked on. This wasn't an interview at all. We chatted about the camp and school. I had never sent anything to the college, so, fortunately, he wasn't aware of my less-than-impressive grades. I had nothing to lose, and a half hour passed before I knew it. I apologized again for my appearance, but then I hadn't planned on having an interview. He chuckled, making some comment about hoping that if we ever met again, I could be clean enough that he could see what I looked like.

My parents were stunned to hear of the interview. My mother couldn't believe they would have let me in one of the offices. I assured her that there was no way I was going to Hamilton College but that I had enjoyed the conversation. The director had generally seemed interested in what I was doing, a fundamental change from how I thought the rest of the world viewed me. We drove down that steep hill and headed toward Hamilton, New York. Thirteen months later, I returned to that steep hill as an incoming freshman at Hamilton College.

The college I had no intention of applying to became the perfect place for me. Over the years, I've worked with many students, all starting to narrow down the mountain of college choices to find the perfect college, but the student fits the college, not the other way around. There is no perfect college, but one can make almost any school the ideal place if one actively works to make it so.

But why did I get in after that muddy interview? I've often wondered what the director must have thought about it. I have no idea what effect the interview had on my admission, but nothing else in my resume should have gotten me in. All other colleges rejected me (as they should have). But then, was what I had at Hamilton even an interview?

I certainly wasn't nervous that day as I had nothing to lose, and lack of sleep and an incredibly physical day made me loose as a goose. I thought an interview consisted of a college official asking me difficult questions, and I had practiced answering those questions all year. However, that day, we just talked and laughed. He seemed interested in me and just kept asking follow-up questions. In hindsight, I realized he knew exactly what he was doing; he got to know the real me that day, not the canned personality I had rehearsed. With absolutely no pressure on me, I relaxed—completely relaxed. If I had walked in wearing a suit and let the nervousness build, I probably never would have gotten into Hamilton or any other college. I also learned an interview strategy that I used throughout my long career.

The most significant moments in life cannot be rehearsed, and chance so often plays a role. One can plan one's life, but life never follows a script. So, the next time you have an important interview, stay up all night and cover yourself with mud and paint. Well … maybe not!

CLOTHES MAKE THE MAN

In the summer of 1967, as I was preparing to head off for my first year of college, my mother wanted to give me cash to help purchase college clothes. "You'll need clothes for college, George, and I want to help out." She dug into her purse and produced a ten-dollar bill. That wouldn't even buy one shirt. No problem! I knew exactly what to do. After a day of clothes shopping, I returned home with a complete college wardrobe and gave her a quarter in change. She collapsed on a couch in tears. "I've completely failed as a mother."

In this world of high fashion, where anything can be marketed and usually is, and where a consumer can pay $150 for a pair of athletic shoes that cost less than five dollars to make, I have never conformed. It's probably because I had to wear a coat and tie to high school. Despite my warnings that wearing a necktie deprived my cerebral neurons of oxygen, I succumbed to authority. Looking at my grades in high school, I must have lost quite a few brain cells. I was horrified entering Hamilton College in the autumn of 1967 to discover that first-year students were expected to wear a coat and tie to dinner. Fortunately, this was corrected quickly when many in the class realized that the dress code only stipulated a coat and tie. This code soon bit the dust after several of us showed up for dinner with a coat, tie, and *no shirt*.

Yes, I am a confirmed slob, a term of endearment to me. Cleanliness is a different matter; it is a necessary and welcome component of health and social etiquette. I dress for comfort, never to impress. Clothes are functional as they should be. I apologize to all who have dealt with my dress over the years. I am quite comfortable with my wardrobe.

When I graduated from high school, my mother pulled me aside and said that now that I was a "man," I would have to purchase my clothes. If that had included suits, I would have been in real trouble, but there was no reason to panic. My parents always bought me nice clothing, which I paid little attention to. I grew up in Baltimore society, where every adult owned a tuxedo and wore it on many occasions. This didn't exactly sound like the life for me. Comfort was always an issue, but impressing others with my dress was never in question. Even though I had little contact with other classes, something always seemed artificial about high society. I balked when I started being invited to parties because of my name (a prominent father and a grandfather who had been a U.S. senator). Something in me said that a reputation must be earned, not inherited. I was proud of my family and enjoyed most people I met, but it didn't seem real. College was a way to escape society and meet people on my own merits.

After my mother's clothes pronouncement, she said she would give me some starter funds for my college wardrobe. I'm ashamed that I had never gone clothes shopping for myself, but I figured I could handle this most "adult" of tasks. Yes, she handed me ten dollars, but I needed a durable winter wardrobe since Hamilton was famous for its frigid weather. My friends laughed, seeing Mom's ten-dollar bill. However, I had a plan. Hopping in the car, I headed off to my favorite clothing store.

Now I realize my mother had never set foot in Sunny's Surplus Army/Navy Store on Greenmount Avenue, but it was one of my favorite haunts. One could buy anything from a hand grenade shell to military-packaged meals, but it was the reconditioned clothing I sought. I then proceeded to load my cart with a complete wardrobe:

- three sweatshirts

- a long, heavy-duty winter coat

- gloves

- multiple pairs of socks

- two belts

- five pairs of reconditioned pants, all four to five sizes too large

- five shirts

The shirts were reconditioned factory shirts with embroidered names: Sid, Floyd, Otis, Mack, and Tyrone. This was great! I could be a different person each day. I decided to splurge, bought an extra blanket and a white lab coat, and went to check out. The clerk rang my cart up: $9.75. Upon arriving home, I gave my mother the quarter change from her "contribution." I remember her sitting on the couch, crying, and saying, "My child can't go off to college looking like that." That Christmas, she gave me a nice sweater and sports coat, which I left at home.

Clothes were always about comfort, never looks. When my future wife first laid eyes on me the following year at college on a blind date, she met "Floyd" wearing his lab coat. My clothes went well with the three-dollar couch I splurged on and bought for my room. It was comfortable, but I never entirely removed the dead rat smell. Jackie married me anyway—poor girl! I did break down and wear a tux for my wedding two years later. I spent more renting that tux for one day than my entire clothes budget for four years of college.

After college, I went into active duty in the Air National Guard. There, a spotless uniform was mandatory. "You mean that people actually polish shoes?" Once again, I lucked out, ending up in the unit Command Post, a top-secret office where only a few authorized people were allowed. The coat and tie could stay off most of the time unless the Commander entered.

Teaching once again brought me back to the world of coat and tie. My supervisor told me he expected his "gentlemen" teachers to dress appropriately. Gentleman—that was my father and grandfather, not me. And I was a life science teacher: animals, outdoors, dirt, and chemicals. I surely wouldn't want to stain my only coat, and it quickly came off and stayed off. A few months into the school year, the outstanding school secretary called my room and informed me that my supervisor was heading down the hall to my room. I knew this was code for "find your coat and tie." Fortunately, my room was at the far end of the building, and I had time to scramble. But where were my coat and tie? I madly looked around the room, hoping that one was lying around, but alas, I was going to be "naked." Then I saw Manny, the classroom pet black rat snake. I quickly grabbed the docile snake (we kept him well-fed with mice) and draped it around my neck. My supervisor that year wasn't quite sure I was teacher material. He was old school, a competent teacher in his day, but relatively rigid in his expectations. He found no humor in a snake wrapped around my neck. The kids were in hysterics, probably enjoying his reaction as much as my new tie. I wore a coat and tie the next day, half expecting to find a termination letter in my mailbox. However, that day's activity was just too rugged for a coat and tie, and the tie soon found its way into the desk drawer. I was beyond hope.

Poor Jackie threatens to buy me a suit each year. It was one of the three things in 1970 that I vowed I would never own. The other two were an air conditioner and a color TV set. Those last two date me, although we did hold off on air conditioning until we installed geothermal heating and air. And do they even make black-and-white television sets anymore? However, I still have never owned a suit.

I can understand teenagers putting importance on clothes; they can be a part of the struggle to define who they are. I had no idea who I was, but I understood clothes were not a part of the answer. One must wonder when an older person is obsessed with clothing and appearance. To me, clothes are a matter of comfort. I'll pay extra for a wool shirt or socks. Cheap shoes are also a disaster. However, when content with one's being, looks are minimally important. I was always glad I never had a job that required a high level of dress. We would think twice about a salesperson showing up at our door dressed in a t-shirt and jeans.

My wife has had to put up with my dress all these years. I do sympathize with her. Attire is more important to her, and I find no fault with anyone thinking that way. Sadly, there is so much more social pressure on a woman to manage her appearance, and I understand that clothing is a part of the culture. I rebel when it becomes a part of social status. That's probably what initially sent me down the "wrong" path. I've always rebelled against social class because it is something gained through someone else's efforts. My grandfather was born on a working farm, the son of a shipbuilder. He rose to be a U.S. senator; that is a status well-earned. But being born into the life he and my father made for me, while nice and comfortable, really had nothing to do with me. I somehow felt more like a "Floyd," needing to earn my way through hard work rather than privilege.

There is also an unnatural aspect to "dressing up." I am most at home working outdoors which involves getting dirty. Nice clothes don't stay nice outdoors; they are soon adorned with dirt and grass stains. One feels closer to our elemental roots when dressed for the outdoors. That's what I like about wool; it's natural and an excellent fit for outdoor life. Years ago, the explosion in wearing jeans was a return to simplicity and earthiness, but now they have become the height of fashion. Once cheap, they are now beyond my "budget." And to think people will pay more to purchase jeans with "manufactured" holes; I can add holes to my pants at no charge. The fifteen-dollar tan outdoor work pants are my choice. They are comfortable, easily replaced, blend well with dirt, are a natural deterrent to mosquitoes, and are natural air conditioning if baggy: reason #542 why I had no career as a model.

No one will have to choose clothes for me once I pass on since cremation will be my choice, and my ashes will become a part of what makes me happy: the natural Earth. However, poor Jackie will lose her final chance to get a suit on me.

Not Ready for Prime Time

November 1966,
High School Essay on the Works of William Faulkner
Grade – 82

Teacher Comments: "Considering the circumstances, you have done a good job here. You discuss the connection between social change in the South and the element of depravity, but you have not always shown the connection adequately.... Stylistically, your writing is generally pretty good. On the whole, though, this is a pretty good essay."

There was one fact unknown to this teacher: *I hadn't read any of the books.*

Such was the sad state of my educational career in my senior year of high school. I was drifting through school, unmotivated, and with no plan—simply living the life I thought others expected. Not that a seventeen-year-old should have narrowed in on a career, but one should have a plan or at least feel a responsibility to make the best of oneself. I was not ready for prime time.

I was amazed that I received the grade I did on the assignment. The eleven-page report was based on three of Faulkner's novels, was footnoted, and included copious quotes to help satisfy the minimum word requirement. I used the CliffNotes versions of the three novels as my sources. This project certainly did not qualify as a high point in my education, but when one waits until ten days before a project is due, a train wreck results.

There is little in this period of my education that I take pride in. I even resorted to minor cheating once on a quiz, using the fact that several others did likewise as feeble justification. I had fallen off the education applecart and was drifting through life, putting out one self-created fire after another. I was accepted into Hamilton College later that year; college admission offices must be allotted one mistake annually. Anyone paying attention to my high school career should have seen this five-alarm fire and acted; clearly, my parents were preoccupied, and the teachers were more consumed with the pedagogical aspect of their jobs than the personal welfare of their students. I fell through the educational cracks.

I was one of my class's top two or three sixth-grade students. Five years later, I was invisible, ranked forty-eight out of sixty-four students. The decline in grades was gradual, which may be partly why I flew under the radar. From age twelve on, my previously good work habits deteriorated. I could no longer focus, procrastination ruled, and my life goal was to crawl into a corner where no one would notice. I figured the only award I would receive was "Most Likely Not to Be Remembered by Anyone at the Twentieth High School Reunion." Most stories of a child derailed begin with some abuse or neglect; however, no one was more loved by a family than me. There's no potential book or made-for-TV movie here; I had a privileged upbringing compared to many. I cared enough to get by and not attract undue attention, and no teacher let my parents know of any concern. I concluded that I was not bright, and that justified my laziness.

If I had been given a social report card, that would have been marginal to unsatisfactory. All knew I was shy, but much of that came from stuttering. My social life until my pre-teen years revolved around sports, but as many left me behind in the dust athletically, I lost many of those friends. My friends evolved, and as the next group became seriously girl-conscious, I soon lost those friends. These were the ones who always had the latest dirty joke to tell or would recount their usually fictional exploits. I then acquired a small group of friends with strong musical interests, and they created a comfortable, non-threatening social life, even though I musically could not have found my way out of a paper bag. Dating was minimal and awkward, mainly consisting of inviting one of my sister's friends to go to a dance. I need to go back and apologize to all of them for my being as exciting as a piece of toast.

I entered Hamilton College in September 1967, completely un-prepared academically and socially. Someone should have yanked the carpet from under me and put me to work for a year. I needed a reality check. I entered college with no real plan other than changing my life. I was self-absorbed and felt no responsibility for my actions and future. I expected the world to care for me as my parents had those early years. I felt sorry for myself but didn't understand that I had the power to change.

I saw Hamilton as a way to upgrade my social life, but I would have to tolerate the academic side of college. I got an academic slap in the face on the very first day of classes. One shouldn't feel lost in a course only ten minutes into the first class. I had somehow aced the chemistry achievement test, and my new advisor had me bypass Introductory Chemistry and instead take Quantitative Analysis, a class Juniors usually took. As the professor discussed the details of Schrodinger's Equation, I looked for a way to crawl out of the class-room and hide. That signaled the end of my pre-med track, as I never recovered. Having a biology professor sophomore year tell me I was wasting his time put an exclamation point on that.

My social life, however, took off. I did not have the self-discipline to monitor my social life, and I was soon wasting study time making new friends. At an all-male college, meeting the opposite sex was a challenge. At the first mixer with a girl's college, every girl was grabbed up before I could even start looking. After standing around feeling stupid for a half hour at a second mixer at another girl's school, I left and joined a small group at a bar. Realizing I was too timid to secure a date at a mixer, I resorted to a blind date for a whole weekend. As terrifying as that was, at least I would have a date. A friend recruited three girls from a local college, and I was paired with one. She was pleasant, but there was little positive chemistry, and she ended up with another guy she already knew. I was okay with that.

At the end of that weekend, I ran into one of the other three girls. She had been paired up with one of our dorm druggies and had left him almost immediately, then spent the rest of the weekend with a friend. She and I met about an hour before her ride left and compared weekend horror stories. She said something that no girl had ever said to me, that she'd had watched me all weekend, wishing she had been paired up with me. Two weeks later, I was visiting her at her school. No one had ever shown interest in me, and I loved the attention.

The relationship gradually soured as the novelty wore off. We both enjoyed the company, but our interests and personalities were mismatched. She was fun-loving and outgoing; I was still somewhat shy and reserved. I could not have been a positive match for her, as she flunked out of college that year. I finally got the nerve to end the relationship and was again alone. Little did I know that I would meet my perfect match four months later.

I went to college at age eighteen because I was supposed to do that but was not ready. My social and academic development had been stunted, and I needed more time to develop. Translation: I needed to stop feeling sorry for myself and grow up. Unfortunately, I initially felt the social pressure to follow the Baltimore society script: go to a good college, get a good job (lawyer, doctor, or banker), marry a Baltimore society girl, and raise little children to follow the same path. I had no genuine interest or goal other than saying I wanted to be a doctor because it sounded impressive. I needed to free myself from that social pressure and find an interest. There was no passion in my life. Nobody would have suggested this, but I needed to take a year off and find myself. I wasted a year and a half of my parents' tuition payments.

I know when the downslide began—at age twelve, Kim was taken out of our home, and Gussie's problems began to surface. I could use these as excuses for my academic and social plunge, but the responsibility for our actions lies entirely within ourselves. I needed a swift kick in the posterior. I was given all the love and tools to succeed; I just failed to use them.

Why relive all these moments? We all stumble through parts of our lives, and learning from errors makes one a better person. We can always discuss "could-haves" and "should-haves" when reflecting on our lives, but there are no "re-dos." Going to college was expected in the family and society I grew up in—not the best reason to go to college. I needed a life experience to give me a reason to attend. Many today make the college decision for the right reason—an extension of a hobby, interest, or work experience. I should have waited a year before attending college—a year of work in the real world. I had grown up in Oz; as wonderful as it was, it wasn't real.

However, I was a lucky one. When I met Jackie in February 1969, I was damaged goods, but she accepted that perfection and I were distant cousins. Her love and support turned my life around. We married less than two years later, even though I was still a "child" in many ways. Anything I have become is because of her.

THE WHOLE WORLD'S WATCHING

In 1968, I celebrated my nineteenth birthday and transitioned to my sophomore year at Hamilton College. There was no more significant year, personally and historically, as all that I had once accepted as the norm collapsed under the weight of several important events. For me and the country, it was one long nightmare. In a short period, chaos replaced sanity in the country, and this mirrored my rapidly unraveling personal life. The United States and I would never be the same again.

I was drifting through college, seemingly with no purpose, and my grades were marginal at best. I had no real goals and was attending college because that was what I was supposed to do. I was wasting my parents' money. Music was both an interest and an escape. I made good friends at Hamilton during my first year but was still largely invisible. I was in the first significant relationship of my young life, and the year would see that relationship unravel and fade away as quickly as it had appeared.

The decade of the 1960s was littered with fear and tragedy as we saw our beloved young president, John F. Kennedy, murdered in Dallas in 1963. The US and Soviet Union had each built an arsenal of nuclear weapons, and global disaster seemed imminent. Now, we were involved in a seemingly unwinnable war costing thousands of American lives. Positive highlights had been few and far between:

the expanding manned space programs and, for us Baltimoreans, the Orioles winning the World Series in 1966.

The 1960s had been peppered with racial unrest as the country struggled to escape from years of segregation. I grew up in a racially isolated area in Baltimore, but I had lived through this period vicariously by following the news. While hardly a social activist, I had become an outspoken supporter of racial equity. On April 4, 1968, Martin Luther King, Jr., the leader of nonviolent black activism, was assassinated in Memphis. Only several years after the horror of President Kennedy's assassination, it was hard to believe we were going to suffer through the death of another young, vibrant leader. Living in a predominantly white world, I was saddened that many I knew reacted differently to King's death than to Kennedy's, with a few pathetic individuals even thinking King's death was positive.

The death of a civil rights leader can't compare initially to the death of a president. Kennedy's death in 1963 marked the end of an age of innocence, but King's death dramatically changed the country, escalating the civil unrest to conflict. I admired his persistent non-violent protests and willingness to sacrifice freedom and comfort for his cause, and his death at the hands of a white assassin (James Earl Ray) evoked both sadness and anger. Adding this to the Vietnam War and the anti-war unrest, the country seemed to explode. I saw dramatic changes almost immediately. While riots erupted nationwide, most notably in my hometown, Baltimore, I saw changes in my life. That school year, I befriended a Black classmate. Brought together by similar musical interests, it was my first genuine friendship with an Afro-American. While we reacted similarly to King's assassination, the resulting months saw the friendship fade, primarily because of the small Black community's reaction on the college campus. Alex Haley, a noted Afro-American author, was a writer-in-residence at the college, and in the ensuing months, he helped organize a Black student union on campus.

There was a nationwide movement to develop a feeling of Black pride and a more militant Black Power movement, and the militant and almost revolutionary Black Panther Party in the country mobilized quickly. As with so much in politics, this caused some white backlash, and the country began to polarize around race. The prejudice had always been there, but reactions became more open on both sides. Two Black Americans protested on the victory stand at the Mexico City Olympics on October 16. Tommie Smith and John Carlos had just placed first and third in the 200-meter run, and on the victory stand with their medals, while the Star-Spangled Banner played, the two raised their black-gloved fists in the air in silent protest. Many in the country were outraged that two Americans would use the Olympics as a stage for demonstration, but it seemed in keeping with the unrest that ravaged the nation. The raised fist with a black glove symbolized the racial unrest, which was increasing dramatically that year.

The Blacks on campus banded together in a close-knit group in this environment. I understood and sympathized with their efforts, but many whites felt rejected by the Black community on campus. Although the other student and I remained friendly, our limited contact cost me a friendship. I never resented the reaction of the Black students; it was a completely understandable and justified move. I always felt our friendship was a victim of the turmoil that ensued. However, since Hamilton was a predominantly white campus, it was terrific that the Black element of the college could achieve a greater identity.

In 1968, the Vietnam War peaked, and rioting and anti-war protests escalated alarmingly. The country had entered the war years earlier to stop the spread of Communism. North Vietnam was communist, and we sent troops to South Vietnam to protect this country. Many supported our entry into the war initially, but a series of events in 1968 made our mission far less clear and noble, causing opposition to explode. Communist North Korea captured the USS *Pueblo* in January, and eighty-three Americans were held captive virtually all year. In the same month, the North Vietnamese launched the Tet Offensive, a series of attacks that changed the face of the war, dramatically increasing American deaths. The Viet Cong, South Vietnamese Communist sympathizers, were also a force to be reckoned with. With the continued exposure of corruption in the South Vietnamese government, it was often difficult to distinguish the "good guys" from the "bad guys." A South Vietnamese official was caught on camera executing a Viet Cong official, and that picture spread worldwide and mobilized anti-war sentiment.

The US Embassy in Saigon, the capital of South Vietnam, was attacked, and the press started reporting civilian atrocities. In the My Lai incident, not exposed until early 1969, American soldiers butchered 500 citizens, including seniors, women, and children. Although the soldiers claimed that the citizens were somehow linked to the Viet Cong, support for the US involvement in the war dramatically declined.

The unrest spilled into the Presidential campaign that year. President Johnson decided not to run for re-election, and his vice president Hubert Humphrey's campaign ran into difficulties as he seemed inextricably connected to the war. Anti-war candidate Sen. Eugene McCarthy immediately became the darling of the anti-war crowd. In contrast, Humphrey, a more than qualified candidate, couldn't free himself from the yoke of the Vietnam War escalation. President Kennedy's brother Bobby announced his candidacy, which seemed to be gaining momentum. On June 4, I had just come in from a date, and the girl and I sat down to watch the results from the California primary. We were diehard Kennedy supporters, and that night, he won those delegates and now seemed to be the front-runner for the Democratic nomination. As he was leaving the stage after the primary, we heard a shot ring out, realizing soon he had been shot. I remember sitting in disbelief, a second Kennedy now assassinated. That was a long evening as we watched the news coverage almost until dawn. It's the closest I've ever felt to thinking the whole world was unraveling. That year, I was not proud to be an American.

I honestly could have turned into a rebel at that point and did get involved with several anti-war protests during the ensuing months. College campuses were embroiled in continuing protests, sit-ins, and occasional violence. In late August, the Democratic Convention in Chicago erupted in chaos as Mayor Daley deployed an army of police and troops to control protests outside the convention, sparking major rioting and confrontation. The whole country seemed to be at war. The Chicago protesters kept repeating the chant, "The Whole World's Watching," which became a rallying cry for much of the unrest that year. And the whole world was watching!

The parallel of the country coming unraveled and my own life spiraling out of control almost pushed me over the edge. Studies seemed less critical, and I felt anger swelling in me regularly. Drugs had hit college campuses in 1968, and I saw friends joining the dangerous craze, with psychedelic drugs such as LSD becoming popular. I thankfully avoided that, as much out of fear as common sense. An acquaintance from high school had jumped out of a dorm at his college while on LSD. Another close friend suddenly became aloof as he got wrapped up in the drug culture. I honestly can say that I sometimes just considered giving up on college as all seemed hopeless and out of control.

Humphrey became the Democratic nominee, with Richard Nixon getting the Republican nod. Nixon chose Spiro Agnew as his VP, much to everyone's shock. Agnew had been elected Governor of Maryland after a relatively unsuccessful prior political life. I am embarrassed to admit I campaigned for him in 1966, but that election saw the Democrats split the vote in the primary with a very biased candidate emerging as the nominee. George P. Mahoney had advocated a somewhat racist policy, and a friend and I heard him respond to a question about race relations with the words, "I don't give a damn about that horseshit." So, I ended up campaigning for Agnew, a candidate I didn't like, to guarantee the defeat of someone far worse. And now Agnew could be our Vice President! To make matters worse, racist Alabama governor George Wallace was also running for president with running mate Gen. Curtis LeMay, an advocate of using nuclear weapons. Was there no end to the insanity?

Humphrey never shook his connection with the war's escalation, and Sen. McCarthy refused to support Humphrey, splitting the Democratic party. Wallace, a Democrat, also took votes away from Humphrey, and on November 5, Richard Nixon was elected president. I had despised him since his 1960 defeat by Kennedy, and I remember watching the returns until early morning. When they finally announced the official result, I broke down in tears. Knowing that the war was continuing and there was a draft, which would probably put me in the military, the world seemed a dark place that night: war, riots, assassinations, racial unrest, the nuclear arms race between the US and the Soviet Union, my life unraveling, and now Nixon. There was little reason to be hopeful at that point. After the election, it snowed forty-five consecutive days in upper New York State, evidence that even the gods were upset by his election.

The craziness was evident everywhere. A new show, *Laugh-In*, dared poke fun at everyone and everything in the most irreverent ways, and *Hair*, a new musical on Broadway, hyped the anti-war sentiment, free love, and drugs. However, there were minor signs behind the scenes that the country had passed the low point. President Johnson ordered a stop to the bombing of Vietnam, and talks to end the war began in Paris (although they seemed to be headed nowhere as the parties couldn't even agree on the shape of the negotiations table).

There was a positive that year, overlooked by many. Years before, President Kennedy had pledged that the US would have a man on the moon before 1970. Despite numerous setbacks, including a fire that killed three astronauts in 1967, NASA launched Apollo 8 in 1968, sending a team of astronauts to orbit the moon ten times. This paved the way for an actual landing the following year. Having humans look back at their home planet was a chance to forget the insanity of the year and to provide a hopeful look into a future where Earth's inhabitants would consider themselves one species rather than multiple nationalities and races. Despite the chaos occurring on its surface, our planet appeared peaceful and hopeful from space.

Although my life was still in turmoil, I had moved on from my ill-fated relationship and was finally about to get my academic feet on the ground. I still had a lot of healing to do, but a blind date early in 1969 put me on the right track. I met my wife-to-be, Jackie, and although the world still seemed to be spinning out of control, there was hope for my personal life.

Finally, the world came completely unglued on November 17, when the New York Jets played the Oakland Raiders. While the Raiders trailed considerably, they began a monstrous comeback in the game's final two minutes. With the team driving in for a score, NBC, who was telecasting the game, decided to cut to its 7 p.m. showing of the movie *Heidi*. Fans were outraged as no one could see the end of the game, which included a fantastic comeback that saw Oakland pull the game out. Aged football fans still see their blood pressure rise as one mentions what is now known as the "Heidi Game." I had no problem with the program change as the American Football League had not merged yet with the NFL, but, to many, the world has never been the same since—so much for the priorities of some Americans.

1968 was a year to remember, or more aptly, a year to forget. In 1969, my social life revolved around a person who, fifty-four years later, is still my best friend. My grades improved for the first time in years, and I now had a purpose. Growing up is not a smooth, gradual process, but more of a "two steps forward, one step back" process, but there are moments when we lose our way. 1968 was such a year for me. The country was bruised but would survive, although many hard times still lay ahead. I now lived in a very different nation than where I grew up. The Oz of my childhood was but a distant memory.

Source: http://cds.library.brown.edu/projects/1968/reference/timeline.html

MY DOG IS A MOVIE STAR

True—although a slight exaggeration. The dog wasn't exact-
ly my dog. Patches belonged to no one, but he adopted me in
my sophomore year of college. He did have a starring role in
a major Hollywood movie ... well ... he was a walk-on ...
more correctly, a run-on. Although the Academy of Motion
Picture Arts and Sciences tragically overlooked him when
nominations came out for the Academy Awards, he remains
my favorite movie star.

The first semester of my sophomore year at Hamilton College
was a low point in my educational career. I still clung to the idea
that I wanted to be a doctor. I had a course load beyond my capabil-
ity—seven courses, including anatomy and organic chemistry, both
major lab courses. I was still proudly wearing my procrastination hat.
My afternoons were tied up with classes and labs, and I was slow to
begin work in the evening since I needed to socialize and watch a
show or two. My roommate John was much more disciplined than I,
and to allow him to get his sleep, I often worked down in the fraternity living room.

Patches knew everyone in the college. No one knew if he ever had
belonged to anyone, but he had become the college freeloader, profi-
cient at finding food and shelter around the campus. He was a mutt
with a capital "M," probably attributing his DNA to a record number
of breeds. He had a pass to access virtually anything on campus and

could sneak into dorms, classrooms, and an occasional dining hall. He was as much a fixture on the campus as the beautiful chapel that sat prominently in the center of this picturesque campus, high atop a steep hill.

Patches began showing up at the TKE fraternity house, which was slightly downhill from the center of the campus. I lived there, which removed me somewhat from campus life. As a part-time waiter and dishwasher, I always saved him some food. As the weather cooled, Patches would scratch on our door by eight each evening. The bountiful food and warm couch made our house his "home" that year. As I worked late into the evening, he was a good companion, and anyone hearing me talking to him would have thought I was losing my mind. I probably was. Many nights, we shared a couch in the living room, and at dawn, I let him out to make his morning rounds.

Author John Nichols, a Hamilton graduate, had written a novel, *The Sterile Cuckoo*, about a fictional couple at a college like Hamilton. I learned they would make a Hollywood movie from the book with Liza Minelli in the starring role. Although early in her career, Minelli was well known as the daughter of Judy Garland and director Vincent Minelli. The movie was filmed mainly at Hamilton, with many Hamilton and nearby Kirkland College students used as extras. Several friends were part of the house party scene, filmed over three days—three days of beer, music, and partying—a tough gig for a college student. My neighbor from Baltimore was hired with his band for the party, but even though paid, their music was dubbed over when the movie was edited. Having a movie crew on campus was fascinating, but I was more concerned with surviving academically. I watched one scene being filmed, but living downhill kept me away from much of the filming.

The movie came out a year later and did surprisingly well, receiving two Academy Award nominations, one for Minelli for Best Actress. Released in a time of social upheaval and growing anti-war sentiment, it portrayed a more innocent time. There was a showing specifically for Hamilton students, and several of us attended. Seeing Hamilton landmarks I passed every day on the big screen was both bizarre and wonderful, and we all recognized many of the extras, especially in the party scene. Toward the end of the movie, as Liza Minelli's character drives away from a fraternity house, Patches charged from off-screen and chased her car down the road. A huge cheer went up as most recognized the beloved Hamilton canine. Undoubtedly, this was not scripted, and as much as he wandered, I was surprised he wasn't in more scenes. And to think they didn't even list him in the credits.

The movie struck another chord with me as it is about a dysfunctional relationship in a boy's college career, similar to my first serious relationship with a girl. During my freshman year, I dated a girl quite different from me. I was captivated, and it took me a while to realize we were complete opposites. Unlike the male character in the movie, I was not studious, but like the movie's female lead, my girlfriend was fun-loving and soon dropped out of college. Seeing the film reminds me of how lost I was my freshman year, but I watch it for a completely different reason—to see that wonderful dog who was my close companion in a challenging year when I needed a friend. I never knew what became of Patches; I saw him occasionally around campus, and he would always stop for a long head rub. He had many friends and probably continued his freeloading ways until his final days. I worry that his last days must have been difficult, and I pray someone was watching over him at the end. I have had many dogs I have been closer to, but Patches was there at a difficult period of my life—my friend and the only celebrity I have ever known. I simply have to play *The Sterile Cuckoo*, and he's up to his antics again.

ADVENTURES WITH FROZEN
DIHYDROGEN MONOXIDE

When I taught school, I gave each class a petition to sign that would ban a potentially "dangerous" chemical from the school. The petition presented the potential dangers of dihydrogen monoxide, including such facts as:

- Accidental inhalation of dihydrogen monoxide can lead to death.

- Dihydrogen monoxide is a major component of acid rain and contributes to the greenhouse effect.

- The chemical is used in dangerous animal research, to produce styrofoam, as an ingredient of toxic pesticides, and as an additive in many "junk foods."

- In its gaseous state, the chemical may cause severe burns.

- It reduces the effectiveness of automobile brakes and accelerates the corrosion of metals.

- We have found dihydrogen monoxide in the tumors of every terminal cancer patient.

After a litany of these seemingly disastrous consequences, every student would sign the petition banning the chemical, shocked that the school system would allow a toxic substance to be present on school property. I then had the students break down the scientific term to get H_2O, our favorite chemical, water. After withstanding the inevitable barrage of boos and wadded paper balls (thirteen-year-olds do NOT like to be shown up), we started a lengthy discussion. In addition to being an excellent icebreaker for starting my chemistry unit, it was also a perfect example of how we can misrepresent information and scientific data, which humans are remarkably adept at. Dihydrogen monoxide also breaks windows in its frozen state, a fact I discovered at a young age.

Winter precipitation events provided some wonderful childhood moments. At the other emotional extreme, my brother and sister were killed in a car traveling twenty-five miles per hour on an icy road. However, I choose to remember and focus on the magical moments the frozen compound has brought me.

When Jackie and I first moved down to the Eastern Shore of Maryland from college in upper New York State, we began teaching in Cambridge in January. In our second week, we awoke to a dusting of snow, certainly no more than one-half inch. We drove into our respective schools early to get organized. After a half hour, I noticed the school was still unusually quiet. Calling Jackie, I found that she was experiencing the same level of inactivity. Some quick investigation revealed that school had been canceled for the day. We were in shock.

I remember walking to school after a fifteen-inch snowstorm in Baltimore; that school had three snow days in eight years. During student teaching in Upstate New York, they closed school one day after a significant snowstorm, only because the custodians couldn't find the school doors buried under the monstrous snow drifts. Hamilton College was in the New York State snow belt where lake effect snow prevailed. We were southeast of Lake Ontario, and the westerly winds always picked up moisture. I'll never forget that it snowed an inch or more for forty-five consecutive days after Richard Nixon was elected President in 1968, an omen if ever there was one.

The winters up north were impressive. The roads became giant bobsled runs with snow piled so high on the roadsides that one could see only white. Jackie had to drive home one wintry evening when fog was added to the equation. The term whiteout took on a new meaning that evening for her. These snow-piled road shoulders provided one positive—one could veer off the road and carom right back onto the highway. We had a fifty-four-inch snowfall during our last winter at Hamilton. I never understood how they could determine a total because no area had fifty-four inches; there might be two inches in some areas and forty-foot-high drifts in others. It wasn't unusual that winter to see a sign that said: "Road Closed Until Spring." And they were!

Most people in that area ignored the snowstorms. Leave your car in the garage, and fire up the snowmobile to ride on top of the snow. The highway departments had great snow removal equipment—snow blowers the size of a combine. These would pick up the snow and throw it a reasonable distance—often on top of the car you had spent two hours shoveling out. And you did have to shovel your car out, or the snow blower might be blowing scrap metal along with the snow. Finding your car after a storm was possible if you knew which lump in the parking lot was your car. We were always the third lump from the left in the second row of lumps. If your neighbor was away, you might end up shoveling out someone else's car until you realized your vehicle now didn't have a blue roof.

After one snowstorm, the drifting was so significant that there were no lumps. The first day, since they couldn't find the doors to the school, we just sat and admired the magnificent snow mountain, which had been a parking lot the day before. The following day, we awoke to a rumbling sound. Jackie suddenly blurted out, "SNOW BLOWER," waking me from my dreams of a summer at the beach. The snow-eating monster was working its way down the road. If it ventured into our parking lot, my Plymouth Barracuda might quickly become scrap metal. Scrambling out into the parking lot with only a broom (I wasn't awake enough to grab a shovel), I crawled over the snow to where our car ought to be. College was on break, and ours was the only car in the lot. The broom, which seemed useless at first, suddenly became quite valuable. I could poke down through the snow, hoping I would strike metal. The blower had rumbled into the parking lot at this point, and the giant fountain of snow identified its location. One poke after another only struck snow as the snow-eating monster loomed closer. I finally hit metal, and with a series of jabs, I identified the outline of our car. I could save the car by standing on it and waving a broom. The monster approached. Then, in a moment of sheer terror, *am I sure this is our car? Maybe someone else drove into the lot as the storm hit us.* It was too late now. I waited for the grinding of metal as my beloved Barracuda would quickly become a modern art sculpture. The monster passed by without the sound of shredding metal, and I took a deep breath. A few minutes of sweeping away snow revealed our car's maroon roof.

During some winters, snow diving replaced ice hockey as the college sport. Students would go into the showers on the second floor, take a hot shower, and then race across the shower room, diving out the second-story window. (No alcohol was ever involved, although it might have helped.) The giant snow drifts cushioned your fall … at least to some extent. One sank quickly before abruptly stopping. It was exhilarating… at least until one's brain registered the freezing temperature. It's great fun, at least for college students whose brains have not fully matured. (And to think Jackie wanted to marry me!) I was not brave enough, and few moved on to the advanced snow diving course. The dormitory across the quad had a third floor! There was a rumor that one student dove out a fourth-floor window, but this was either never verified, or possibly they are still digging to find him. Note: This somewhat risqué activity was made possible because Hamilton was not coeducational then, so the dorms were male only.

The college "bobsled run" was crazier still. Hamilton was often called the "Hill," as it was situated on an extremely steep hill. If the area had been subjected to mudslides geologically, every house on the

Hill would have been at the bottom long ago. An acquaintance often rode me to and from town during my freshman year. His car needed a significant maintenance overhaul; there was a hole in the gas tank. This was not a problem since he would never fill the tank more than one-third full. Going down the steep road was easy, but returning was different. As the car started up the steep incline, the gasoline ran toward the back of the tank and out the hole; the tank would soon be empty. The solution was simple: just back up the hill. Enough people had seen him do this, and no one even batted an eye as they passed. The hill was so steep that once, the college had a twenty-four-inch snowstorm while the town two miles below had a whopping two inches. In severe icy conditions, a twenty-mile detour up the north side of the hill was sometimes a better move.

The sidewalk down the hill was an impressive incline. It passed through a stone archway, which rumor said had been erected in memory of students killed sledding down the hill. So, of course, this motivated students to sled the hill. I had sledded some impressive hills in my days. The Baltimore Country Club near my home had the most exciting hill. Unfortunately, there was a vertical metal pipe sticking up near the bottom. Apparently, a child had been killed running into it, but that didn't faze us; just avoid the pipe. A child's brain is advanced in many ways, but noticeably retarded in growth is the portion that said, "Hey, be careful. You might be the victim of the next accident." We built up enough speed that we never saw the pipe, The real challenge was to stop before the stream at the bottom of the hill. This I did every time except one, and that was a long, cold walk home.

Returning to the Hill in my junior year, I finally built enough nerve to navigate the hill on a sled. Two glasses of wine might have helped motivate me. It began like any sled run, but I lost my nerve as I built up speed. There was no pulling off the sidewalk; I was on a bobsled run, which kept me barreling down the course at ever-increasing speed. The stoned archway started racing toward me, and

I decided to try braking. Dragging my feet seemed the logical next step until the friction ripped the sole mostly off one of my shoes. Before I could figure out Plan B, I noticed the archway trailing away behind me. Relief! If someone had been walking up the Hill sidewalk (and no one would have been that foolish), a hospital visit for both of us would have been a certainty. It was one of the most terrifying moments of my life. No wonder more females survive to middle age than males!

And now, in Cambridge, a few millimeters of snow closed schools. I realize now that schools bow down before the Mighty L—liability. A school bus accident nearby, which killed the driver, pushed all local systems over the edge. Caution is not a bad idea, but our obsession to make any accident impossible leads to excess. Accidents happen! We'll never live in a world where they don't. With their jobs on the line, school administrators always side with caution these days. I can picture this scenario several years in the future. "Our County has decided to close schools today because a cloud has been sighted within five miles of a school!"

I know many moan and groan about winters in our area, but many wonderful memories are tied to winter snowstorms. I remember very few dates growing up, but I remember all the years that significant snowstorms occurred. 1957 saw the first monster storm in my life. I remember Gussie and I pulling Bill out of a snowbank, which had him immobilized. It was his snowsuit that made movement an impossibility. These remarkable body-length strait jackets kept one toasty warm. This way, you would just take longer to freeze to death since you couldn't move. And, of course, one could only lie down on a sled since sitting in a snowsuit was impossible. That was the winter we discovered snowmen and, better yet, snowballs. Snowmen were soon pushed over to become the beginning of a snow fort. We chose sides, and each side erected an impressive fort, which not only had to protect one's army but also be able to hide an immense stash of snowballs. The defense did no good if one had to leave its protection to run out for fresh snow to make a snowball. We spent most of the day building these monstrous structures, often so much time that there was no time left for the snowball battle.

When the battle finally commenced, it was impressive. Snowballs flew at a furious rate, and one could expect to be hammered, even if mostly protected. The opposing army had an older brother, giving them a distinct advantage. He could build snow "cannonballs," which he was strong enough to lob into our fort; our impressive walls did little to stop these. I devised a plan to sway the momentum back to our side. I made the perfect ice ball. I was a decent baseball player and knew I could nail him with a baseball-sized snowball. I carefully shaped and packed it for several minutes, letting the warmth of my hands turn the snow into ice. Then I waited for the perfect moment when the brother was exposed, building one of his giant cannon balls. I saw the opportunity, took a deep breath, and let my perfect ice ball fly. And did it ever fly! Right past the brother's ear and through Mrs. Cockman's window. You must understand that Mrs. Cockman was not our favorite neighbor. The poor woman lived alone and spent her entire day waiting for one of the many children in our neighborhood to take even one step into her precious yard. Over the years, this yard had become a graveyard for balls from errant throws. And no one dared try to retrieve one. Having a ball roll down the sewer was a better fate; all of us had climbed down sewers to retrieve balls on many occasions and, fortunately, thought nothing of it.

As I heard the glass shatter, my short life passed before me, and I was confident it would remain short. Our army was retreating anyway, as my friend's brother was leading a charge that would see our fort leveled, but this was not my concern. I saw Mrs. Cockman staring out her window. Maybe she hadn't seen who had thrown the snowball. Retreating to my house, I tried to convince my parents to go to her house for me. Kids try to do that—get your parents to bail you out. But this didn't happen. I soon climbed her steps with my parents waiting for me on the sidewalk below. I could hear my heartbeat. At least with my parents watching, she might not kill me (and we knew that she had a gun). I wish I could say that this all had a happy ending, that she forgave me, and a new friendship began. But this wasn't a made-for-TV movie. She screamed and yelled, told me how bad I was, and said that I would not only pay for the window but would owe her more money for pain and suffering. My father, the lawyer, intervened later, and they settled for window payment. It took six weeks of allowance to pay for that great shot of mine. And worse still, we lost the battle.

In the winter of 1966, my ordinarily cautious parents went to Washington for a law conference and left me in charge. At age sixteen, I was more than capable. I would be responsible for my younger sister and brother, which was no mean task. The predicted two-inch snowstorm turned into a twenty-four-inch monster, a nightmare for my parents and heaven for three young kids. We began the evening inside, watching our favorite spectator sport … through the picture window in our living room. Our house was at the bottom of a steep hill, which all the locals avoided in snow. If they failed to brake sufficiently, anyone driving down that road would soon be sitting in our yard. On a snowy evening, we opened the shades and waited for some poor soul to fail to negotiate the stop. Heading up the hill was equally hazardous as the car would spin out, ending up wedged against the curb. In both scenarios, the Radcliffe family gave a standing ovation … and then went out to assist.

As the storm intensified that evening, so many cars were getting stuck that we stayed outside. Performing rescue after rescue, we had the time of our lives, oblivious to the wind and cold. That's when we discovered it was 1:30 a.m. Unbeknownst to us, Mom (with her doctoral degree in worrying) had continually called the house to see if her babies were all right… getting no answer each time. Suspecting the worst, she slept little that night. In the morning, my parents got special assistance to get out of the hotel garage so they could head home to rescue their children, who undoubtedly were in dire straits. When they arrived home, we wanted to tell them all the great stories from the previous night. Strangely, that's not what Mom wanted to talk about.

Yes, winter evokes such great memories. I don't remember all those times I was bordering on hypothermia; I remember the fun. Most today moan and groan their way through winter. It will be twenty-five degrees, and many act like we're wintering in the Arctic. My response is always, "Hey, it's winter! It's supposed to be cold." And twenty-five is not cold; in my freshman year at Hamilton, we got down to forty-five below one night, and this didn't factor in the significant wind chill (the wind chill charts didn't go that low). That entire week, we never got above ten below! People dream of living in Hawaii, where the temperature rarely varies—however, wonderful summers and winters give us the best of both worlds. I could do without frozen pipes, but winter sets the stage for a super and welcome spring.

One memory from Hamilton occurred in the nearby town on the first spring day when the temperature got into the sixties. Late afternoon, everyone spilled outdoors, and the frisbees, baseballs, and barbecues came out. It was a spontaneous celebration, as if everyone's biological clocks were in sync. The long winter was over, and now we were on the home stretch to summer. Nature, of course, had a few more surprises. I remember one year working to erect the dock at the camp, standing in the water while there was still snow on the ground or finding snow in July in a deep crevice—a snowball battle on a ninety-degree day. We have friends moving to Florida to escape the snow and cold. How sad to have a year without snow. Variety is the spice of life, and our weather is quite spicy. But canceling school for five millimeters of snow? Come on! Let's get a life!

PIZZA PIE

During the summer of 1971, I sweated enough to lose fifteen pounds in Air Force Basic Training at Lackland Air Force Base in San Antonio, Texas. As we waited in line every morning before dawn to get into breakfast, our drill sergeant would share stories and advice. One morning, Sarge was more cheerful than usual and told us how he had fooled the local pizzeria the night before. Interrupted by fits of laughter, he explained how he had gotten more pizza without being charged any additional money. He had asked the waiter to cut the pizza into twelve slices instead of the usual eight. "An' they didn't charge me a daggone thing more!" We stood in silent shock, each thinking the same thing, "And this is our leader for the next six weeks?"

There are threads that run through one's life, connecting moments in time and acting as hooks to hang our memories. For me, that was pizza.

In the late 1950s, our family discovered pizza, or "pizza pie," as most called it then. There was no Pizza Hut, Domino's, or Papa John's, but pizza had gradually gained popularity in this country since its introduction early in the century. Frozen pizzas would not hit supermarket shelves for a few more years, but one could buy a pizza in a box. Chef Boyardee packaged all the ingredients needed to make a pizza. This pizza, TV dinners, and chicken pot pies provided an arsenal to protect us from my mother's cooking. Cooking to my mother was what enemas are to the rest of us, and she loved passing on the meal preparation to us.

I was the one in our family who discovered Chef Boyardee pizza kits. I could spread the dough across a pan, layer on the tomato paste, sprinkle on the cheese, and then drop on the pepperonis, concentrating them on my slices. This soon became a staple as I could now "cook" dinner myself. My parents often went out on Friday nights, and when my mother handed me the expected can of tuna, I told her I'd prepare a pizza for the three of us. I always withheld that it was a pepperoni pizza, a minor violation of the Catholic "no meat on Fridays" rule; I reasoned that no animal was called a pepperoni.

If there were pizza establishments at that time, we never frequented one. The earliest reference to what might have been a pizza traces back to the writings of Darius the Great (sixth century BC), where he referred to baked bread covered with cheese and dates. I'm not sure Pizza Hut will feature that one any time soon. Excavations of Pompeii proved the existence of pizza at that time, but it seemingly grew in popularity once tomatoes were exported from the New World in the sixteenth century. In the ensuing years, pizza became quite popular in Naples, and in 1905, the first license for baking pizzas was granted to Gennaro Lombardi in New York City. The first Pizza Hut in 1958 opened the floodgates, and the rest is history.[1]

In the US, we consume over three billion pizzas annually, and the average person consumes over twenty-three pounds of pizza a year (so my bathroom scale isn't broken after all). That one Pizza Hut has now grown to over 70,000 pizzerias, and 350 slices of pizza are sold every second in this country.[2] So it turns out that I was a trendsetter, after all!

Pizza took on a new dimension in Cooperstown, NY, when I was a counselor at Hyde Bay Camp. A restaurant in town sold an excellent pizza for under three dollars, and a counselor rarely returned from town without a pizza. Usually, it was for the kids in the tent we supervised, although a few "friends" always suddenly appeared. We'd wake the kids if the smell of the pizza entering the tent had not already done that. Usually, one or two were barely awake and often wouldn't remember the pizza the following morning. But this was camp ritual, and they would obediently, if not eagerly, woof the slice down. One morning, however, I remember seeing one of my campers sleeping soundly with his head resting on the uneaten pizza slice. It was not wasted, as he consumed it as soon as he awoke.

One night, I purchased a pizza and headed to the minibus, which would take us the seven miles back to the camp. I was informed that the movie many had gone to see was running late and that it would be another hour. This pizza would never stay warm, so I needed a plan. This, ironically, was the only time my wife-to-be ever made it to Cooperstown and the camp. The minibus was parked beside a laundromat, which gave us an idea. Dryers have heat. After running the dryer through its cycle, we placed the pizza into the hot dryer and quickly closed the door. When we returned a while later, there were two possibilities: there would either be a still-warm pizza or an irate patron wondering why his previously cleaned clothes were now covered with cheesy tomato paste. The pizza survived, and the campers were thrilled.

There was another place to get pizza in Cooperstown, the Regent Hotel. Located off the main street, this somewhat disreputable-looking place had a small kitchen serving a remarkable pizza. The Regent pizza was a monstrosity, weighing more than five pounds and containing two pounds of the greasiest ground beef imaginable. Costly for its time, you certainly got your money's worth pound for pound. The hotel had a deal: the pizza would be free if one could consume it entirely (without vomiting) in one hour. College kids love challenges. The pizza was cut into eight slices, and I saw many a truck driver quit by the fifth slice. Several at the camp went into "training" for the confrontation with a Regent Pizza. This would consist of overeating for several weeks and gradually increasing the amount of water consumed at a meal to expand one's stomach. Dave took the training seriously, and we finally thought we had a winner. I often wondered how much time he spent in the Kooks, our name for the marginally mechanized and supremely primitive outdoor bathroom.

The day for his attempt at a free pizza came, and he entered the Regent with his multiple trainers and cheering squad. I could identify with what he was going to go through. In previous forays into Regent Pizza land, I knew how fantastic that first slice would taste; I have never had a better slice of pizza. The second slice went down quickly, but something always happened on the third. Whether one's digestive system was beginning to rebel against the grease, or the stomach was nearing capacity, that piece lost its appeal, and one's enthusiasm tanked in a hurry. I never made it to slice number four. Dave was psyched and convinced he could obliterate one of these pizzas and, with his training staff, had developed a plan. He would use the entire allotted sixty minutes, almost eight minutes per slice. Complete with his impressive staff of advisors, a trainer, and a timer, Dave made his run at the record.

10 Minutes – Dave was all smiles and well into Slice # 2.

20 Minutes – As Slice # 3 disappeared, Dave grinned and talked trash. His coach continually guided his every bite while the training crew, complete with towels and water, watched his every move. He knew he could slay the beast.

30 Minutes – Dave had slowed down on Slice # 4, but he reassured everyone that this pizza was a done deal. A new strategy was evolving—slow down and pace himself, leaving the last two slices for a sprint at the end.

40 Minutes—Dave was on Slice # 5 but slowing still. The smiles were gone, as all enjoyment of the pizza was history. Dave uttered, "Whose dumb idea was this anyway?" We knew this venture was now in jeopardy.

50 Minutes - Dave, now on Slice # 6, had his head on the table. The training crew gave him a massage while the coach was in serious pep talk mode. Much of the crowd had dispersed as all thought this another in a long line of failures. He suddenly sat up, with a second wind, finished off that piece, and picked up the next to last slice. He was ready for the sprint; however, his stomach was not—off to the bathroom, knocking over several chairs in a different sprint than the coach had planned. The Regent Pizza had another in a long line of victims.

That next year, when I was a junior at Hamilton College, pizza would again play an interesting role. The first term was not going well, and I decided to remain at college over Thanksgiving break. Sophomore year had been an academic and personal nightmare, although meeting my future wife Jackie later in the year started a considerable rally. In my junior year, I was beginning to get my academic legs but was still working through many bad work habits developed over the years. Four intensive study days would set me on a positive course for the upcoming exam run. While I had a stockpile of great music, there was no one else on campus, and the fraternity house I was living in was empty except for Alexis, the wild cat, who lived in the earthen basement, and campus freeloading mutt Patches, coming off his unplanned cameo role in the recently filmed *The Sterile Cuckoo*. He had joined me many late nights in our house and would often sleep downstairs in our fraternity house. With no one else on campus to feed him this weekend, Patches would undoubtedly be moving in; I would not be alone.

No one was more family-oriented than me, and missing a holiday meal was not setting well; several times, I came close to hopping in the car and heading south, but the commitment to studies won out. But what was I going to do for a Thanksgiving Day meal? I had full use of the fraternity house kitchen, but cooking a turkey for Patches and me seemed like a royal waste of time. I headed to the local market, waiting for divine culinary inspiration. And there it was – Chef

Boyardee was staring down at me from the supermarket shelf. Pizza! But this was Thanksgiving, and not just any pizza would do. Thoughts of the Regent Pizza from the previous summer surfaced, and I had my plan. I was going to make the pizza to top all pizzas. If I made a monster pizza, I would have food for the weekend. I began filling my cart, starting with four Chef Boyardee pizza kits. With several pounds of ground beef, a large can of tomato sauce, and multiple blocks of cheese, I was ready to put the Regent Pizza to shame. The Guinness World Record of a 13,000 square foot pizza[3] was safe (I'm assuming that was not oven-baked), but I did have use of a big commercial oven.

Thursday morning, I started constructing this gargantuan culinary masterpiece. Fortunately, I had found a gigantic square pan that would just barely fit in the oven. I first made the crust, having enough dough to line the large pan completely, and then the fun began - tomato sauce, cheese galore, onions, and mucho hamburger. I could barely lift the pan. This would be a feast to remember. All longing to head home for turkey faded as I gazed upon my work of art. Patches' nose had brought him into the kitchen earlier, and he was as excited as I was. I figured I would need at least a half hour to cook this monstrosity. The local TV station was running a *Rocky and Bullwinkle* marathon, perfect fodder for a mindless college student, and I retreated into the TV room to await the feast. Incredible odors permeated the house, and I headed in to check on the pizza. After a few more minutes, I removed the masterpiece. I sat it high up on the counter, making sure that it was out of the reach of Patches, a legendary food thief. Taking Patches back into the TV room with me for added insurance, I gave it a few additional minutes to cool.

Finally, the time came for the Thanksgiving feast. I had skipped breakfast that morning and couldn't wait to dig in. I was missing family, but this pizza would make up for it. Patches returned to the kitchen with me, and I went to the refrigerator for a soda. Patches was lapping some tomato sauce off the floor. I couldn't believe I had missed some as I cleaned up. However, I sensed something was wrong when he found some ground beef. I looked up, and the pizza pan was empty!

Completely bewildered, my mind raced as I couldn't believe what I saw. I was the only person in the house, and Patches had been with me the whole time. Pizza didn't evaporate, but it was gone. Had I lost my mind and already moved the pizza? Was some unseen stranger playing a cruel joke? Do I call the campus police and report a stolen pizza? That request would probably warrant a sobriety test. I looked around as if I expected it to surface magically, but the pizza was nowhere to be seen. I saw several more tomato sauce marks on the floor and, knowing that I had mopped the floor, realized something was seriously amiss. The tomato spots seemed to be heading for the basement door, and I soon ran down the stairs. Before I could even find the light switch, I noticed a pair of eyes staring at me. Alexis! Turning on the light, I finally saw my pizza, but it wasn't Alexis eating it. Numerous kittens surrounded her, all now wallowing in THEIR Thanksgiving feast. The feast I had dreamed of all morning was not to be.

Now starving and disappointed, I had to get something to eat. Hopping into the car, I had to find food somewhere, and the local pizzeria seemed a logical destination. It wouldn't be the same, but I had pizza on the brain. As disappointed as I was, I had already found the humor in the situation. That was one happy litter of cats, and after that meal, Hamilton College was due for a population explosion of wild cats. Five minutes saw me pulling up in front of the pizzeria. Getting out of the car, I walked up to the door. The sign on the door read: "Closed for Thanksgiving."

Sources:

1. www.pizzafacts.net/pizza-history/pizza-timeline/
2. Brandon [Gaille], "29 Great Pizza Consumption Statistics", brandongaille.com/27-great-pizza-consumption-statistics/
3. Guinness Book of World Records www.guinnessworldrecords.com/world-records/largest-pizza

A Simple Twist of Fate ...
Times Three

At age ten, I had my life planned to the smallest detail:

- *Since I had been a good student in elementary school, I would excel in high school.*

- *I would go to Princeton as my father had.*

- *I was going to be a doctor or lawyer, like my father and grandfather.*

- *I would avoid military service since there would be no further wars after the Korean conflict.*

- *After law or medical school, I would marry and settle in Baltimore. I had visited Cambridge for vacations and decided that this was the last place on Earth I would want to live: mud, mosquitoes, farmers, and none of the excitement of city life.*

- *My three siblings would all settle nearby, and their families would create a great network of family around me.*

Years later, not one piece of that plan had materialized. All my childhood dreams had disintegrated, and the planned life was "gone with the wind." Ironically, this is not a tragic story but one of pure joy. How could a child's plans have unraveled so quickly? And why wasn't I the most disappointed person on the planet?

I did not excel in high school, and Princeton wisely rejected me. I did not have the grades to pursue medicine or law as a career, and I ended up in the military amid another war. My siblings passed away early in their lives, and I settled in Cambridge, where I live happily with the best wife anyone could have ever had. I never imagined any of that as even a possibility.

No, it's not the life I planned, but sibling deaths aside, I wouldn't have it any other way. It's as if my life played out how it was meant to. So much of the hand we are dealt in life is far beyond our control, but we have total control over what we do with that hand. The mirror image of myself as a doctor or lawyer living in Baltimore would be far less satisfying. I wonder how it would have felt to be that person; that's natural curiosity. And any image of life without my wife, Jackie, pales in comparison. Life presents itself with so many turns, and we can wonder where the alternative turn might have led us, but once we turn, we change, and there is no going back, just more choices down the road.

Many believe in fate—their life is meant to play out a certain way. They don't like the thought that events are random. We want to believe that there is a divine purpose. My brother and sister were killed in a car accident years ago. There was no divine purpose; they were not wanted in heaven. It was a tragedy, but it was random. Life throws us the occasional curveball, and it is up to us alone to deal with it and proceed. However, small events can have significant repercussions. Predicting the future is far more complicated than predicting where every pool ball will end after a break. Even an indiscernible piece of dust on the pool table could drastically affect where every ball stops. A lifetime is countless events, all impacted by almost imperceptible phenomena.

Undoubtedly, the paramount event in my lifetime was meeting Jackie, my wife of fifty-four years. It was not "meant to happen," but thank goodness it did. It was a highly improbable meeting and would not have happened but for a chain of events beginning in 1962. My shyness and stuttering likely caused me to pass over opportunities early in my life, but life is never about looking back at missed opportunities; it is about how we choose when the next one presents itself. The key is being attentive to those partially opened doors and willing to open them when they appear. Many believe fate and destiny play a key role in our lives, but our decisions are at the steering wheel. If we make the best of the chosen path, whatever that is, our lives should be complete and rewarding.

In 1962, I made a rare and completely out-of-character rash decision, which would completely alter the course of my life. Summers were periods of freedom for me, and I cherished my independence. My parents had sent me to a summer day camp several years earlier, and I had hated it; prison might have seemed a better alternative. This traditional "whistle camp" left no positive memories, but I have evidence that I hated it. I did not return the following summer. My only concrete memory was running down the gravel driveway to the camp from the bus, falling, and splitting my knee open. I sat in the infirmary for hours before my mother drove out there, and to this day, I still have a significant scar on my knee where a decision was made not to use stitches. I also have this recurring dream of a tremendous, bald, hairy-chested, and frightening counselor from the camp. Without the knee incident, that would be my only recollection of several weeks of camp. This was hardly a ringing endorsement of where a parent should send their child for the summer, but I was not the typical kid. I valued my freedom. A place where at 10:15 one goes to archery and at 11:00 it's on to basket weaving is not my idea of independence.

Some people need to be kept busy with serious parental scheduling. Each day, I needed a blank slate that I could soon fill with many projects—building a clubhouse, playing baseball, building a go-cart, or biking around the neighborhood with my friends. Those glorious summer days all ran together, but this was heaven to a young boy in Baltimore in the 1950s and early 1960s. "Whistle camps," as I called these summer factories, were just school in the outdoor heat… summer prison. I knew one summer of a whistle camp was enough, and I would never go back again. The following summer had been another period of freedom and bliss, with three weeks spent at the family farm, crabbing, exploring, and spending time with family. The summer of 1962 would be more of the same: a chance to rewind and reconnect with my world before moving on to the dreaded eighth grade.

My life had changed dramatically since the previous summer as my little sister Kim had been diagnosed as mentally retarded and removed from our home. Eight years my junior, she had become a treasure to me. Even though she couldn't talk, and we had little in common due to the age difference, I had taken over a lot of the responsibility for her as the stress of dealing with her frazzled my mother. Every day after school, Kim and I would go for long walks, play with our beagle, Nickie, and build forts in my bedroom. There is no sibling rivalry when the age difference is that great, and we bonded most uniquely. She loved my stuffed bears, and they became the principal players in the world we created. Her temper tantrums and communication difficulty frustrated me greatly, but there was magic when we were together.

I don't know whether it came from the responsibility of being the big brother or her adoration for me, but I treasured the time we had together. Then, with no warning at all to me, she was gone. My parents had decided that my mother could no longer handle her, and, leaving me out of the planning to protect me, they decided to put her in a private institution an hour from our home. I was devastated and began a long downhill spiral that affected me socially and academically. Seventh grade saw massive changes as I kept more to myself and fell rapidly from my status as an exemplary student.

In the early spring of 1962, I was playing with my friend Chris in our neighborhood when he invited me to his house to meet a friend. I balked at first, but he pressured me into it. In his living room was an older man, and I quickly realized he was discussing a camp that Chris might be interested in. This was fine if I wasn't a target of the sales pitch. A team of wild horses couldn't drag me back to a camp; worse yet, this was a month-long overnight camp. I guessed they would even be scheduling what and when you dream. No thanks, not for me, but I was only a spectator. The gentleman introduced himself as "Mouldy," and that certainly seemed out of the ordinary. However, I only partially listened to the talk, waiting impatiently for this to pass and to return to fun and games. Chris was a close friend, and I would put up with anything for him. That's when my parents suddenly entered the room, and I smelled conspiracy!

They said they were just there to listen as my father had been taught by the gentleman's father years earlier. Relieved somewhat, I soon found myself listening, and that's when I heard words that caught my attention, "Each camper makes his schedule each day, and if he wants to sit in his tent and read comics all day, that's fine—just as long as he passes a basic swimming test." Maybe this wasn't prison after all, but there still was no way I was giving up my freedom. Photos of the camp in the Adirondacks were inviting, and the stories Bob Pickett shared that day were entertaining. Still, the meeting soon ended so that Chris and I could return to our usual fare of exploring, writing plays, playing board games, and biking. The next day, he told me he had decided to go to the camp, which meant I would lose my closest friend that coming summer. I told him about all the fun he would miss, but he was bent on attending. However, the shock came that evening when my father asked me if I also wanted to go. "No" flew out of my mouth before he finished the question, and the subject was dropped. My father was the master of when to apply pressure and when to back off. In hindsight, he had to know the turmoil I was enduring after the loss of Kim, and while he was grasping at straws to help his son, he knew that pressure in this instance would only backfire.

I thought about Kim that night, reminisced about all the wonderful summers of past years, pictured a summer without my friend around, and thought of Mouldy and those words he had spoken: *Each camper makes his schedule each day.* After an hour or so of lying in bed, I suddenly sat up with the thought, "I'll do it." Running downstairs, I told my parents my intent to go and returned to bed. As I lay there, I suddenly panicked. What in the world had gotten into me? I was sacrificing my freedom for an unknown camp and ... overnight ... and for a month! Had I completely lost my mind? No problem; I would reverse my decision in the morning.

I had every intention in the morning of changing my "yes" back to a "no," but as we were almost late for school, there was no time to talk. It would wait until the evening. Later that day, I realized that a couple of classmates also went to the camp, and by the time I returned home, I was reconciled to going, although I knew it would probably be the biggest mistake of my life. Pride also kept me from admitting that I had made a poor decision the night before, and Chris's excitement about going helped alleviate some of my fears. He was also an independent guy who knew what he was sacrificing.

The school year passed, and I had almost forgotten about the camp. When the last day of school arrived, real panic set in. I would be heading off to the camp in a week. There was no getting out of it now since the money had long ago changed hands. Like it or not, I was going back to camp! I wondered if the huge, bald, hairy-chested councilor would be there. There was a lot of shopping and packing to do to pass the time, and before I knew it, I was sitting in a packed car heading north with Chris and his family. I will never forget the June drive from Baltimore to Cooperstown, NY. I know the seven-hour drive lasted at least a week. I was miserable and just kept wondering what I had gotten into. What had possessed me to agree to something I didn't want to do, and why had I not backed out when I had the chance? I still remember every town we passed through and every landmark we saw, as I hoped we would never reach our destination. We stopped for lunch in a small Pennsylvania town, and I remember staring out the window, regretting my failure to back out months earlier. That must have been akin to a condemned prisoner's last meal; the whirling thoughts numb one's taste buds as the impending execution dominates all. Once we got to Hyde Bay Camp, I was introduced to my counselor, unloaded my footlocker, and sat in the tent that would be my home for the next month. I was miserable, homesick, and desperate. I could spend a month without my parents, but I was sacrificing the freedom that was dear to me.

We slept on war surplus beds in large military tents on wooden platforms at the camp. As I sat alone on my cot, hearing the screams and laughter of busy campers in the distance, I could not help but think I had made the stupid move of the millennium—and I would be there for a month. I could survive four weeks, I guess. My counselor returned and told me to dress in my swimsuit to take the swimming test, and I soon walked down to the dock. The green wooden buildings were rustic, and many were adorned with artwork done, as I later found out, by Jack Garver, a teacher at my school. Otsego Lake, nestled in the foothills, was beautiful, and I now noticed all the canoes, sailboats, and the large camp powerboat, the Hacker, pulling a camper standing on a board. Things were looking up, and I reminded myself that *each camper makes his schedule each day.*

I easily passed the swimming test and quickly joined all the aquatic activities around the dock. Chris was there, and I soon realized several classmates were in the group. After dinner that evening, orchestrated by legendary camp cook Henry, many of us went up to the ballfield for a game of Capture the Flag. Hitting the sack early that evening, I heard my first rendition of the classic camp monster/ghost story, William Clark. At the critical point in the story, just as

William was invading the camp for another chance to wreak havoc on a group of innocent campers, another counselor came up from under the tent flap, grabbing me with an impressive scream. The whole tent bailed out of their beds as the two councilors laughed out loud. Yes, this place would be all right—no boring whistle camp here.

For one month in 1962, I escaped the incredible home stress I had been under; sometimes, it's hard to know the weight of the stress on us until it is removed. One month later, my only regret was that I could only stay one month; the following year, I was coming for two, and I would return until 1969, when the camp had to close. I was different and had discovered a world I would live in for years. Hyde Bay Camp was the antithesis of a whistle camp. One was never forced to do anything or sign up for any of the fantastic overnight camping trips, but no one sat on their cot for long. However, summer reading was quickly put aside during the mandatory rest period after lunch for the collective Library of Congress of Comics, which seemed to exist throughout the camp. A sense of theatrics and humor permeated everything in the camp. Launching a newly repaired sailboat was done with fanfare that would dwarf even the Nobel Prize Award ceremonies in Stockholm. Nicknames abounded, and no one was spared from good-natured teasing, much like what one would see in a family. And Mouldy, probably the most serious individual in the camp environment, lovingly continued the family environment his father had created years earlier. His wife, Betty, was everyone's summer mother, and the administrative staff was all part of this large, all-encompassing family.

Most important to me was the opportunity to get away from the indoors for the summer. Expecting to lose freedom, I found a new kind of freedom in the natural outdoors. Living in an outdoor tent for a month, trekking up through the woods to a noxious two-seater, going on the frequent camping trips, where we fashioned our tents out of ponchos, canoeing, sailing, and exploring natural places such as

Shadow Brook (literally the source of the Susquehanna River) made a convert of me. I had always wanted to be a doctor for reasons I never clearly could elucidate; however, after Hyde Bay, the course was set for me to be a science teacher with a strong focus on the environment (although it would be several years before the light bulb went off). Years later, my classroom would be laced with the same creativity and humor that the camp had been based on, and the Ecology Corps that I started and ran for years included camping and canoeing trips similar to those I had engaged in at the camp. I went on to be a counselor at the camp, and several years into my teaching career, my teaching style evolved into a role much like that of the counselor I had been. Kim had given me a passion for working with younger children, and Hyde Bay opened the door for how to do this. As a teacher, rather than a purveyor of information, I became a director of experiences driven by student creativity. And to think I almost didn't go to Chris's house that winter day in 1962.

Fate also intervened in 1966 as I was leaving the camp. We decided to look at some colleges on the way home. My father somehow drove onto the wrong campus, a rare move for that twentieth-century Daniel Boone. I had never heard of Hamilton College and had no intention of looking it over. However, we did, and fifteen months later, I was sitting in a Hamilton dorm, ready to start my first year. Hamilton was an all-male school my first year, and a sister school opened the following year with only a few females. Dating opportunities were few and far between, and a relationship in my first year had gone sour quickly. Occasionally, a friend would offer me a blind date, but I had seen enough of these horror stories to steer well clear. In February of 1969, my roommate offered to set me up with an acquaintance of his girlfriend, but when I went to say "no," for reasons still unclear, it somehow came out "yes." My thinking was probably stunted from an all-nighter studying for an organic chemistry test.

Why would someone accept a date for a three-day weekend?

There is no backing out once the "date" starts, and I looked back on the many disastrous dates I had witnessed others endure. But three days? Once again, I could not summon the courage to escape it. Expecting a wreck rivaling the sinking of the Titanic, I decided to be myself. Knowing my date had already arrived, I returned from a biology lab unshaven, hair badly needing to be shorn, and wearing my reconditioned shirt labeled with the name of its previous owner, "Floyd." What a great first impression I must have made. On the second date, a couple of weeks later, my date and I discussed the possibility of marriage. This was Jackie McCann, now my wife of fifty-four years. It is fair to say that the blind date worked out well.

These twists of fate transformed my life, leading to my passion for the environment, education and career, and, most importantly, my lifelong companion. What is so ironic is that the three turning points are all connected. Without going to my friend's house in 1962, I never would have gone to Hyde Bay Camp, which would have meant I never would have gone to upper New York State and found Hamilton College, and without Hamilton, I never would have met Jackie. Losing Kim that year also put me in the frame of mind to go to the camp. The smallest domino can eventually topple the most significant object. Many would enter the word "destiny" here; they would say Jackie and I were destined to meet, and those other pieces were meant to play out to reach the destined outcome. As attractive as that might be to a romantic, our meeting was not preordained. There is no predetermined course that our life must follow; like a board game, each decision changes the game, but chance is the engine that powers the course of events. Each decision sets the stage for the next decision. Rarely can one know how life will play out. I had my life planned out at age ten, and thankfully, none of it went according to plan. While having a plan gives direction and purpose to what we do, it's those partially opened doors we pass that need to be opened. It's a rare ten-year-old who knows what they want.

What makes life so remarkable is that there is always a surprise around the next corner; yes, I am the eternal, and sometimes naïve, optimist. I am in my seventies now, but I know many unexpected and wonderful turns are still ahead. "Getting old" means one is resolved to the fact that the game of life has already been played out, and one is just awaiting the end. I am not old! (That may come as a shock to those who have to look at me!) It's fun to look back and reflect on what has passed as long as one knows that the best still lies ahead. I remember that winter day in 1962 when Chris called me to his house. That one tiny, seemingly insignificant door opened a lifetime of beautiful memories. I haven't seen my old friend in years, but I doubt he realizes he set off a sequence of events that led to my wife, Jackie, the love of my life.

My Dog Doesn't Like
Joe Namath

We know that our beagle, Maizie, is intelligent, or at least we pretend she is. Doesn't every dog owner think their dog is canine Mensa material? Beagles are supposed to be smart, but then they are so eccentric that one could argue that they simultaneously reside on both ends of the intelligence spectrum. She is our first dog to watch TV but doesn't always like the commercials.

Interestingly, she howls at almost every car insurance commercial, ... but so do I. How can company A be cheaper than company B, which is less expensive than company C, which is more affordable than company A? Maizie is obviously a mathematically inclined beagle. But then she also howls at every commercial hosted by Joe Namath, the famous Jets quarterback. That proves she is intelligent because Joe Namath set off a chain of events that cost me $5,000.

1969 was a challenging year for Baltimore sports fans, made infinitely more difficult because I attended a college in New York State. Growing up in Baltimore, we considered the New York Yankees the lowest form of life possible. We lived in frustration most years because they invariably ended the year above the Orioles in the standings. 1966 had been a pleasant change as the Orioles won the World Series that year, beating the Los Angeles Dodgers in four games. In 1969, I was at Hamilton College in upstate New York, and there was not another Baltimore sports fan in sight.

That winter, the Baltimore Colts made it into Super Bowl III, where the National Football League champion Colts played the American Football League champs, the New York Jets, with Joe Namath as their quarterback. Namath had been a college football star, but everyone knew that the AFL was an inferior league; they had lost the two previous Super Bowls. The Colts were heavy favorites to win the game, and I was looking forward to a blowout that would silence all my New York friends. One asked me to bet on the game, and he was so convinced the Jets would win that he offered a straight bet even though eighteen points favored the Colts. I never bet, but this could be the most effortless five dollars I ever made.

Before that moment, I don't think I had ever made a bet. Sports betting was not commercially acknowledged as it is today, but billions exchanged hands under the table. Unfortunately, it is big business today, with many making it a career. I initially balked at the bet, but my friend was so arrogant that I finally decided to teach him a lesson. I would be more than happy to take his money.

On January 12, 1969, I sat down with a large group of friends to watch the Colts silence all the New York fans around me. By the end of the third quarter, Namath had led the Jets to a thirteen-point lead, and I was the silent one, sitting in a room with twenty fans laughing and jeering. The Colts would score once, but the die was cast as the game ended 16-7. I was five dollars poorer.

I had gotten over the humiliation by fall and now had a chance for revenge. The Baltimore Orioles were the American League champs, winning 109 games and finishing nineteen games in front of the second-place Detroit Tigers. Led by future Hall of Famers Brooks and Frank Robinson, Boog Powell, a young Jim Palmer, and 1969 Cy Young winner Mike Cuellar, they swept the Minnesota Twins in the league championship series. In the World Series, they would face the New York Mets, a team that had never had a winning season before 1969. I smelled victory, and the recipient of my five dollars earlier in the year asked for another bet.

How could I refuse? I could not only shut up the New York fans, who were still razzing me about the Colts, but I could also get my money back. The Mets were "amazing " in that series, and the Orioles were not. Losing in five games, my Orioles set me up for another year of ribbing. At that point, I made a decision that I have stuck to until now. I would never bet again. Not that I ever usually bet, but Joe Namath and the Amazing Mets cured any propensity I might have had. I have never wagered on anything, and the Maryland State Lottery has not even wrestled one dollar from me all these years. I received a lottery ticket once in a basket of goodies associated with an award; I gave it to a friend who promptly won five dollars.

Soon after the Orioles lost the World Series, a friend approached me with another chance to make a bet, but this was different, not a sports wager. The United States was conducting its first Selective Service draft lottery to see which men would receive an all-expenses-paid vacation to Vietnam. The United States was at the height of the unpopular Vietnam War, and the lottery was supposed to be a fairer way of drafting needed recruits into the military. The 366 days of the year were randomly selected, and those born on the first day drawn in the lottery would be drafted first, and so on.

I could bet five dollars in a pool involving multiple colleges, with the winners of the lottery receiving all the cash. I'm not sure "winner" was the appropriate word for such a victor, but these individuals would split the money, supposedly payment for a plane trip to Canada, to avoid the draft. I was not a big fan of that war, nor any war, and I never wanted to enlist. My father enlisted during World War II, as did most of his contemporaries, but the country had been attacked in that war, and world order was threatened. I briefly considered buying a ticket to support the individual who would be the lucky "winner." However, I was "cured" and would never bet again, thanks to Joe Namath and company.

On the night of December 1, 1969, I returned from studying at the college library. With exams a few weeks away, my thoughts were on upcoming exams, not the news. Walking down to the fraternity house, I was finally starting to feel good about my schoolwork and life. The cold night air felt refreshing after several hours of studying in the library stacks, and after having skipped dinner, I dreamed of digging into some leftovers. I was not prepared for the surprise as I entered the house.

"YOU WON!"

"Huh?"

"George, you won!"

I now remembered the draft lottery. "OK, seriously. What happened?"

"No, your birthday was picked number one."

I didn't know anybody knew my birthday. "Really?"

Several had joined us in the hallway. Yes, September 14 had been the first date drawn. Confusion suddenly evolved into panic as I knew I was headed toward the military after my student deferment ended. I couldn't picture myself wielding a rifle. I had never held a gun before, and as clumsy as I was, no one, including our troops, would be safe. Medical deferment? I was too healthy. Trip to Canada? I was staying here with my family. There was one certainty—I was going to walk right off the graduation stage into the grasp of the military.

I remembered the draft pool. I had debated paying my five dollars to enter. Had I given in? No, the Jets and Mets had ensured I had purchased no ticket. Adding insult to injury, I later discovered that if I had bought into the draft pool, I would have won $5,000. Somehow, the lost money was soon forgotten as schoolwork dominated my thoughts.

I joined the Maryland Air National Guard and happily never reached Vietnam. Even after briefly regretting not entering the draft pool, I remained committed to never betting again. Sure enough, the Baltimore-New York sports rivalry was back center stage several months later. The Baltimore Bullets played the New York Knicks in the National Basketball Association championships. And, yes, the Knicks won, icing my sports humiliation.

The Orioles went on to win the World Series in 1970, and the Colts finally won the Super Bowl in 1971—at least partial redemption for 1969. Years later, I'm incredibly proud to have a dog who howls at Joe Namath. I always knew beagles were intelligent.

WHERE ARE MY PANTS?

I was thirty minutes away from walking down the aisle to marry the love of my life. I was not nervous; marrying Jackie was the easiest decision I ever made. In fact, I was too relaxed. That's when horror struck; I had NO pants, and this was not a dream.

I should have been as nervous as a human could be. I was twenty-one years old and getting married in a couple of hours. However, Jackie and I were already married in spirit, and the ceremony would make it official for the world. How many couples talk about marriage on the second date? If I had any common sense, I would have realized I was young and probably didn't know what I was entering, but I knew this was the most logical thing I had ever done. I was marrying my best friend and soul mate. I had been through one semi-serious, failed relationship earlier, so I knew what a mistake felt like. Jackie and I were a perfect fit; after a couple of hours, we had seemingly been together for years. And now, we would finally be married. It seemed like the most beautiful dream, and I never wanted to wake up.

Jackie had completed her college career at Elmira College a half year early, finishing her last exams a few days before the wedding. I was halfway through my final year at Hamilton College and was fresh off my next to last semester, still groggy from writing a forty-page summary of my student teaching. We both stumbled home to celebrate Christmas with our respective families, and suddenly, the big day arrived. There had been no time to get nervous, not that we would have been anyway. While deeply immersed in college work, preparing for a wedding dictated that the wedding would be simple, and that was exactly what we wanted. Other than picking out the music (entrance song – Bach's "Jesu Joy of Man's Desiring" and Nino Rota's music from the Franco Zeffirelli version of *Romeo and Juliet*), the wedding would be simple: church wedding, simple reception in the parish hall, and dinner back at her parents for immediate family… absolutely no frills.

Compared to so many weddings today, this was an econo-wedding. There was no elaborate bachelor party. A couple of friends briefly joined me at the Hamilton Pub for one beer, and then we returned to studying for exams. The reception was held in the Danbury Congregational Church parish hall, where a few women threw together some hors-d'oeuvres—no wedding planner, band, DJ, or alcohol. The most significant expenses may have been the fifty dollars paid to the minister and the tuxedo rental. The church was still decorated from Christmas, so any flower expense was unnecessary. It is sad to watch couples today going into debt to fund their wedding; today's average wedding cost is over $40,000. And there was no honeymoon in Aruba, just a three-night stay in the world-renowned vacation resort in Washington, DC—the Howard Johnson Motor Lodge. Interestingly, we were curious about the strange office building our room overlooked; two years later, Richard Nixon and acquaintances made that one of the most recognized structures in the world.

What possessed me to head out that wedding morning with Jackie's brother-in-law, Michael, I do not know … probably mostly a matter of the family getting me out of the house while Jackie and the bridesmaids got dressed. I had already learned that sometimes I was just in the way … even on my wedding day. I don't remember where we went or what we did. At some point, I looked at my watch and realized there was less than an hour before the ceremony. Now, I'm the master of the quick shower and change, but I was dealing with a tuxedo, not a garment I was familiar with. The best man, ushers, and I had been fitted the previous day, only then to find out the small fortune that all of this would cost ... hundreds of dollars so we could be in strait jackets for a couple of hours. Barely getting wet in the shower, I rushed to dress. The best man, John, and my ushers had all dressed and were on their way to the church. My tuxedo and shirt lay on the bed, and I threw on the shirt, fumbling with the buttons as if I had never worn a shirt before. I grabbed the trousers from the bed, jumped into them, and almost fell backward. That's when horror struck. Either my butt had grown five sizes since the previous day, or something was terribly wrong. Panic quickly set in.

Jackie's mom realized something was amiss and entered the room. After calming down, with her excellent logic, we reasoned that John had put on my tux. Grabbing the remaining monkey suit, I jumped into my jeans, ran to my car, and sped off to the church. Unfortunately, most of the crowd was seated, and John was waiting for me ... in the front of the church. Jackie was soon to walk down the aisle to be greeted by ... no one.

The problem was getting into the church and signaling John without attracting too much attention from the mostly assembled crowd. When I suddenly darted down the side aisle in a pair of jeans, he and the rest of the church must have thought the groom was backing out. The preliminary music was already playing, and I told him of the dilemma. We were similar in size, but while John had broad shoulders, I had a wide posterior end, a situation I have always blamed on genetics. We hurried into a side room and quickly began changing our pants, finishing just in time for the two of us to make our grand entrance as "Jesu, Joy of Man's Desiring" began to fill the church. Walking out into the front of the congregation, I was too winded to be nervous. As I stood there waiting for my beautiful wife-to-be to appear, I could only think how I was the luckiest man in the world, and as the organist played the piece we had chosen, I suddenly thought, *in hurrying, did I remember to pull my zipper up?*

A lowered zipper had already become my trademark in those first twenty-one years of life, but this was my wedding. Usually, I could distract whomever I was with, turn, and raise the zipper in one swift motion, all of which could go unnoticed. However, as the second most important person in the church that day, many eyes would be on me. I broke into a sweat for the second time in a brief period. Anyone close to me would have assumed I was just a nervous groom, but I was potentially close to making this a memorable wedding for the wrong reason. I had to find out very inconspicuously if the zipper was even down without looking like I was suddenly groping my crotch, not the best move for a groom. I clasped my hands together and dropped them in front of me, trying to feel with the back of my hand. I hadn't figured out how to pull it up, but after a few seconds ... relief, the zipper was up. I was saved just as Jackie was now approaching the altar.

The wedding ceremony went off without a hitch, and I was again on top of the world. I didn't like being the center of attention, but this one day, I didn't care. I had married the girl of my dreams. We retreated to the parish hall for refreshments and the cake, and soon, it was time for us to leave the church under the traditional barrage of rice. The more appropriate use of birdseed had not occurred at that time. We both went into a room to change into more comfortable clothes before making our hasty exit. I finally exited the dreaded tux and returned to my usual casual attire. Putting on the pants, I was going to ensure the zipper was up this time. No one would be looking at photos years from now, laughing while they pointed at the groom's crotch. I grabbed the zipper of the jeans and gave it a good tug. That's when the zipper clasp broke off completely. My fears were now reality... there was no pulling up this zipper. As I fumbled with the jeans' zipper, trying to get it up, word must have leaked out that I was having issues. Suddenly, someone appeared with a large hat pin, and with some assistance, the opening in the pants was somehow held closed, and we could head to the family supper. In hindsight, I should have known that this temporary solution was a disaster waiting to happen, and it did.

I met Jackie in the church, and we prepared to run the gauntlet. We knew we could survive the pelting by rice. With help from Jackie's parents, we avoided the mandatory decoration of the newlyweds' car with shaving cream, cans, and signs. We switched cars with them, leaving our vehicle hidden further from the church. We made it through the rice-throwing crowds to the car, where we would have to pose for one more picture. I got Jackie into the vehicle as quickly as possible to minimize the build-up of rice and raced around to the driver's side. Opening the door, I leaped in and ....

I should have remembered that the stick pin was a temporary solution and that movement might work it loose. It did! I assume that when acupuncture is done, the testicles are generally avoided. The pain was immediate and intense as the two-inch hatpin quickly found its mark. I don't remember if I screamed or just exhaled every bit of the oxygen in my lungs. I had forgotten about the hat pin, and it took me a second to connect the searing pain with it. I was able to free it, but not before one of the most painful experiences of my life. There is a picture of me in that car, a photograph of a groom so happy with his new wife that he is shedding tears. Looking closely, however, you can see that these were not tears of joy.

Despite the jaw-clenching pain, we drove away from the church as happily as a couple could. The pain soon passed, and all was right with the world. As we drove from the church, we passed another car covered with shaving cream and toilet paper, cans clattering behind it, and adorned with a large, showy "Just Married" sign. Jackie's mother sat in the passenger seat with Jackie's wedding dress piled high in her lap. Cars would honk as they passed by, and the elderly "newlyweds" just smiled and waved to all the world.

THE PROMISE

Some say promises are made to be broken, but I take them seriously. In 1971, I made an unusual promise, one I have adhered to religiously for over fifty years, and I can say with certainty that I will honor it to my grave. The promise has cost me participation in one of the most popular activities in our area, but I don't miss it. Most importantly, because of my promise, the world is far safer.

1969 was the only time I won a lottery or contest, winning an all-expenses-paid vacation to boot camp in the summer of 1971 following my graduation from Hamilton College. My birthday, September 14, was drawn first in the first draft lottery, ensuring our country's military would suffer a significant setback with one George Radcliffe in its ranks. The Vietnam War was not progressing well, and putting me in uniform would ensure the country would lose the war. My father served brilliantly in World War II, but I was anti-war, a klutz, and hardly the lean, mean fighting machine our country needed.

A year and a half after the fateful lottery, I was basking in the sun at the Lackland Air Force Base vacation resort in San Antonio, Texas. Basic training so far had not been like the horror stories my father had shared about his basic training: two men dying during training, avoiding water moccasins, and machine gun bullets passing overhead while one crawled through the mud. The food was as bad as he had recounted; everything tasted the same. We'd get up every morning at

4 a.m. to stand in line for two hours for breakfast, which was usually cold by that point. I remember one morning when we were surprised and delighted to find blueberry pancakes as a choice. After we all woofed a truckload of these down, someone noticed that each blueberry had six legs.

It was hot, and in the words of Robin Williams as Adrian Kronauer, "It was damn hot!" It did go below 100 degrees one day … I think. The base had one safety measure: if the temperature reached 115 degrees, there would be no outdoor exercise. In late summer on the base, it would reach 110 degrees quickly, and then the temperature would creep up while thousands of America's finest fixated on the thermometers all day.

But 115 never happened. The thermometers must not have been able to show that temperature. We reached 114 several times but never 115. A thunderstorm occurred once, but that simply made it 114 degrees and HUMID! The days and the weeks went by, and finally, the day came to report to the rifle range. One had to pass three tests to get out of basic training: a one-mile run in under eight minutes, a pathetically simple written test, and the marksmanship test. This was the last of the tests, and it would then be bye-bye to basic training.

Now, up to this point in my life, I had never held a gun before, not even a BB gun as a kid. My father didn't hunt, and guns frankly scared me. I had enlisted in the Air Force partly because I didn't want to hold one of these contraptions. I had trouble killing a mouse; firing at a human would not happen. This wasn't an excuse to stay out of the military. That would only happen if one were a "conscientious objector," and religion prohibited it. I had no medical reason to avoid the draft, and I wasn't going to try the antics of a couple of my friends. One ate a partial roll of aluminum foil bit by bit, figuring that the X-ray at his draft physical would show he was "near death" and unsuitable to serve. They'd seen that trick several times before. Another ate a five-pound box of chocolate the day before his physical, knowing he was somewhat allergic to chocolate. It was not a pretty sight, and after the horror show his body went through, the medics sent him home to retake the physical when he "felt better."

So here I was at the rifle range, with no clue how to fire a gun. We were assured that anyone could pass the test because the target wasn't that far away, and the M-16 sight made it almost impossible to miss. We were given the usual safety orientation and time to practice. I was terrified. I imagined someone turning around with the weapon and accidentally touching the trigger, wiping out the whole group before he realized what was happening. We had three chances to pass the test, needing to hit a target 54 out of 60 times. The first group moved to the line, lay down, aimed, and fired. Their scores were read off: 60, 58, 57, 60, 60, 59, 58...; not one score below 57 on their first of three tries. The next group contained the "dorm klutz;" I knew I could do better than him. He scored 57, and once again, there was no lower score. This was going to be a cakewalk. Then, my group moved to the line. I don't remember firing the weapon. I must have hit the trigger, but all 60 shots went off before I knew it. I had carefully aimed so this would not be a problem. Sarge read off the scores, and that's when I heard, "Ratliff ... 42." (After six weeks of basic training, he still couldn't pronounce my name. I think the two syllables got him.) *What! 42; I'm sure I misheard him.* The laughter from behind me assured me I had heard correctly.

No one else had failed, but I had two more rounds to pass. With everyone watching me, I lay down to try again. Taking several deep breaths to calm myself, I fired again. "Ratliff ... 48." I heard the snickers behind me, but that wasn't what was bothering me; it was the thought that if I failed this last round, I would spend another six weeks in basic training with a drill sergeant who couldn't pronounce my name, more 114-degree days, my wife 1000 miles away, and more blueberry pancakes. I lay down and concentrated like never before. Sarge came up and handed me another rifle. Maybe that was it; the first gun had a defective sight! My spirits lifted, and I aimed ever so carefully. I knew I had it licked this time. The shots went off, and I waited for Sarge to retrieve the target. At first, he said nothing, then walked over close to me and whispered, "48." My heart sank. This couldn't be happening. I would become the "Charlie and the MTA" of Lackland Air Force Base. People would come to see the old man who was perpetually stuck in basic training, and now that he was old and couldn't even see the target, he would die in San Antonio, Texas.

That's when Sarge whispered, "If you promise never to hold a gun ever again while we're on the same planet, I'll pass you."

"Hey, no problem," I enthusiastically responded.

He turned and announced to the group, "Ratliff ... 54." That response was met with applause, which I appreciated, although I knew what everyone was thinking. *How could anyone be that bad of a shot?*

To this day, I have honored that promise. In my six years in the Maryland Air National Guard, I never got near a gun; working in the Command Post ensured that. I also think Sarge sent word back to Maryland to keep me off any rifle ranges since no one ever called me for the mandatory annual marksmanship certification. And I've never hunted. This was not a difficult promise to keep; I don't have the stomach for hunting anyway. The other night, I met with a group, each recounting his most remarkable hunting exploits, from quail to alligators and big game. I didn't have much to contribute to the conversation. I'm not a "normal" guy, and I'm okay with that. How could I ever shoot a goose or duck? My ancestors, who hunted to survive, are all shaking their heads, saying, "What went wrong!" I kept my promise, and I am all the happier for it. The promise got me out of basic training and home to my wonderful wife; her blueberry pancakes don't have legs.

Show Me the Way
to Go Home

Basic training was over, and this rookie airman was finally on his way home. Sitting on a mesh of straps passing for a seat, I waited impatiently for the C-124 cargo plane to take off. A captain stuck his head in the door. "Airman, there's been a small delay. We're still waiting for the pilot." That's not what I wanted to hear, but dreams of a home-cooked meal helped me pass the time. Finally, I heard a jeep drive up. A voice outside said, "Major, glad you're here. You've got some recruits eager to head home." Finally! I could hear footsteps walking up the portable staircase. Turning around, I saw our pilot. Panic struck, and I immediately looked for a way to get off the plane.

It was late September 1971, and I had completed Air Force Basic Training at Lackland Air Force Base near San Antonio, Texas. After six weeks, I could only think of returning home. The rest of my active duty training would occur at Martin State Airport near Baltimore, and I looked forward to living at home. Jackie and I had been married for eight months before my departure, and the six weeks had seemed an eternity. I was fortunate as others served extended tours of duty in Vietnam. Basic training had been intense but had wound down during the last two days, turning instead into a waiting game, hoping my orders would come through. Jackie had moved to her home in Connecticut after two weeks of staying with my parents in Baltimore and had just returned to Baltimore to await my return. All I could think about was seeing her face at the airport and throwing my arms around her.

I had flown down to San Antonio by commercial air and expected to return home the same way. My orders had not come through, and as others left Lackland one by one, I thought I would never go. Finally, after hours of waiting, a group of us were sent to a building to get our orders. Of course, we had to stand in line a little longer. Standing in line was a given at Lackland Air Force Base; whatever one needed, there was a line before one could get to it. After another thirty minutes of waiting, I was handed my orders. I was scheduled to fly back by military air, and the plane was scheduled to take off in just ten minutes. Wonderful—since I was at least twenty minutes from the airfield, I would miss my flight and be forced to spend another night at Lackland.

The sergeant didn't seem concerned about getting us to the plane; he had to smoke a cigarette first while we waited to board the bus. I tried to let our fearless leader know that my plane was due to take off any second. "What's your problem, Ratliff? It ain't goin' nowhere without ya." Finishing his last puff, he headed for the bus. I had already called Jackie to tell her I'd be home that day, and I dreaded having to make another call, telling her I'd been delayed again.

We pulled onto the airfield and parked beside a C-124. These cargo planes had been an Air Force staple in the 1950s and 1960s but were now relegated to the state Air National Guard units. Relieved I had not missed my ride, I grabbed my gear and headed for the plane. Not quite a luxurious commercial jet, but if it got me home, any ride would do. I walked up the stairs and entered the aircraft. Where were the seats? There was just an empty hold with a few straps hanging down. There was a short ladder leading up to what I guessed was the cockpit, but there was no seat to be found. I had already decided they could have pulled me behind the plane on a rope as long as the aircraft made it to Baltimore. I soon discovered that the straps were our seats; it would be a swingin' ride as the plane worked its way north.

A small group of us were going to take this "VIP" flight home, and we managed to climb onto our straps. And then we waited … and waited… and waited. No one was in any hurry to depart for a plane take-off already overdue. The engines hadn't even been fired up, and no flight crew was in sight. Finally, someone spoke up, "Has anyone seen a pilot?" Another of our group finally got up and walked off the plane to speak to a ground crew. Returning, he informed us that we had no pilot at this point. As if my six weeks of basic had not included enough waiting, we were in for another round. Time ticked by, and I suspected I might spend another night at Lackland, this one sleeping on a plane.

After another half hour, we heard a jeep pull up beside the plane. Being a cargo plane, the windows were too small and dirty to allow any visibility. We could hear voices outside the airplane, but no one seemed headed up the steps. Maybe this wasn't our pilot. The talking continued, and suddenly, one of the voices broke into a loud and raucous song:

Show me the way to go home.

I'm tired, and I want to go to bed.

I had a little drink about an hour ago,

And it's gone right to my head.[1]

The singer was inebriated and had trouble climbing the steps, as he needed coaching from a second individual. Puzzled, we listened in disbelief. This certainly was no commercial airline. Finally, the intrepid singer reached the top of the stairs and fell through the door,

---

1 Campbell, J. and Connolly, R. "Show Me the Way to Go Home, London, 1925.

landing in a pile on the floor. After retrieving his spilled beer, he got up with difficulty, and I couldn't believe what I saw. He was dressed in his undershorts with no shirt. He wore a Pickelhaube, an antique German military helmet with a protruding spike, and was carrying the remains of a six-pack of beer. He turned and spoke (or tried to), "Hi, fellas, I'm Major Duncan. I'm your cruise director, and if you give me a second, I'll get this piece of sh*t in the air." With that, he turned and, after three attempts, managed to stumble up the few steps to the cockpit. He disappeared, and we all sat in shock. We heard him yell from the cockpit, "Captain, where's the key to start this piece of sh*t? Goddamn it, I shouldn't have had that sixth beer." None of us spoke. Was this for real? Next, we heard a monstrous belch from the cockpit, and he resumed singing the song. And this was our pilot? I needed to get off the plane ... NOW!

Survival trumped thoughts of home, and I was sweating more from fear than the excessive heat. Finally, one of the others spoke, and it was clear that all thought exiting was the best strategy. That's when the outside door closed. We were all now securely locked in this death trap. We had been through six weeks of obeying orders and not questioning authority, but we needed to get off the plane. We then heard the propellors firing; this guy was going to try to fly us home, and we were going to die. If only I could talk to Jackie one last time.

That's when Major Duncan appeared again. He stuck his head out from the cockpit and was now dressed in full uniform, his Air Force blues. Flashing a big grin, he (coherently this time) went through all the flight procedures, weather, and our ETA. With a "Welcome aboard Flight 1752, airmen," he returned to the cockpit. We had been duped. Although we thought ourselves men of the world, we had completely fallen for this gag. Several others then explained they had known it was a ruse, but their expressions a few minutes earlier had spoken otherwise.

It was a beautiful joke, but one could not pull it off today. There have been too many airline disasters involving hijacking, terrorism, or a pilot bent on self-destruction in the news since then. While briefly terrorized, I appreciated the joke once I realized a drunk would not fly us home. This country has lost much of its sense of humor, which is understandable considering a couple of decades of terrorism, most notably the Sept. 11, 2001, attacks on the World Trade Center and Pentagon. 1971 was a different time. Although amid the Vietnam War, the military had not lost its sense of humor. My father had seen his share of pranks during the Second World War, sharing numerous stories with us when we were growing up. It was obvious that duty came first, but during down periods, a sense of humor kept soldiers from succumbing to the mental nightmare that came with war. This practical joke was an excellent diversion for us; no one on that plane thought it inappropriate. I always appreciated a good practical joke. The flight ended up being one of the smoothest flights I've ever had. The major and the captain, who had been in the cockpit the whole time, were utterly professional and got us home uneventfully. Now, whenever I hear the song "Show Me the Way to Go Home," it always elicits a smile as I remember back to that glorious day when I finally got to go HOME.

X-Y-Z

It was my first day as a teacher, and I had spent hours prepar-
ing an introduction, as making an excellent first impression
was essential. I entered the classroom the day before my debut
to ensure everything was in place. I rehearsed the lesson mul-
tiple times. However, no education class in college could have
prepared me for what was about to happen. A minor class-
room disturbance would become a Category 5 catastrophe.

The first day for any classroom teacher is both exciting and traumatic. How many jobs require one to do 100% of the job on
the first day? One can prepare a lesson inside and out, but children
are unpredictable. This is what makes the job exciting but also what
can make it quite a challenge. Working with adults is not a cakewalk,
but they are generally more professional and predictable. Most leave
their problems outside the job; children wear them on their sleeves.
However, there is no more rewarding profession.

I was confident as the students trickled into the classroom, looking with curiosity at the new figure in front of the classroom. I could
see that they were sizing me up, and I had been told often in teacher training that those first few moments set the tone for the year. I
wanted desperately to make a good first impression: amiable but firm,
caring but consistent. I never dreamed I would be doing this job;
when one stutters, standing in front of a class and delivering a lesson
is more of a nightmare than a dream, but I knew this was now the
career I was destined for. I was going to be a good teacher.

I waited for the class to settle and began to speak. All quieted quickly; so far, so good. I had a short introduction planned. Wisely, I was going to limit my talking that first day, knowing that preteens would be too excited that day to listen for long. I just wanted to set the tone and have them leave excited for what was to come. Not even three minutes into the class, I noticed several girls in the front row giggling. Unphased, I forged ahead, knowing that twelve-year-old children can be silly. The giggling continued, and I was soon rattled. Something was amiss. I plodded on and finally realized the reason for the giggling. My zipper was down! I panicked and concocted a quick plan to cover up the clothing malfunction, hoping that most in the class had not noticed. That's when a minor clothing malfunction evolved into a nightmare.

You will have no difficulty if you ever need to tell someone how to identify me by sight. I have brown eyes, but someone might feel uncomfortable staring at me closely, trying to determine the color of my iris. My hair is no longer brown, and since I always wear a cap, one might not notice I am balding. There is nothing extraordinary about my height (six feet and shrinking) and nothing remarkable about my body shape ... other than it is rounder than years ago. There are, however, a couple of reasonably reliable clues that one could look for: socks not matching, holes in my pants, shirt only partly tucked in, if at all. And to think I'm passed over yearly for the "best dressed" award. But there is one highly reliable characteristic that would make me stand out in even the largest crowd ... the zipper on my pants is probably down. I could blame this on absentmindedness; it does run in my family as my grandfather even went to work one day dressed in coat and tie, but missing one essential article of clothing ... his pants.

The zipper might be one of the great inventions of all time, and males are incredibly thankful for its existence. Running to the bathroom after waiting for an eternity, we would die, or worse, trying to unbutton those cursed buttons. The zipper allows us to quickly discharge unneeded baggage and resume our pathetic attempts to look important. Little kids might have difficulty learning how to get a zipper started, but without zippers, the snow would have melted before Jackie and I could have buttoned up the snowsuits of our three children, and they probably never would have gotten an education as the school would be dismissing before we could get our "three under three" out of the house.

The name of Whitson Judson has largely been forgotten by history; he should remembered along with Edison, Bell, Whitney, and Howe. Although Judson never used the term "zipper," his invention, the "clasp locker," patented in 1893 and revealed to the world that year at the Chicago World's Fair, has simplified our lives in a significant way. In 1851, Elias Howe, inventor of the sewing machine, came up with an "Automatic, Continuous Clothing Closure" but failed to market it. Gideon Sundback perfected Judson's device in 1913, but the name "zipper" would come four years later when the B.F. Goodrich Company would use Judson's fastener on rubber boots.[1] As wonderful as Judson's invention is, it becomes our nemesis when it malfunctions. I will have spent two years trying to unstick non-functioning zippers. But even sadder is that I have never mastered the essential operation of Judson's marvelous device.

I had zipper malfunctions throughout my school career as I was frequently seen with a zipper in the wrong position, and my mother, to destroy any remaining self-esteem that I may have had, explained that I was having this problem because my posterior end was large, forcing my zipper to head south frequently. Now large butts are a genetic certainty in one line of our family, but at age fifteen, feeling as if I was a mutant anyway, I did not need to hear this particular genetics lesson. With time, I became adept at ensuring the zipper was "locked" as much as possible.

Returning to that fateful first day of teaching, I had a problem: how to pull up a zipper with thirty middle school students looking my way. Inspired, I concocted a foolproof plan. I would become demonstrative while making a point, and while whirling toward the chalkboard to write something down, I would quickly alleviate the problem, then continue spinning to face the class with the problem solved. That's when my other confirmed trait would fatefully intervene; I have a doctoral degree in clumsiness. "Klutz" is my middle name. The move began well as I emphasized a point and started spinning to write a word on the board. I rotated off center and soon was stumbling to the side, and with my hand on my zipper, I could not right the spin. I stumbled against the large trash can beside me, and struggling to regain my balance, I fell backward ... right into the trash can. The class erupted, and I lost all composure. I got myself out of the trash can with some difficulty and quickly got back on my feet. I had now lost my train of thought, and after finally getting the kids to quiet down, I finally attempted to regain my form. That's when I noticed I had only gotten the zipper halfway up.

Being older is terrific, and I love to play the part. A lowered zipper might be embarrassing to a younger man, but people expect these things from an older person, and I delight in living down to their expectations. I realize now that my whole life has been a dress rehearsal for being the absent-minded older adult. Now, when Jackie leans over and quietly reminds me to "X-Y-Z" (examine your zipper), I can smile and say, "I'll get to it in a moment." And sometimes I even do.

Source:

1. About.com "Inventors," The History of the Zipper, inventors.about.com/library/weekly/aa082497.htm

BIGFOOT IS ALIVE AND WELL IN CAMBRIDGE

It was 3 p.m., fifteen minutes before dismissal. Most of my students were starting to clean up their laboratory experiment, and several stared at the clock, hoping their gaze would speed up the second hand. The classroom windows were open, letting in some fresh spring air, accompanied by the odor of freshly cut grass. Two students stood to gaze out the window; they were the first to hear the screams. Soon, all were glued to the windows. This was not the usual enthusiasm of middle school students; there was terror in the air. Thirty students were sprinting across the athletic field toward the building, and their elderly teacher was emerging from the woodland trail they had been walking. As they passed our window, one of my students remarked, "Look, Emily and Mary are crying!"

The yelling and crying continued, and we soon heard what precipitated the chaotic charge. "Hide everybody. Big Foot's coming!"

My students turned toward me with big grins. "Mr. Radcliffe, it worked!"

Yes, our plan had worked, but none of us could have ever guessed what would happen next.

I was an unorthodox teacher, only sometimes appreciated by the principals I worked for. It is amazing that I chose that profession—a shy kid who stuttered and one who rarely enjoyed school. I always thought a typical school was an unnatural learning environment, no more conducive to learning than prison incarceration was to rehabilitation. My strategy was always to harness the students' energy and creativity. Children learn from play, experimentation, and trial and error; learning is a cooperative venture, not a top-down flow of information.

I adhered to the curriculum, but I challenged and empowered students. One principal referred to my classroom as "chaos," yet she could not explain how my students achieved at a high level and excelled on standardized tests. My students were active, and I encouraged a moderation of mischief, probably a relic of my earlier Hyde Bay Camp experiences; the students would have ensured the mischief even if I hadn't.

The students and I had built a mile-long nature trail on our school property. My extracurricular Ecology Corps had done much of the work, but I wanted all 150 students to put some muscle and sweat into the project. I wanted them to take ownership; by placing part of themselves into the project, they would hopefully connect with the natural world, something that cannot happen by immersion in a textbook. Learning must also be affective, not just cognitive.

Someone had vandalized the students' trail signs and bridges earlier that month, upsetting all. While the damage was a setback, I loved how the students reacted. They cared. They invested considerable time restoring the features. Some in my extracurricular group then added an unnatural twist to the environmental project. They made a giant footprint in a pan of sand, filling it with plaster of Paris, into which they inserted a broken shovel handle. Two days later, after school, they stomped a trail of giant footprints through a wet section of the woods. This had no redeeming educational value, but I allowed it as a reward for all the hard work.

Poor Mrs. Smith. The prints were not intended for an elderly teacher who never took her classes outside. However, as chance would have it, she ventured out on this beautiful spring day, the only time she took a class into the school forest. Her terrified students made it back to school in record time. Yes, Big Foot was alive and well at Mace's Lane Middle School. Surprisingly, no one in her class noticed Big Foot had two left feet.

My students knew about the footprints as the guilty parties had shared their deed with classmates, but the seventh grade had two sections, and Mrs. Smith, the other science teacher, ventured out with a class of unsuspecting students. How observing footprints could have escalated into terror is beyond me, but no one was prepared for what would happen later that day.

The middle school was to have a dance that evening. That event is quite a spectacle, one that would send aliens quickly back to their spaceship to return to their home planet—gangs of boys roaming through the dance doing more eating than breathing, a large group of girls discussing the fact that Steve said "hello" to Sue and comforting Betty who was completely being ignored by Fred who was busy showing off for Sally who was crying because Helen said Arnold didn't like her ... while only four couples were dancing. Ah, yes, to be twelve or thirteen again.

There had been some talk during the dance about Big Foot's appearance earlier in the school day. By this point, two students claimed to have even seen the monster. While most laughed, a few grew uncomfortable.

"I saw him coming after us as we ran out of the woods."

"What did he look like?"

"He was really tall; he ...."

(*Why are monsters almost always a "he?"*)

"He almost got Alice when she tripped and fell. He got so close that she could hear him breathing. It was horrible."

I always chaperoned the dances, which allowed me to see another side of my students. Invariably, a high school student would try to get in to see his eighth-grade girlfriend, so I would have to play policeman. That evening, one persistent character was determined to get in, finally giving up halfway through the dance. The dance was winding down, and all seemed to be peaceful until ....

"It's Big Foot!" a girl screamed. "He's trying to get into the gym." A stampede of students from the gym soon followed another scream. I tried to work my way back into the gym, but the river of students slowed my progress. "Mr. Radcliffe, Big Foot's in there!"

Going up to a student who didn't seem to be in any hurry to leave, "Where is this Big Foot?"

The student laughed and pointed up to one of the gym windows. These large windows rose above the bleachers, making darkening the gym for daytime activities impossible. Outside one of the windows, a shadow of a figure was standing, backlit by the outdoor security lights. Somehow, someone had climbed on top of the entryway and was peering into the gym. I immediately guessed it was the student I had worked much of the evening to keep out.

"Well, it's certainly not Big Foot unless he's only five and a half feet tall."

Another student stopped beside me. "It's him, Mr. Radcliffe. I saw him."

"Susan, stop and look again. That's no giant beast."

"But Evelyn says she saw him up close." And off she ran.

Soon, the music was playing in a mostly empty gym. The principal was swamped with students wanting to call home. This was well before cell phones; the school had only an office phone and one pay phone. The use of the pay phone was slowed by students having to find the correct change, and soon, the dime became a rare commodity. The line to get into the office was long, and I could see that the principal was quickly losing patience. Seeing me, he came out. "What in the world is going on? Big Foot? I know these students have active imaginations, but this is ridiculous. Who started this rumor?" I guessed he hadn't heard about the charge out of the woods earlier in the day, so I didn't volunteer any additional information.

The swarm around the phones was a buzz of speculation and exaggeration. Big Foot was now in the school and had chased several girls into the bathroom. He was terrorizing people outside the school, and the police had been called. The last part was correct, as a police officer always showed up near the end of the dance to control traffic. His presence pushed the panic to another level. In true form, several boys were unphased and continued to feast in the cafeteria. The stories got better with every passing minute. Fortunately, we were close to the end of the dance, and a few parents had arrived early and were waiting outside. Soon, the parking lot was one massive traffic jam, but within fifteen minutes, the school had thankfully cleared. I breathed one big sigh of relief as the last car pulled away. A dance never ended so quickly, with every student getting picked up on time. At one prior dance, I had waited almost two hours for the last student to be picked up. We needed to hire Big Foot to chaperone all our dances.

I had forgotten about our exciting visitor by the following Monday until a student mentioned it. "Mr. Radcliffe, do you believe that was Big Foot here last week?" As a science teacher, I never felt that my opinion on controversial topics was appropriate. I had the students list the facts of the incident and then suggest other possibilities. I asked them to invoke Occam's razor: given multiple hypotheses or explanations for a phenomenon, the simplest one, or the one with the least assumptions, is most likely correct. The class finally decided there had been no Big Foot. We then launched into a discussion of UFOs, applying the same thought process. It was a great discussion that explored other paranormal phenomena, such as ghosts and ESP. I let other classes launch into the same conversations.

Later that day, a note in my mailbox from the principal asked me for a meeting. I knocked on his door, thinking I would be reprimanded for Friday's nightmare. "George, I noticed today that you all were discussing UFOs and whatnot, but that was not what was on your lesson plan. You need to stick to the curriculum." My efforts to explain fell on deaf ears, and with a simple apology, I left the office. That principal never learned how Big Foot made it to our school. There are some secrets better kept that way.

Today, most seem to have forgotten Occam's razor as conspiracy theories abound. We live in a country where to question is patriotic. We are blessed to have access to all the relevant facts … if we take the time to look. We live in a fast-paced world where time is often a precious commodity. When I was a child, my father spent nearly an hour every morning at breakfast, reading the paper: collecting the background information to a story and comparing alternative viewpoints. Now, we listen to a thirty-second sound bite as we grab our coffee and donuts on the way to work. And everyone wants to have a position on an issue. To keep our country strong, we should question everything; there is no place in a democracy for baseless conspiracy theories.

I always harnessed student interest and questions in my classroom; I referred to it as opportunistic teaching. As long as they were not trying to stall a quiz or needed activity, I let them talk and ask questions. Driving home that evening, I realized how we had turned the school upside down with our "footprints." I should have felt remorse, but no one was hurt, and some tremendous unscripted learning occurred. I was never to become the "favorite teacher" in the eyes of any principal I worked for, but I certainly took some of the boredom out of the schools in which I worked. I remained a "child" all the years I taught. There were better information deliverers and funnier instructors in my schools. As a stutterer and shy person, I maybe wasn't cut out to be a teacher, but as a curious and sometimes spontaneous child, I could engage students and communicate well on their level. I probably should never have been a teacher, but I certainly chose the right career. But bring Big Foot to school? Maybe I did go too far, but no one complained about school being boring that Friday.

THE WRONG PERSON
WROTE THIS BOOK

By all accounts, I shouldn't be writing a book. My high school English teachers would be shocked that I'm writing at all. However, my brother Bill was a gifted writer whose writing was even commended by author James Michener. He was a talented journalist who was rocketing to the top in his career when his life was cut short in a tragic car accident in 1982. While a significant personal loss for me, we all lost a writer who could put a unique spin on even the most ordinary story. This should be his book.

In 1979, Father Bernard Pagano, a priest at our local Catholic church, St. Mary's Refuge of Sinners, was charged with several counts of armed robbery of convenience stores in the Wilmington, Delaware, area. He became known as the "Gentleman Bandit," a polite gunman who had committed these robberies over several months. He often visited his half-sister in the Wilmington area and was identified in a line-up by several individuals. Father Pagano was an unusual priest, intelligent but frequently controversial. He once upset many of the parishioners when he participated in a charity wrestling event as "The Mad Monk." Many locals quickly wrote him off as guilty.

Bill was a local reporter at the time, working for the *Daily Banner* in Cambridge. After an initial interview with him, he befriended

Father Pagano and became one of his strongest advocates. Bill maintained Pagano's innocence throughout the following months, even admonishing me on one occasion when I, like many others, started to doubt. After all, the priest looked like the composite sketch that witnesses had helped construct, and numerous eyewitnesses had identified him. Bill covered the story with many objective articles. Toward the end of the trial, another man turned himself in and confessed to the crimes, and Father Pagano was cleared. However, he had already left the Cambridge parish and moved to New Jersey. Bill kept in contact with him for a while. Two years later, the story became a major television movie, appropriately titled "The Gentleman Bandit."

I will never forget Bill's unbiased defense of Father Pagano. He repeatedly criticized the numerous parishioners who had abandoned the priest. Bill said it wasn't so much a matter of guilt or innocence as the need to get out all the facts. "Just give him his day in court." I remember all the gossip that year; as with many issues, everyone quickly became an authority on the story. Bill researched while everyone else talked. It made me proud of my brother for being such a vocal advocate of "keeping an open mind." We always say someone is innocent until proven guilty, but most still rush to judgment. Like a good reporter, Bill always kept an open mind and worked hard to unearth the facts.

That year was the first time I looked up to him. Four years younger, he had always been the kid brother but stood much taller than me that year. He died three years later, along with my sister Gussie, in a car accident, and I wish I could have seen the heights to which he would have risen in his career. He moved from the *Banner* to the *Delaware State News*, and several days before his death, the *Philadelphia Inquirer* had hired him. My little brother became a giant in 1979 and taught his older brother an important lesson. We lost family; the world lost a gifted writer.

I've always referred to my family as lovingly dysfunctional. We were close but had more than our share of issues: Mom's bouts of depression, Gussie's mammoth medical issues and resulting behavioral problems, and the youngest, Kim's severe intellectual disability. In many ways, Bill was the heart and soul of the family, always upbeat and laughing. We always called him "Nature Boy" since he was always outside, collecting some organism. He loved our beagles and once had a pet skunk, Izzy, that he walked around the neighborhood on a leash, watching most run to the other side of the street when they saw him coming.

He was the ultimate practical joker, pulling one prank after another. My father always shared stories of his childhood pranks; I listened and laughed while Bill tried and often succeeded in outdoing them. He knew how to tease his older brother. He would lead me on until I lost patience and retaliated. Of course, I, as the older brother, got in trouble because I was "older and should have known better." Bill would walk away victorious with the world's biggest grin. All knew his sense of humor well, and he never used it to disparage someone. One of my last memories of him was at a family function where he was joking about a pointless education meeting he had covered that day. He launched into a replay of the meeting's absurdity, playing the multiple roles of those involved. This may have been the hardest I have ever laughed. He could mimic our elderly grandfather perfectly and, although hysterically funny, did it with such kindness and respect that my grandfather laughed heartily. He could have been a gifted comedian; combining this with his impressive writing skills, he would have gone far. If he were still alive, there is no doubt he would have authored multiple best-selling books.

When someone dies, we usually focus on what was lost, not what we had, the memories that could have been, not those we are left with. Bill departed over forty years ago, more than half of my life. He is not just a distant memory but a part of me now. When we were young, he was Nature Boy, and I was the bookworm. I was the essentially serious child; he was the jokester. I was the worrier, and Bill sailed through life with the carefree attitude of a child. Over the years, I have assimilated the best of him, becoming a nature lover and finally learning how to find humor in the trials of daily life. I don't have to strive to retain the memories of one we lost long ago; they are the best part of me.

Although Bill's professional career was cut short, his gift shone through often. When first hired by the Cambridge paper, he was given the human-interest stories no one wanted to cover—the closing of an old store, someone's two-headed chicken, or a hen acting as mother to a small litter of puppies. He tackled each one, and with his characteristic caring and sense of humor, he created memorable stories that gained him recognition and awards. When working at the *Delaware State News*, he often highlighted a little-recognized job by performing the job for a day, everything from a postal carrier to a refuse worker, riding and working on a garbage truck for a day. While writing with humor, he wonderfully detailed the job's difficulties and the workers' dedication. After a day of handling garbage and being doused with rancid milk and diaper contents, he shared, "Who needs to 'work' for a living when you can work for a living."1

Bill did not avoid controversy and often took on the paper's executives on which he worked. At one early paper he worked for, he uncovered a memo instructing the staff to avoid putting any story involving an Afro-American on page one. He confronted and exposed the paper owner and editor and would have lost his job, except that a larger paper had just hired him.

He got to know James Michener while beginning his research for the novel *Chesapeake*. Michener interviewed Bill's grandfather, Sen. George L. Radcliffe, at Spocott in 1973 and followed Bill's career from there. When *Chesapeake* was published in 1978, Bill covered the book's release. Michener wrote Bill after his article was printed, "Everything you wrote was accurate and just the way it happened. You have an acute ear and a good eye." Bill also received several journalism awards in his short career. We can only imagine the heights he could have attained in his career.

How sad that someone who so loved life would depart us so early, at age twenty-nine, but how blessed I was to have such a brother. I carry him with me every day. Bill had a gift for writing, and I should be reading his books rather than writing one myself. I end with an editorial of his that captures what he was so capable of:

May 32nd?

It's possible that my distaste for February was planted in my brain when I was an impressionable child; I was brainwashed if you will, but nothing I have seen since grade school has altered my view. "If we can make it through February," a friend of my grandmother's used to say, "we'll live another year." She died in February.

Despite its mercifully short length, February is the worst month of the year, the Kansas of monthly geography. I once saw a tree in Kansas, at least, I thought it was a tree. I should have known better. On closer inspection, it turned into a vine-covered telephone pole. Birds, mammals, and every other form of wildlife have escaped from Kansas, a state overrun by wheat fields, wheat fields, and an occasional corn field. To be truthful, I must admit I once saw a dog in Kansas. Standing by the side of Interstate 70, he appeared to be a coyote at first glance, a coyote with a collar. His ribs were showing, naturally, and a dull, lifeless look highlighted his demeanor. I suspected he was contemplating suicide, so I passed him by. I suppose Kansas has, too.

February, despite what Washington and Lincoln's Birthday, and Valentine and Groundhog's Day aficionados might claim, is the Gregorian Calendar pits. A look at its 11 monthly counterparts puts the undisputable fact in stark perspective.

January is the start of the new year, the first flush of winter. February .... March has the first signs of spring, and April has spring and the return of baseball,"The Summer Game," and May

may well be the top month of the year. For good measure, it closes with Memorial Day. June marks the start of summer. July is another in a series of summer baseball tandems (topped by a Fourth of July weekend), and August is, well, more summer, for a lack of anything better to say. September brings the first touch of fall colors, October carries the World Series and Indian Summer, November touts Indian Summer and Thanksgiving, and December is armed with Christmas. Which brings us back to February ....

February has, well, let me think .... February has the year's best cold and flu viruses (one's always going around), brown grass, and pasty-white "tanless" people. While a December snowstorm is marked by excitement, February's storms are dispiriting, winter's last straw. February's snow is the grey-black lumps that hang above your rear tires, just waiting to fall and melt in your shoe. In short, February has little, if anything, to justify its existence. To top the month's irony, pictures of baseball players frolicking in the Florida sunshine highlight the month's sports pages.

Which brings me to the point of this diatribe on the month's obvious shortcomings. If it's necessary to add one day to the calendar every four years, why pick February? September, April, June, and November have 30 days, and who would complain about a 32-day May or July? But February, come on now, Gregory....[2]

Of course, after reading that, you will put this book down, saying, "The wrong person wrote this book."

1.   Bill Radcliffe, *Delaware State News*, Dover, DE, 2 Nov 1981, p. 11.
2.   Bill Radcliffe, *Daily Banner*, Cambridge, MD, 4 Feb 1980, editorial page.

AN UNUSUAL SEPTEMBER DAY

It has been fifty years to the day since I sat in this same Mc-Donald's, eating an Egg McMuffin. Today, I am using it as a place to write, but on Monday, Sept. 10, 1973, I sat here in complete shock at the end of the most unusual twenty-four hours of my life, a day that changed my life forever.

Returning from a Maryland Air National Guard weekend on Sunday, September 9, 1973, nothing could have prepared me for what the next twenty-four hours would bring. I was partly through my six-year military obligation, the result of winning the first draft lottery in 1970. That morning, I had reported for duty at 3 a.m. and was getting home at 10 p.m. I was so tired on the way home from Baltimore that I constantly got out of the car and jogged the highway to stay awake. I dreamed of my bed the whole way home, not the best way to stay awake. Jackie awaited me, and I wanted to talk to her before collapsing. She was eight months pregnant with our first child, due on October 7. I knew she was starting to get extremely uncomfortable, not that any male can comprehend pregnancy, and I had thought about her all weekend.

We had wanted children almost from the moment we met; it was part of what connected us immediately. Jackie had miscarried the first child the previous year, making us more nervous about the second pregnancy, but all had gone smoothly up to this point. We were planning natural childbirth and had gone through a series of Lamaze classes. Jackie was a natural mother and handled pregnancy with such grace. I felt useless as I watched her progress through each stage of pregnancy. While relieved that I would never have to go through this hijacking of my body, I marveled at how she was getting to know our child before it was born. We neither knew nor cared about the gender. Being pregnant during a sweltering summer without air conditioning had been no picnic.

As I turned into our half-mile driveway, I was so glad to have that trip and weekend behind me. Fighting sleep even down the driveway, I finally reached the house. Jackie was in excellent spirits and filled me in on her weekend. I had little to share since my weekend was uneventful. Working in the unit command post would be busy and stressful during a war or an exercise, but nothing happened that weekend, as I spent more time gazing at the clock than working. Jackie did share that she was having some gas pains but didn't seem to make much of them. Pregnancy was hardly a walk in the park!

We talked for over an hour, and I soon got ready for bed. It was quickly apparent that Jackie wasn't going to sleep. She was clearly in another uncomfortable phase of the pregnancy, where finding a good sleeping position was impossible. The fetus pressing against the bladder made her feel the need to urinate twenty-four hours a day. It's times like these when a husband feels wholly inadequate. Even my feeble attempts at sympathy fell way short of the mark. The gas pains were making sleep impossible that evening. Somehow, I managed to stay awake so that we could talk. Random words were finding their way out of my mouth, but I knew I needed to stay awake; it was the least I could do. The minutes ticked slowly away, and Sunday the ninth soon became Monday the tenth.

I don't know when I first thought about it, but it finally occurred to me that there was a pattern to Jackie's gas pains as they came and passed. I remembered from our Lamaze natural childbirth classes that timing the interval between contractions was vital. A three-minute interval meant that the uterus had dilated to ten centimeters, and birth was imminent. I decided to time the interval between gas pains for fun and awaited her subsequent pain. "Three minutes!" This had to be just a coincidence. I'd time it once more. Three minutes again, and then again for the third interval. We both started laughing. She couldn't possibly be in labor since our child was projected to be born in four weeks, but the gap was three minutes each time. Finally, at 2 a.m., we decided, as a precaution, to head to the hospital. If nothing else, we could get something for these gas pains, which were becoming more than an annoyance.

I'll never forget driving through town, both of us laughing uncontrollably. Either her gas pains would become a classic family joke, or we were in for one big surprise. In retrospect, I am amazed that Jackie could laugh through the whole episode. I was slap-happy from lack of sleep, but she was, at best, horribly uncomfortable. We were too tired to worry about a possible problem; this was surreal. Jackie had been a trooper throughout the pregnancy, and I marveled at her composure. We were still laughing when we reached the emergency room, and we soon found that the staff wasn't laughing at all. She WAS in labor, and events were on a fast track. So much for gas pains!

They whisked her off to one room and me to another. Finally, we were going to put all the Lamaze training to work. Some time went by, and I began to worry. Didn't I need to be with her, helping with the rhythmic breathing? I hoped nothing was wrong. There was no falling asleep now – quite the opposite. A nurse soon came in to inform me that the baby was in the wrong position and that a Caesarian Section would be necessary. I was too tired to be worried, and all seemed healthy with the baby. But wait a minute; this was still a month too early. For the second time in twenty-four hours, the second hand of my watch seemed to go backward.

I have no idea how much time passed as I sat dazed and unprepared for the moment. The first child was often late, and I had figured

I would start preparing mentally when October hit. Suddenly, a nurse entered and informed me that I had a son. You can picture this scene repeatedly, but nothing prepares you for the reality. I knew his name would be John Scott; that had been decided long ago. He wouldn't be stuck with my name, "George," for which there is no suitable nickname, a fact I had learned the hard way. He had two names, both of which lent themselves to good nicknames. If conceived without a Y chromosome, he would be Mary McKim, after my little sister. As it turns out, there never was to be a Mary.

I sat there dumbfounded, trying to process the situation mentally. Nothing registered. I finally got to see Jackie, who was exhausted, and then John Scott was wheeled in. I know that fathers aren't the brightest people, but there should be no surprise when you see your child for the first time. You see your wife grow more prominent over the months, and it's not a turkey growing inside. But the reality of seeing one's child for the first time is a significant shock. The mom knows only too well what is living and moving inside her, but the father never fully comprehends what is happening. *Oh my God, I am a father. That's my child, a real human being! Jackie really was pregnant!* Like I said, I'm not too bright. Scott weighed 8 pounds; whoever gave us the October due date needed to return to math class.

My father had shown up at the hospital by this point, and we decided to leave mother and son alone for a while. A McDonald's was nearby, and we decided to get a bite to eat. My feet never touched the ground as we walked out to the car. *I'm a father. I'm a FATHER!* Wasn't a father an older adult? I was just a young guy, only a few years removed from my teddy bear. Likely, this was a dream, probably the result of a coffee overdose from the twelve cups consumed trying to stay awake the previous day. Throughout the whole gourmet Egg McMuffin breakfast, I sat in total disbelief. This was more than my feeble mind could comprehend. *I was a father!*

By the time we had left McDonald's, my father had pulled everyone in Cambridge over to our table to share the news. I, of course, could say nothing because all I could do was think, *I am a father*. My thoughts soon turned to Jackie. She had been given a spinal for the Caesarian Section, and I knew that would be wearing off. When we returned to the hospital, she was feeling significant pain. Once again, her husband felt utterly inadequate. She would force out a smile occasionally, but she was in pain. A male cannot possibly understand how a woman feels at this time. The spinal was only partly effective, and she remembered feeling the incision. That thought made me cringe.

I was so proud that day, but I had a problem when people came up and congratulated me. Congratulate me? I had done nothing except eat an Egg McMuffin nine months after contributing one-half of a cell. My wife suffered months of discomfort, from morning sickness to labor pain at the end, got no good sleep for several months, and felt the incision. And you want to congratulate ME? I was the proudest person on Earth that day but also the most inconsequential player. But as they say, my life would never be the same. I had married the most wonderful person on Earth, and now we could be a family. What a fantastic day!

THE FINAL RESOLUTION

Mom was growing weaker by the day, and I visited her more frequently. I always asked about family, avoiding the one subject that had become a wall between us. Dad's phone call that morning made me drop what I was doing and head directly next door. Time was running out.

"How are you feeling, Mom?"

"Hi, honey; I'm doing OK. How are Jackie and the boys?"

"We're fine, but Dad says you feel much weaker."

"Father Ray is coming over, and we're going to pray together. Will you join us?"

"Sure, Mom." This was the last thing I wanted to do, but I would do it for her.

"You know, George, you're leaving the Catholic church hurt me deeply. I always prayed that you would return. What did I do wrong to drive you away? I tried to be the best mother I could."

"You were the best mother, Mom, but it's your religion, not mine. Just because it's unimportant to me doesn't mean you failed in any way. You gave me the love and guidance I needed, but I must live my life my way. The Church was important to you, but it's not me. Look at how I'm living my life. Be proud of that."

"I am proud of you. I just wanted ...."

"Mom, I'm not changing, just as I never wanted you to. It is who I am, and you are who you are."

She smiled, and I hugged her. These conversations had historically ended in her leaving the room, engulfed in tears. Today was different; she seemed at peace.

"George, I understand, and it's OK. You are a wonderful son, and I am so proud to be your mother."

"You're the best mother. Thanks for understanding. I just needed to know if you approve of me. I always felt you were disappointed in me."

"George, I could never be disappointed in you."

"Love you, Mom."

Sadly, that was the last time I saw her as she passed that night. I knew she had finally accepted me, and I felt peace.

That was the final resolution I had dreamed of for years. Unfortunately, it never happened.

How often do we see a show where two individuals quarrel only to resolve the conflict at the end of the story? And, of course, it's resolved immediately after the last commercial. Life is complex, following no predictable pattern, and some things resolve themselves nicely while others stay messy. I thought my differences with my mother would evaporate at the end, putting aside years of strain and emotion. But as it often does, fate intervened and created a different ending.

My mother and I were always close; there never was a more caring and devoted mother, and I have only the warmest memories of our early family. Every child should grow up in an environment as warm, protective, and all-encompassing as I had. Even her religious teachings were comforting when I was young. It provided a fairy tale structure to life, answering a young child's ultimate questions. Being told that life here on earth was just the first chapter was comforting. I was a kid who went to bed worrying that the Sun might not rise the next day. I also was enamored with the ritual of religion. There was something supernatural about sitting in a church with a rainbow of light streaming down from the stained-glass windows, hints of incense wafting through the church, and Gregorian chants emanating from the inner sanctum that could make any young child believe that this life was all part of a greater plan. But I grew up, and my scientific mind painted another picture.

However, while Catholicism was rooted in love, it also utilized fear to structure my moral character. I didn't need the fear because my parents' example alone steered me down the right path. The religious structure should have evolved as I aged and viewed the world through a more questioning eye, but Mom's Catholicism remained that simple, unforgiving dogma.

By age eight, I decided I was already headed to hell. The complex system of classifying actions as venial and mortal sins and using confession to wipe clean the slate conflicted with my logical mind. If there were a God, he would never have set up such a complicated system, and why were Catholics the chosen ones? I knew many non-Catholics who were better people than some of my Catholic friends. I also found confession ridiculous. Lie, cheat, and steal, and with a few "Our Fathers" or "Hail Marys," all was absolved. I needed proof, something that faith does not require. Church lost meaning, and I soon found hypocrisy in organized religion. Eventually, I did not need God to explain my life and the universe. I wasn't put here to serve Him, and why was God a "he" anyway? Gussie stayed religious but quickly changed God's gender.

Mom, however, saw strict Catholicism as the only path. Her parents and grandparents had been devout Catholics. Her great-uncle had been a renowned priest in Baltimore, two great-aunts were nuns, and her grandfather had donated the money for the magnificent communion rail in the Baltimore cathedral. Mom was never one to question her faith and, to her credit, practiced it until her last days. When life turned difficult, her faith carried her through.

Finally, a series of events put a massive strain on our family, significantly impacting both mother and son. The significant medical and psychological problems gripping my two sisters drove my mother deeper into religion as she grasped desperately for an explanation for their condition. She found the answers she needed in her faith. She became so desperate for the comfort her religion provided that she started attending church every day. Science and math provided a different mindset for me, as I found my answers elsewhere. I understood why she needed the refuge of religion, but she couldn't comprehend my chosen path. The tension built between us as Mom never kept her thoughts to herself. She saw herself as a failed mother, and even though we remained close, she awaited the return of her Prodigal Son. Clearly, in her mind, the fact that her child had abandoned religion trumped any other positive. The comments began:

"If you truly loved me, you would go to church."

"Why don't you love me anymore? How have I failed you?"

"Don't you want to go to heaven?"

Over the years, the comments escalated in intensity. "You must go to church. You're hurting me so."

Dad tried to stay out of the discussions, but his concern was always for my mother's welfare. The fascinating thing was that he was not even the same religion as my mother and, according to her interpretation of her faith, was not going to heaven. This statement did not sit well with her children when they were young, as we envisioned our father burning in hell simply because he wore the wrong uniform. He did join my mother's team in later years, solidifying her position. I could not accept my mother's beliefs, but I always understood it was a critical piece of her; without it, I'm relatively sure she would not have survived. The problem was that there never could be a rational discussion between us. Naively, I tried to argue my position, constantly reminding her she was a great mother. There was no common ground, and every discussion quickly ended with my mother running to her bedroom in tears, not to appear until later that day, if at all. My father counseled me not to upset my mother because she was "so fragile." Time passed, and stubbornly, I would try again to find some resolution.

The whole matter intensified when Jackie and I announced our engagement since I was marrying a non-Catholic. I couldn't see why this would be a problem because Mom had done the same thing years earlier. Jackie and I, desperately wanting our wedding to be an entirely peaceful event, agreed to meet a Catholic counselor and have a priest present at the wedding. Family peace was paramount, and Jackie was so understanding. We were happily married at Jackie's Congregationalist Church with a priest present. Ironically, soon after, the priest left the priesthood and married.

Children further complicated the matter as Mom insisted they be baptized and brought up Catholic. The only way to maintain family harmony was to agree, and we rationalized that our children should probably be exposed to some religion anyway. I have forever felt guilty for caving in, but it was the only way to keep peace. When my little sister died soon after, my mother took another big step into her religious sanctum. Later, my other two siblings were killed in a car accident, and Mom became too fragile to confront. With only one remaining child of four, Mom turned the heat up on her Prodigal Son, and only his return would satisfy her. She now suffered from depression. I was torn between pleasing Mom to minimize her depression and raising my family as I chose. I was forty but had to bow to my mother's pressure. My boys were subjected to years of church and Sunday school.

The arguments intensified. My father made it clear that I should not bring up the subject of religion as my mother was near breaking. I avoided the issue, but she frequently broached the subject when we were alone. Nothing I could say appeased her; even my conciliatory comments sent her running to the bedroom. Few saw these moments, and I started to avoid being alone with her. This only increased my guilt because I knew too well that I was her only remaining child. Nothing I could say brought her any peace. As she aged, I wondered how this would ever find any resolution. Would she finally accept who I was on her deathbed? In my mind, I began to play out this potential final scene to find peace.

Time didn't ease the pain I was causing her; if anything, the opposite was true. Jackie and I finally decided that we needed to call my father over for a talk to get his help. He wasn't Catholic; indeed, he would understand. I'm unsure how we got him away from Mom since they were inseparable, but he came for dinner one night. Jackie and I had rehearsed what we would say countless times, and both of us were hopeful that with Dad's help, we could at least diffuse the tension. He entered, and we got him his ritual glass of wine. Jackie and I looked at each other to see who would first break the ice, but Dad said he had an important announcement to make before either could speak. "After much thought, I have decided to become a Catholic." Our jaws dropped; Dad would not be the mediator we needed.

I took Mom out to lunch periodically to reassure her of her special status, and many of those times, we did get through the meal without mentioning religion, but it was always the elephant in the room. I knew she was proud of me, but the hurt always seemed to dwarf anything I could say. Only my "return" would bring her the peace she sought. Periods would pass when there were no confrontations, but I knew she still wore her feelings right below the surface.

Then came the fateful Christmas dinner some years later. Our boys were grown, and we assembled for a wonderful family holiday get-together at our house. I had not gone to church in a while and knew the tension was building again. I stayed home that morning to help Jackie with the large dinner we were hosting. The dinner went nicely, with laughter and sharing of good times. That makes the holidays special; a family reconnects after a year of going their separate ways, finding nothing has changed. As usual, it was the best of holidays, and Jackie had outdone herself in preparing the feast.

That's when it happened! Mom dropped the C-bomb that ended the festivity. "George," she said, "I'm sorry you didn't go to church with your father and me today." I panicked; how would I get out of this without a scene? I mentioned having to help Jackie with the meal, but before I had much of it out of my mouth, she pronounced, "I have lost three children and suffered so throughout my life, but nothing has brought me the hurt that you did when you left the Church." As they say, you could hear a pin drop. Everyone gasped, and I desperately looked for a hole to crawl into. There was no reply to that accusation, and I sat utterly silent. Someone quickly killed the deadly silence by changing the subject. Everyone chimed in, and the moment passed. I quickly raced into the kitchen to start washing dishes. Any other memory of the day was lost. If there had been a life-size cross in the house, I would have been nailed to it.

Ironically, that was one of the last times I heard her use the religion conversation-killer. She had become best friends with a Roman Catholic priest. Always outspoken, he quickly sensed the tension between my mother and me and intervened in a way I had always hoped my father would. I will forever be indebted to him for standing up to her, but then he had the proper credentials to do this. However, the tension remained right below the surface, and Mom and I were relegated to trivial conversations, nothing that could elicit a repeat of the fateful Christmas Day nightmare.

There still had to be a resolution. I couldn't have my mother pass on with this great wall between us. Either I had to pretend to be a Catholic for the rest of her life, or she had to accept that I could still be a loving son outside of the church. To say I was feeling guilty was the understatement of the century. I will die still feeling guilty and thinking I was selfish for not caving. I did what I thought best, but never did a few days go by when I didn't have second thoughts. I could only hold out hope for that final resolution.

Mom was now in the home stretch of her life as medical problems began to build. In 2004, she was given six months to live. Indeed, in her final days, she would see that I had always been a devoted and appreciative son. I never forgot a birthday or Mother's Day and visited her and Dad at least once a week. Then life played one of those cruel tricks that seem to be so much a part of it. Dementia set in, and Mom's memory began to crumble. Her short-term memory suffered first, and she regressed to an almost childlike state. Then, one day came the horrible realization that there could be no final resolution. Although she was far past the six months she had been given to live, her mind was dissolving fast.

Then, another shock—Dad, who had been in perfect health, died suddenly in 2009 of bacterial meningitis, and Mom moved in with us. Dad made me promise to put Mom in a nursing home if anything ever happened to him, but I never intended to honor that promise. I retired and helped Jackie take care of my grandchildren, and Jackie and I became Mom's caregivers. Our conversations with Mom never progressed beyond when dinner time was or whether she could have a second glass of wine. Soon, she failed to recognize who I was. There would be no resolution; the time for any possible reconciliation had long passed. Dementia is a cruel fate for anyone. I realized that even if I brought up the subject, she would have no memory of it two minutes later. We had long since stopped telling my mother that my father was deceased. Why inflict pain if the memory would not last? The consensus was to keep her comfortable and happy those last few days.

When I think objectively, I realize there never could have been a final resolution—no storybook ending. My only consolation is knowing that in her last couple of years, she no longer worried about whether her Prodigal Son would return. This was sadly replaced by wondering where she was or even who I was. In the end, I'm not sure there was any thought at all. She passed in 2014, and I still wonder how this irreconcilable difference could have been surmounted. Maybe a "good" son would have put up a good front and attended church all those years. I'll go to my grave feeling like a failure as a son. She had to know I cared, but this was not enough for her. Jackie and I kept her home with us for her last five years and sacrificed a lot to make her feel special. It doesn't seem enough; it's not what she wanted. I can certainly rationalize that I was a good son, but I can't help feeling I failed her. If I could relive all those years, I probably would do nothing different. It was her weakness, I understand, but you'll never convince me I was the son she wanted or needed. At least one of us is at peace now.

As time passed after her death, I have come to understand that my mother was a much stronger woman than I gave her credit for. Many women never could have survived the loss of three of their four children. Add to that, Mom suffered from depression, likely intensified by a range of physical problems. Living in that household as a child and visiting often as an adult, I saw the depression firsthand. I was surprised later to find that others saw only a charming, loving person. Whenever someone came to the house, Mom rose from the bed she spent much of her day in and cheerfully greeted them, engaging them with upbeat questions and genuine caring. She became the person she actually was. I now consider her one of the strongest individuals I have ever known. To continually lift herself out of the depths of depression must have taken incredible strength. While likely her religion partly fueled this, she was able to become again the loving individual I saw daily as a child.

In Oz, I was the dutiful Catholic son, but Oz faded when I started questioning religion. I grew to understand and accept the importance of her religion to her. Few people lost as much as she did in her lifetime, and religion was the constant that kept her afloat. She even lived long enough to see the death of a grandchild. I will always treasure the love she showed. A less loving mother might have thrown in the towel on me. There never was that final resolution I so desperately fought for, but in later years, I found the peace it would have brought. So often, we let someone pass on without letting them know how special they were, which can haunt us for a lifetime. I told Mom how special she was; I just couldn't compromise who I was to please her. If there is a heaven, she'll be in a seat of honor, and I'll probably be outside with the dogs. This story probably ended the only way it could, and while not the happy ending we dream of, it is how life plays out its ironic self.

THERE IS AN AFTERLIFE

How nice it would be to leave these mortal coils behind one day and bask in a worry-free land devoid of hardship and pain, surrounded by all the people we have loved. I like my mortal coils, even if they sometimes ache. What I look like is everyone else's problem; I've never been one to gaze in the mirror. I enjoy being me. Dreaming of a hereafter for a soul doesn't work for this somewhat scientific brain. I was raised as a Catholic and promised eternal bliss in heaven if I did not die in a state of sin. To a young child, heaven was the ultimate reward for doing everything my parents instructed. To my six-year-old self, it meant an eternity of ice cream, baseball cards, teddy bears, dogs, and my family.

My first disillusionment came when Mom told me my beagles would not join me in heaven; heaven lost much of its charm that day. There could be no heaven without Nickie and Dixie. The idea that our bodies would not go with us was a bummer. How could I play ball and ride my bike? Then Mom shared that my father could not join us in heaven because he was Episcopalian. God seemed picky and lost much of "his" aura since he discriminated against non-Catholics and beagles. My sister had already decided that God, if perfect, could not be a "he." The tale of my soul going to heaven sounded too much like a ghost story, and time further eroded that fairy tale. The idea of no heaven makes death even more terrifying, but I need proof before I could believe; faith is risky.

I don't need the ultimate reward to live a good life. However, I do believe in an afterlife, but not what so many hope for. It's right here on this good old Earth that we've loved and toiled through all these years, but it will be for those left behind, not me. Each person lives on in the hearts and minds they have touched throughout their brief time on this planet. I have lost all my grandparents, parents, siblings, and a son. But that is incorrect—I have not lost them; I just incorporated them into myself.

My parents and grandparents lived long and productive lives; their deaths were the natural order. But losing a son and my three siblings when they were starting their life journeys rocked me. I am enriched by the love they gave me, and they walk through each day with me. Would I be the same person if they had never existed? I would have been spared the shock and sorrow their deaths caused, but I would be so very different. I am, in fact, a composite of all the unique individuals who have impacted my life.

After a death, we focus too much on the fact that the deceased is not physically present. People say that you can never "see" them again. If there were a heaven, they would also have no physical presence since our mortal coils are temporary. While I might not be able to reach out and touch them physically, I feel them more significantly. I have memories, but my relationship with them can continue to evolve as I learn more about them. We have their memories, but these can fade over time unless we actively work to continue to learn more about them.

My relationship with my brother and two sisters was like that with any sibling: a mix of love, competition, jealousy, laughter, and often conflict. Sadly, I had little time to know them as adults since their lives were cut short. I needed to know them as people, not just as a sometimes-annoying sibling, which I also was to them. If I let my knowledge of them freeze at the moment I lost them, then they have died. To forget is the real tragedy. I have a responsibility to them in death as I did in life: to get to know each better and to introduce them to others.

The same process works for my parents. There has never been a parent who didn't annoy their child numerous times; ask my sons. I can remember my mother and father as parents, or I can get to know them as the remarkable individuals they were. My mother has been gone for ten years, and I remember our battles over religion as if they were yesterday. But I want to know her as an individual, not just a parent: her hopes, dreams, and fears. She is not dead if our relationship evolves. To focus on the loss is a disservice to a loved one. Remembering brings a touch of grief, but letting our understanding of and relationship with them evolve is a joyous process. Focusing on what could have been is destructive, and that causes part of us to die.

It is tragic to be several generations removed from an individual when no one remembers them, and the stories about them are long forgotten. They lived an entire eventful life of loving, coping, and achieving, but all we retain is a name, birth date, and death date. That's when they are indeed dead. Each person goes to an afterlife on Earth, and the glory of that "heaven" shines if they remain a part of the lives of those still battling "down here." They live on in their letters, photos, artwork, and stories. Pictures are what most of us retain. We love these because they elicit those beautiful memories, but the photos will mean little to future generations because they don't capture the individuality of those who have left us. That was always one of the reasons I didn't like history in school; too often, it was a collection of names, accomplishments, and dates, but each historical figure was a real person with hopes, fears, strengths, and faults. And the characters in our family tree are no less important. My great-great-grandmother Radcliffe lived an entire life and birthed a considerable family, with many achieving remarkable success. I have a portrait of her, but I know nothing about her because her descendants let her "die." Like many women years ago, she was relegated to the home, and birthing was her most significant accomplishment. However, she had to be unique as her children achieved so much.

To those wanting a child's eternal reward for a good life, such an afterlife is not comforting. We'll all be forgotten when the Sun expends its finite supply of hydrogen, but who knows—we may have spread through the galaxy by then. For now, those who knew a deceased loved one are responsible for keeping them alive. As did my grandfather and father, I do it with the stories I share orally and in writing. Memories of my siblings could have faded over the forty years since I last gazed upon them, but I feel like I saw them yesterday. They are alive and well, bringing a smile to my face daily. I wish I could hug them, but they are still here, both with their positive and sometimes irritating traits. They remain real, and I get to know them better every day.

My little sister Kim only lived with us for four years, leaving our home to be institutionalized. While that loss devastated me, her smile is ingrained in me. I have very few memories of her after age four. However, over seventy years later, she constitutes a significant part of me—the little kid who is so much at my core. She lives on in the teddy bears that adorn our house. Some could say that I am in denial and never accepted the loss. In fact, I am carrying all three of my siblings with me through the physical life they were mostly deprived of. They will live on through me. When someone close to us dies, we can let the necessary mourning evolve into a state of self-pity; that means the individual is gone. Many today make a memorial service a celebration, which is terrific, but it is so tragic if it ends there. We have a responsibility—we owe it to them—to keep them alive. To grieve, although painfully human, is somewhat selfish; it's about us, not the one who has physically departed.

I have physically left Oz, but it is at my core. You won't just be meeting me when we connect; that would be boring. You'll meet my four remarkable grandparents, a loving mother, an inspirational father, my sister Gussie with her zest for life, my talented brother Bill with his infectious sense of humor, and my blessed sister Kim, that little blonde-haired fireplug who STILL brings me so much joy.

RETURN TO OZ

I turned up the narrow street for the first time in over sixty years, wondering how much it had changed. This neighborhood had been the centerpiece of my Oz, the magical world of my childhood. Nostalgia and curiosity motivated the visit, and as the only survivor from those marvelous days, I was curious how quickly the memories would flood back. It didn't take long.

Before turning onto the street, I passed a familiar apartment building and its pharmacy, where I had frequently purchased baseball cards with pennies earned from recycling bottles. The first house on the street had a hedge that Jack and I hid behind with our basket of snowballs, waiting for cars to turn up the road. Only once did someone get out of their vehicle to chase us. Most expected the attack and waved as they drove by; several would even jump out to playfully lob a snowball our way. Across from that house was the neighbor who hosted a community Christmas Eve party each year before we went out caroling. Soon passing Jack's home, I remembered many days spent there, although it usually served as a launch pad for our next adventure.

Next to Jack lived one of the rare girls in our neighborhood. By chance, most of the families in the neighborhood had only boys, with two homes having four boys. This was great for ball games but is probably one of the reasons I showed no interest in the opposite sex in those early years. Boys outnumbered the girls by more than five to one. This one girl was older, and with her constant make-up overdose and condescending attitude toward the neighborhood rabble, she became the butt of jokes. We were the only home with two girls, and Gussie didn't count as she was rougher and more aggressive than any boy in the neighborhood. She only had one friend on the road, much younger, but Gussie was happiest roughhousing with the guys.

I then passed the neighborhood bully's house; every street must have one. Ed was older than most of us and enjoyed the power bossing around the younger kids gave him. I remembered finding a five-dollar bill on the street, a gold mine in the 1950s. Ed immediately insisted it was his and took it from me. I was powerless to argue or resist. His yard still had the large tree from which he had hung me upside down one day for no reason until his parents cut me down an hour later.

Every house was still there as years ago, fixed up considerably but structurally the same. Our old home looked the same from the street, although a large, elevated porch had been added in the back. I was tempted to knock on the door but chose to remember it as it had been. The property seemed almost smaller than I remembered it. I had jokingly said the side yard was so small I could cut the grass with scissors; I hadn't exaggerated much. Two houses away was Mrs. Cockman's house, where she stood watch over her tiny yard lest some kid enter to retrieve a ball. Officer Jones lived directly across the street, and she must have had a hotline to his house, calling him regularly about the urchins who lived in the neighborhood. He always listened to her but then "admonished" us with a big smile and pat on the back.

My friend, David, lived next to him, and I spent many days and nights there as we spent many hours playing ball. His mother made the most delicious fudge, and visiting David's house always meant sneaking into a small sewing room where she hid this chocolate gold. Since it was not known to evaporate, she must have known what we were doing. And the fudge was always there; it magically reconstituted itself. His older brother, unlike us, was serious, and we spent many hours tormenting him mercilessly. To his credit, he never lost his cool.

Continuing up the road, I passed the house where I got my first dog and remembered all my adventures with Friskie that year before we moved. The dog quickly became my best friend, and no one saw me without that four-legged clown trailing behind. Leaving the street, I went into the alley behind our house. Barely wide enough for a garbage truck to pass, it was a dirty thruway but part of our bike loop we used several times a day. I stopped and remembered that seven-year-old boy on his new bicycle, careening down the alley without knowing how to stop it. I saw Dad racing behind the bike, out of breath, trying to give directions as he panted. The rose bush I had ended up in was long gone.

Returning to the street, I started up the hill again, finding a rare parking spot. I squeezed into a spot barely long enough for my car and rolled down the windows. I had no memory of hearing birds years ago; that sense was not operating then, but birdsong emanated from the many trees lining the street. I remembered how dark the road seemed sometimes, in the shadow of trees and adjacent apartment buildings. However, something was wrong, dramatically different from what I remembered.

It was early afternoon on a mid-September weekend, and the road was eerily quiet. I closed my eyes and traveled back to the 1950s. I knew what was missing. There were no dogs outside. Our dogs ran wild, charged through neighbor's yards, chased cars, carried off balls, and toppled garbage cans. What also struck a chord was the absence of children. Where were the children who biked, roller skated, and ran screaming years ago as they played tag, hopscotch, and capture the flag? Where was the stickball or step-ball game?

A superficial look at the neighborhood indicated I was back in Oz, even with the remodeling of some of the houses, but Oz was the children, not the homes. Other than the birds and distant traffic, the street was quiet, never the case years ago. I wondered whether there were still children in the neighborhood as there were no signs of young life: no bikes, balls, bats, or gloves cast aside awaiting the return of play. Years ago, there would have been a maze of chalk lines on the street and numerous hopscotch grids, but the pavement was bare. There were no open windows, and houses were undoubtedly air-conditioned now. Was there still a Good Humor Man, equally likely to be a woman now? Would anyone even hear the truck today with no one out playing and the sounds of air-conditioning and televisions probably masking the sounds of those glorious bells?

That street was alive years ago, pulsing with the sounds of laughing, screaming, and sometimes crying children, more of a large family than a neighborhood. Today, I was looking at a street with thirty houses but a community devoid of life. Summer nights had often been a celebration with neighbors congregating in someone's yard, attracted by the smell of a barbecue. Crime now had so many afraid to go out at night. Were the fireflies we chased with abandon still there?

The neighborhood had become more affluent and was now largely inhabited by John Hopkins University professors and grad students. My parents bought our house for $8,000 in 1951 and sold it in 1958 for $19,000, allowing them to upgrade to a larger home for our growing family. That original house recently sold for over $600,000. Today, our family would have been unable to afford it with my sisters' medical bills.

Sitting in the car that afternoon, I traveled back to Oz, but only in my memory. I heard Gussie racing around the neighborhood, terrorizing everyone with her toy bow and arrow. I listened to the argument as a runner had been declared out in a stickball game. Mrs. Cockman was screaming at someone to get out of her yard. Bikes zipped up and down the street, and children were roller skating down the slight incline. In one of the houses was a shy little boy with his collection of teddy bears and baseball cards, utterly unaware of what life had planned for him. He would have been terrified if he had known that twenty-five years later, only he would be alive of the four Radcliffe children.

In reality, I don't have to return to Oz; a part of me still resides there. I have kept the best of it and rejected part of it. I don't just remember it; I can go back by simply closing my eyes. I can see and hear my family as if they are with me. While it saddens me in some ways, it also is like returning to the womb, a warm, nurturing blanket. I never want to stay there because I live in the present and eagerly await the future. But visiting Oz always restores me when I feel myself drifting; it's an oasis in the insanity of daily life. I still have the teddy bears and the baseball cards, and Jackie knows she is married to a child-at-heart. She travels with me back to Oz and is so patient. She met all the principal players so that we could enjoy the visits together.

The street is integrated now; no Black could have or would have lived there in the 1950s. Many rode a bus to a nearby stop and walked up the street to work as maids, no longer a politically correct term. We knew them all and enjoyed their company, sense of humor, and different perspectives on the world. However, their presence did nothing to shatter our mistaken belief that we lived in a white-privileged world. We would have to leave that street and the 1950s to see that the world differed from what we knew. Oz was nurturing but not the real world, which is infinitely more remarkable with its diversity.

I am sad that Oz no longer exists on that remarkable little street. How unfortunate that children today cannot experience the bliss and freedom we had. It is now a residence-lined avenue, no longer the pulsating community family we knew as children. Television programs, video games, and carefully scheduled activities are the menu for many children today. What will they be able to revisit in years to come? I had my Oz and will forever treasure it.

www.ingramcontent.com/pod-product-compliance
Lightning Source LLC
Chambersburg PA
CBHW070437100426
42812CB00031B/3319/J